Praise for Will Alexander's *The Combustion Cycle*

With a bird's tetrachromatic vision, Will Alexander lights language up with all its possibilities to accommodate a larger vision of the self, cosmic in its capaciousness. No longer are we only allowed the shapes given to us by petty expectations--instead, in *The Combustion Cycle* (which, for a fuller experience, I recommend reading with an excellent dictionary by your side), each word opens to an incredible new way of seeing and being in the deep and many-dimensioned universe itself. Alexander finds hope for a powerfully beautiful *now,* simultaneous with all our long histories and our potential futures.—*Marcella Durand*

Will Alexander's *The Combustion Cycle* stands as a towering monument to the imagination. Each of its three major phases is narrated by a shapeshifting first-person voice roving through landscapes of cosmic scale. Flying 'in advance of neurological infinity,' Alexander's traveling eye concatenates diverse facts of science and history into dazzling kaleidoscopic patterns. Over these lines hover the spirits of Aimé Césaire, Erasmus Darwin, and the compilers of vast Renaissance compendia. But the metaphysical weight of this tome will bend spacetime around it. The first and best epic of the Anthropocene has arrived.—*Andrew Joron*

Entheogenic, ecstatic, shapeshifting – this is the poetry Plato warned us about. In Alexander's incantatory cycle, the transcorporeal, explosive "I" cohabits with planets and plants, birds and sharks, weather and fire. Every line is a psychic and physical threshold. Each syllable traverses multiple alphabets. Alexander's poems piece together galvanic epiphanies into materials for a decolonized generation starship. "Embarkation is resistance." To read is to be propelled.—*Joshua Schuster*

Will Alexander is by far the most original poet working in the United States today. A major force in the dissemination of Surrealism, there is absolutely no one who sounds like Alexander and he, most emphatically, sounds like no one else.—*Justin Desmangles*

THE COMBUSTION CYCLE

THE COMBUSTION CYCLE

Will Alexander

Roof Books
New York

ISBN: 978-1-931824-96-5
Library of Congress Control Number: 2021930645

Drawings by Will Alexander:
"The Henbane Bird" cover image
"The Proto-Avian" for "The Henbane Bird"
"The Alchemical Androgyne" for "On Solar Physiology"
"The Carbon Placenta" for "The Ganges"

Acknowledgments:
I want to thank to staff at Beyond Baroque for allowing me the space and time to do the initial typing of this book. Let me mention former directors Fred Dewey and Richard Modiano as well as its current director Quentin Ring and former assistant the indefatigable Tetra Bellestri for putting this book on disc. Also, I want to thank my close collaborators (amongst others) Janice Lee, Heller Levinson and Carlos Lara for the seminal yield spawned from spontaneous conversation and Clayton Eshleman for helping me ignite my first foray into print. Additionally, would like to thank poet Brenda Iijima for helping shepherd this work to the wider world via Roof Books and to my partner Sheila Scott-Wilkinson for providing me with the germinal powers of her technical expertise and critique helping me polish and accurately render the closing particulars in this volume. As the cover image on this volume, I want to thank the owner of its original manifestation Nesa-Ron Weir.

Roof Books are distributed by
Small Press Distribution
341 Seventh Street
Berkeley, CA. 94710-1403
Phone orders: 800-869-7553
www.spdbooks.org

Roof Books are published by
Segue Foundation
300 Bowery
New York, NY 10012
www.seguefoundation.com

This book is dedicated to my late parents

Will & Birdie my genetic co-authors

THIS CYCLE INSTIGATES AN INTERPENETRATION

OF LINGUISTIC POWER CREATING IN ITS WAKE

A SUPRA-RECOGNITION EVOLVING WITHIN THE

OCCULTED PANORAMA OF THE COSMOS, CROSS-

WEAVING, THE ANIMAL, THE HUMAN, AND THE

PHYSCHIC ELEMENTS, POETICALLY ENGENDERING

GNOSTIC RECOGNITION.

Will Alexander

Absolute fearlessness is required,

because at every step, at every second,

you must wage war against everything

that is established.

The Mother

Table of Contents

Author's Note

Shamanism not merely a regional articulation but a global resonance that occurs across a syllabus of regions from Patagonia to the northern polar wastes, to western Africa, there exists this inner technology of burning sans Occidental machinery with its in-built delimit. Springing from unknown genetic powers the being articulates themself beyond any semblance of a pre-planned destiny. So many times in the Occident we hear the person articulate to the world: I want to be, say, a nurse or a fire fighter. Not that this is bad, but a shaman seems to be intrinsically calibrated by an impalpable calling.

The Combustion Cycle was and remains a felt experience. Not that considerable study and research was not included in the gathering of the materials at hand but it was above all that my poetic instinct allowed me to meld their disparate forces into a form of lingual orchestration. For the record I was never an apt or outstanding student or scholar in the official sense. In fact, I was barely passable across my tenure as a student. This is not some sort of defense but an articulation of a mind that remains intrinsically non-linear.

When leaving the bondage of official scholarship, I felt enabled to explore my curious tributaries of imagination. I felt enabled to explore my inner lingual voltage, a voltage not unlike the powers of lightning or water or water on earth that was freed to carve for me a lingual canyon. What transpired for me was a charismatic license that has allowed my imagination to enact its power over a protracted time. It remains pulse as instinctual awareness that has allowed me to explore regions beyond the expected grasp of my seeming capability, for instance, my verbal investigation of African lingual geography in "On Solar Physiology," the connecting poem in this volume.

Let me say in closing *The Combustion Cycle* was written not as a literary exercise but attempting to clear what I consider to be obstructive self-detritus, helping me render unknown regions of myself not as anecdotal exercise, but as attempt to connect this poetic endeavour with unknown beings that continue to propel the human diaspora.

Will Alexander

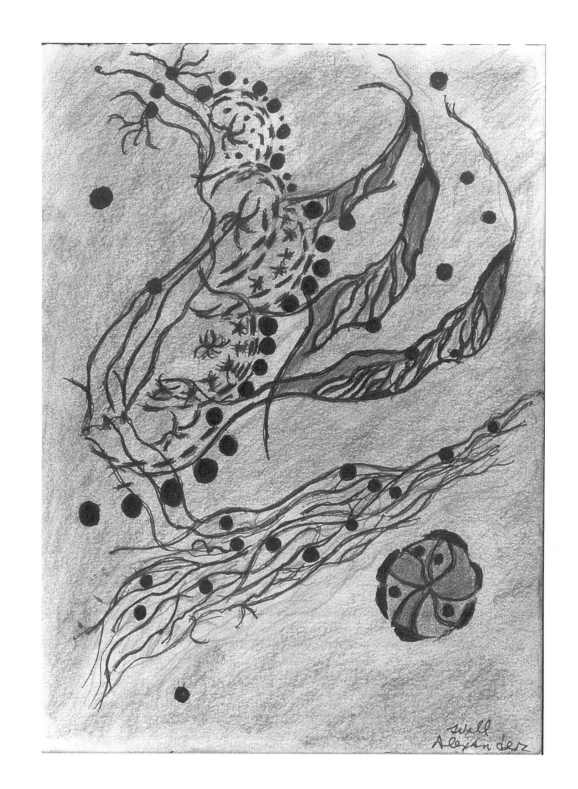

Concerning the Henbane Bird

"...any fragment of the cosmos can give rise to a hierophany, in accordance with the dialectics of the sacred."

Mircea Eliade

"Poison?
the mystification by poison?

no

but life as seminal cladistics
not prone to involuntary slumber
or to the eye of measurable destruction

but the equidistant barriers surmounted
as movement through centripetal transparency
like a flask of mirrors
as centigrade in rotation

I exist as incessant cylindrical magenta
inside my black vertiginous eye
never ceasing to vibrate
so that I am diaphanous
transpicuous
less given to accessible opalescence
or distortion by skiagraphy
as I hover inside the Andes
as the fuel of an interior lightning subspecies
as an ark
as a sun on a tremorous ruby
not being subject to tribes
or genera
or toxins

being the shamanistic Hillstar I am nevertheless subject

to an iridescent shrillness

to a faultless hurricane taxonomy

being the flight that is vapourous

cleansed

& undividable as transfusion

my molecules ghosts

my genetics in abstentia

of the avians

I am the pre-existing Hillstar

not collapsed into form

I am obscure

& proto-endemic as voltage

like a sun minus saffron as weight

aligned

with the first Vulcanian satellities

rising from ghostly eruption

they are 3 in number never subject

to calendrical zones

to continental weight

I am sunless

according to the scribes who've pored over texts in Chaldea

who've negated various weights of salt

according to sound by inverse rotation

according to mountain chains

according to various beasts

born before gravity was founded as law

a law implied & imploded

as various dimensions of surcease

making me sullen & untoward

climatological & variform

therefore

I merge & cease to merge

with manifestation & its rifeness

one could call my wingbeats aloof

my presence

3 suspended suns anterior to shining

anterior to promulgation as mass

anterior to the quavering of hawks

one thinks of titans whose glory is translucent

whose voids are akin to weightless hovering funnels

& this is not to condone

a monotheistic sacrifice body

but to fully engage a transcendental seepage

as a swan emitting sounds

whose fundamental gift is disorder

whose zone revolves as darkened mental largesse
to engage a living
no longer embrangled by outcomes or collapse

what informs me can never be classified as edict
as bound by circular drachmae

yet I exist as a dark interior spinning gale
as a mirage in an avalanche of portals

those portals which equate & cease to equate
the ruins which dazzle the breathing
by geographic isolation
by cataclysmic land forms

for instance
protozoic glacial blindings
whirring about an inclement carbon
like a gloaming centaur
in a primeval water field

& this primeval water field
mnemonic before existing
before the core of intangible ethers has transmuted

thus
I fly in advance of neurological infinity

before rocks
or the velocity of diamonds

vectors exist before me
instabilities
atoms
which exist by re-erosion
by a purely seismic lithos
which implicates a prior solar osmosis

& because of this solar osmosis
I float
I inundate foci by broken solar connective
which haunts the nectar across a river of sage
being a light which seeps from greenish ocular mists
seeping from my shrillness
from my stunning interior drainage
as if my dialectic
were a simple extrinsic organic
a winged blazing in Peru

I would never contemplate chondrites
by provoking the void which antedates matter

if such were the case
one could speak of a cured thin bill
of 'large eyes...retracted between shoulders'

one could speak of my family as Trochilidae

with my 'sharply pointed talons'

with my 'feathers firm...adherent to each other'

removed from the magic of a sub-genetic plumage

if visible

I would consider myself incarnadine

my blood alive & indescribable with salt

describing myself with an echo of nouns

say

the 'Paramo Sapphire-Wing'

the 'Green-backed fire-crown'

the 'Plain-bellied emerald'

or perhaps the 'Purple-throated mountaingem'

or the 'Black-throated mango'

I could speak of the 'Trainbearers'

the 'Heliothrix'

the 'Starthroats'

you see

I cease to be concerned about the explosive use of oxygen

about the width of my 'bronchi'

about darting by melancholia

imbibing a belly of arthropods

flying in rapid spiral movements

I am that isolate warfare
that gulf of isolate gems

I could speak
of 'black umelanin'
or certain types of 'phaeomelanins'
& I would find myself in bloodless worlds of scholarly
anti-frothing

because I exist in abstentia
I could post-exist an Irazu
as a Juan Fernandez Hummingbird
alive
in a common singing ground
by means of solar fuel
by means of aboriginal mating
with my instinct collected
at a flawless depth of anthracites

perfect in the sense that interior hamlets accrue
at a height
beyond no known biologic
beyond dark technologies as pivot

& these technologies mine uranium ballistics
mine each extrinsic geognosy
as a segregate concatenation

or a specific human gene

which acquiesces to explosion

the unleashing of poison

the diameter by horrific

in this degree I am vatic

I am seasoned by unalterable methane which deepens

I've lived prior to carbon or the implicated ion

the first Archean rocks compounded

with the first pre-cellular fires

my proto-wings being stunned by pre-calescent meteorites

by scars twice the size of the boiling Imbrian basin

here I am

upon this complicated precipice

before & after death

never declared as a singular substance

but as a fire which exists

inside miraculous non-entity

not 'variety in morphology'

but cataclysmic vapour

not height in certain vapour gardens

but dense nucleic trance

which allows me to probe by traces
navigational de-location
blank intensity in movement
like a pulmonic volcano
emitting a curious rotation of codes
arising form its cinders a series of compound mandible trees

I could speak of the 'La Plata River'
of Venezuela & the Andes
of sudden mutability & confinement
of listless flowering mules

I could speak of spinning Andean Lakes
of the incredible blankness at rainfall
of their cold ingemination as regards Martian tectonics

Laurentia being its shale as an implicate lightning mass
as precursor to the trilobites

& I am speaking of only one chemical diction
of one circumstance evolved
from an optimum habitat of light

& this light
above a geometric manna
is a green & osmotic tremendum
totalic as an invisible cognomen
is a syntax of deities

is Anubis
is Thoth
is Ishtar
is Shiva

I am these given names
these holographic flamings
these interior tediums by Yak

again
I am implicate
scorching
phonemic as trespassing mineral
being of 'compound reaction'
I am 'not the simple reaction to a stimulus'
nor am I a blank unflowering exposure
plunged through a soma by equivocal isolation

no
never a stunning technical maintenance
 or simple colour by melancholia

for instance
a diagnosis by glass
comprehension by agitation
is a glimpse of my emptied optical movement

by feathers

glintings

squares

each branch of biology void

each cortical synapse

by diminished saturation

because I have assumed a bickering of masses

& then derived a phobia by concentration

I fly

before existence is founded

before

its depolarized incessance

became message derived from proto-anxiety

I stress as vocable

hounding by isolation

as if

each lunar shell were compounded

as depth by inverted spectra

say

3 magenta intaglios

burning

as blackened germinations

throughout a species of light

wafting

from enigmatic suns

at the same time simultaneous

with a mongoose

a hawk

or a vapour

those aggressive occupying vapours

alive as anarchic clepsydras

then

those implicit scaling realms

like an aleatoric vector known as turiya

which include the blindness that I grasp

the rays which live with optical instability

their codes

their marshes

their emblems

pointed

towards an emblematic deafness

spinning with opthalmic tendrils

with invisible empires on Venus

teeming with an empire of microbes

no longer bound to barriers which ignite reversals

that causes each cell to subdue

according to random teeming

32

to barriers which revolve liquids

which reverse

giving them

the action of lines emitted as rays

as eruptive photon gardens

or a cloudy phlogiston motif

or a barren axial trail

without causes

without sudden incendiary surface

such as that which spirals or deracinates itself

diminished in its power

by rigid algebra or notation

no

by a sense of omniscient vertigo

by levels omniscient with vertigo & nostalgia

which adds or burns itself

with a paradox through liquid

as though one sun

the blackly cratered moon

became barbarity by index & phantom

by mountains

which circle themselves

baffling

the thrust of their physiognomy

their strength

as Sabbatarian fulfillment

as vitreous arsenal ballet

like & unlike the floating methane above Neptune

like & unlike the tornadoes swarming in the Hirayama asteroids

in their colony of vacuums

destroyed

as if

in a suffix of declaration

analogous

to the flux in a purifying dharma

yet they exist

without diagram or projection

without collocation or boundary

I have not created their witness

their calescence

their supernal thermodynamics

their shift in combustion by alembic

because

I

as Hillstar

as force in the Andean substrates

am not the syllogistic imperator

but he

of ventriloqual stamina

of convexity electric with voyage

nautical through invisible agoras

alive

with post-existing obscurity

those beings which post-exist by quantum nomadics

who exchange their essence by ambivalence

the bird-gods communing by insuperable resurrection

so that nothing ever accrues in itself

all the time

without answer

without growth which exhales

all the while implying

the curious mathematics of stony oregano & skin

if I exist as curiosity by technique

it is true

I still exist as a presence

an equation traced by blizzards

by an action absolved of the hyper-dimensions of brooding

absolved of one simple dogmatism as status

of embryology which ignites by commandment

no

not religious deliverance gregariously instilled by

abstruse misnomer

by wretched clinical incitement

but by osmosis

by a template

appearing & disappearing without any known origination

in austerity

neither is it the quest for annihilation

or for dogmatic catalogue only quenched by catastrophe

but by nature

I am inclement

I partake of air before the sun explodes

quaking

in my present double form

I exist without advantage

without a sense of lakes forming in my region

invisible

yet verbally visible

I speak

so as to detonate winds

to take by possession an anti-nuclear form

thereby

withstanding edicts

as if my wings were a great clairvoyant equation

& this equation exists in the source of speculation

in an ecology which generates an incalculable

sorcery by verb

yet I cannot advance creation

nor give it protracted numerological invasive

that equates

with one dimensional vibration

paralleled by counted activity darkened as separate illusive

that is

the serial persistence by which a deductive bridge

is founded

I can say that all separations exist by lower ingestion

that unity is avian in form

is totalic in suggestion

because

it evinces height

it is empyreal scintilla

much like black rotational invasives

& these invasives

undetectable

like darkened radon candles

electric with soaring

insidious with that which obscures

& re-angles its anomalies

according to eclectic gravitational criteria

& all the forms

all the various equational instincts

in motion throughout fissures in the proto-implicate

throughout the great mangers of fire

& these mangers

suns

suns struck

with darkened cellular nomadics

with perfect occult saturation

which hyphenates the power of spells

spells

that hyphenates being

become radial integers that transfix

simultaneous with parallels that waver

& these parallels are tendencies which vibrate

which never coalesce into a bloodless carpentry of atoms

into a field of statistical prominence

into a field of somatology

my universe

never one of corporeality or capture

say

each ration of drift prevailed by pre-calescent heat

being no more than a dozen or 20 solar masses
with a tendency towards formation

for instance
flames through a black dimensional window
light through intrauterine nomadics
irregular amplification

being of Andean climatology
I know the precarious kindling of space
I know its dense subjective bleakness
far beyond the ozone systems
far beyond its sense for capacity of heat

you see
I fly as a floating pontoon coil
as an invigourated distance
spliced as differential confinement
& each sum that I echo
I challenge with a fire of the ungraspable

I make up methods
as if the one-celled beings were congealed out
of heresy
as if the first mountain chains were an isometric error
no longer sought or cherished
as signs of the uncontainable

yet they are the first unnumbered oracles from the Archaen

the first fragmented sepia vocality

like a flashing dominance discharged through the eons

& all this from the caliginous

from the vector of the gyroscopic grain

occluded

enhanced

by the first explosive cataract

by the first ravine of glaciers

knowing the first nucleic tensions were grounded

in the firmament

in this realm of the vitreous

each song that I sing

rife with anathema & aversion

that is in turn spun into the power of vatic investment

never destruction & correlation as simple gestation & flaw

but flight which irradiates suspension

which transforms as vertex the miraculous soil of the erratic

as pre-suggestive biology

never the graphic eikon as dysfunction

but boats of lava burning as mythic suns

so in this degree

I can foretell chasm

I can challenge conjunction with the essence of rhetoric

of dialectic

40

first: a needle

          three missing pyres

          a mountainous investiture

secondly: a stunning tribe of lorikeets

          mapping a plain of dark electrical rivers

now

the synthetic riddle which floods its lagoon like an asp

like a blackened celadon pyre

then from this

a viridian prairie with a dearth of inhabited vultures

with subdivided coves

from which the cells of the Bantu Pharaohs rose

I think of charging rams

I think of unsullied cobras

of course

I claim no hierarchical advantage

as specifically concerns the range of my voice

yet its sub-equal distance

a barrage of ciphers

being a glistening depth

that unfolds as an enormous carbon hieroglyphic

& this carbon hieroglyphic is random

combustible

like a torrent of infernos

of calcareous errata

that will never exist as form

that will remain as central tendency

as corruptive spore in transition

I cannot define

or lend any definitive occurrence to its depth

or re-map the cosmos

& its display of extraneous psychic terrain

there is a law of forges

a primal inquisitor's prism

that possesses no other urge

than to speak of a power which increases its friction

through fragment

I mean by fragment

that which condenses into burial codes

that spins with depth & horizon

which impels a fertile isolation

beyond the geometric

for instance

a tense coronal rain

that appears 'as dark absorption features'

as 'heliographic latitudes'
like the sparse ignition in frenetic polar fields

which ascend & project from a radius of diamonds

& for want of increasing reason I assemble a diagrammatic

the Andean sun:
vectored with Eunomia

Proxima Centauri:
vectored with Hidalgo

Canopus condensed with Achilles

& from these arbitrary mergers
dialectical blindings
dazzling obscurities

the application of combining
the intensive flow of rocks through the ether

because I precede the primal solar infernos
I am witness as draft
as cataclysm through stillness
summoned from empty location of forms
from telekinetic intangibles

never subsumed into a base informing
prone to didactic inscription

perhaps
I am 2 or 3 kelvins removed
flying through the language of the epochs
no longer mired in one central explosion
in one definitive struggle
which has informed its activity
through human mental advance

for me suggestive opaqueness
sealed in tumultuous dodecahedra

this being the pressure on the proto-plane
on the habitat of haunted mural imbalance

much like ice from darting vacuums
from simultaneous foment
before the spark that unseals tremendums

therefore
I am vatic as regards nucleic coronas
I can predict signs a billion zodiacs ago
when a universe ignited
from collapse from random photon exposure

then of course the arrow of each galaxy

the sonar from Andromeda

the molecular soundings from M 31

they are general relays that invade

that give to me

a porous territorial climate

which changes according to the powers

of one particular kelvin or another

say

of 2.7 to 1.6

or

1.4 to 3.7

these are temperatures projected from intangible ejecta

projected from my domain as voice

my ability

to overleap the eons

to imply by singing eclipse phonation

unknown states of the palpable

because I as Hillstar

am prone to that which inscrutable shifts

roaming imploded kelvins

like a radical cinder unpredictable with pions

I

being the void of greatest liberty

who understands the core beyond the central firmament

its greatest hurricane as wilderness

ubiquitous with phoneme upheaval

with classical disruption

so as to create from a prior solitary rubric

without zeal which invades toxic interconnection

I cannot say that I am phenomena by model

capable of adapting to 12 minor igneous ponds

like a dwarf that blazes night after night

as birdless magenta inscription

I exist

I live by means of hyper-intensity

my wingbeats anarchical

unlike a mean or calculable squamosity

bus as echo like dazzling juggler's liquidity

each of my feathers being an uncoloured rebus

lifted

from recondite contagion

as if description had vanished to a faultless non-transference

so as to meander through vacuums

frayed with diagonal omens

for me

cosmologies of exotica:

the leptons & photons that vanish

the quarks & their ghostly mesmerisms that spill & regather

46

in odd cryptographic ambrosia

so that I am ventriloquially able to emit my condition

from the organics of the snow line

suddenly existing

billions of years in the blankness

the Andes:

ruined & magnificence

my perch:

ruined & magnificence

so if I speak of blood across the tropics of Neptune

it is unfixed as regards historic detonation

but always merging with mirrors which glaciate & spin

their motion cataclysmic

non-concurrent with exertion

because I roam the vastitudes

I no longer hail from simplified concussives

because I have emptied the poles of their fever

& spun from emptiness the dialectics of longevity

certainly

not a tragic carrion treatise

holding nothing but the scales of gravitational dictation

scales less detectable than mirage

than the translateral crystal of the ocean bottoms

all the silver
all the land gales
never super-imposed as ornaments
as calliopes that humans sometimes offer as sound

no
life seethes with metamorphoses
with subtrahends emptied at lesser known boundary
of cartographical scale
of the amperage of rocks
of heightened mountain voltage
of snow that fouls volcanoes

such motion intensifies at the liminal
at an earth split in two
by indetectable transgression
not in terms conveyed by a sudden moral creature
plagiarized by terms such as sheik emir pasha

no
I am not a potentate
or some skilled adversarial candidate
formed at his essence by diplomatic juvenilia

I am condoned by the 'Emperor Seamount Chain'
the 'Labrador Basin'
the 'Murmansk Rise'

or

the Cordilleras in Peru
the Orientals
the Occidentals

nor do I specifically hail from Chiclayo
or Chimbote
or Callao

nor do I partake of the exosphere
by which habitat is measured
be I of the Guianas
the 'Lower Andean slopes'
or camouflaged like the 'Eutoxeris Aquila'
'completely spectacular'
partaking of the powers of Ecuador

one cannot describe me
with '8 pairs of ribs'
an 'extensible' tongue
lateral nostrils
'alular feathers'

again
not a 'murmurer'
a 'Heliomaster'
a consumer of fructose

true

I have passed into invisible ignition

oblate with coma

I exist

by neither night nor day

not with an 'iridescent gorget'

nor with a flare of enlarged irradiation

on Earth it is true

that I am listed by variegation

as cinnabar

scarlet

cochineal

vermilion

condemned in my breeding

probed as if I were a magnetic arachnid

or an incubation from grain

spun between zodiacs of water

these zodiacs of such complexity

rise & descend by intrinsic oscillation

so much the case

that tendency obliterates tendency

emitting from seeming stasis a universal power

swaying stars

like a 'Blue-white subgiant'

or a 'White super giant' like Alpha Persei

in the former star a legendary cleansing
in the latter the strength of musical clairaudience

because I am thought to sing at a dull interior pitch
I am able as sigil
I am able to imbibe the torch of crepuscular edenics
to awaken unknown matings in the abyss

to extract miraculous waves from subatomic juncture
from flaws in unscalable nephrograms

a mathematics so unsullied
that during each of my wingbeats
beings emerge
micro-theories resound
concerning the first retro-causal terror as summit
the first kinetic thought as contractive
being mesmeric magnification
by latent quantum elevation

such is intensity by microscopic chronicle
by particles which exist as dictation

corrosion
subterfuge as confine
subterfuge as drift
being collisions which form in transfigured deduction

as to why I exist

as to why my wings fly as perusal

I cannot speak as extrinsic scar or emotion

perhaps a charred victory

or a sacrificial geyser

this intense shamanic coma

only partially dwells within neural tourniquets & surcease

alive as regards a lateral investiture as climate

I am affected by the fact that I am condensed with affect

with osmotic irradiation

like a sorcerous ignition of pinnacles

a spinning synergy of vapour

which envelopes my flight by intransigence as weaving

the pure economy of crystal

only suggested at its core by pure refractive invention

like meridians or twilight

or sunrise on Europa

where the conclave of dysphonia had never experienced

itself within the upright vocality of sapiens sapiens

within the voltage of its day to day theatrics

where protagonists erupt

upon a stunned locale of spiders

taking into their blood a ravenous cartographical nectar

at times

attempting to sustain a vibrational rapport with elevation

I am entwined with hypnosis & magnification

because

I elicit harsh winds

burning suns

spawned in blank arroyos

even in coma I can preach of the 'angles of iridescence'

like diamond as the index of water

saffron then unleashed into stillness

into phantoms that blur

& each bird that I am

accrues to one arroyo or pavilion

landing like angels upon flaming ideologies

at this level I could concur in Patagonia

or sing as if from Tierra del Fuego

flying off to Saturn & the southern pole of Rhea

therefore

I cannot reason with myself as regards negated evasion

or rise to concurrence of pitch

can I determine myself as one spare signal or law?

can I consist of utter complication?

as unrefined potential?

as a spurious background static?

I can reveal myself as nervous solitary power
dispossessed & skilless
knowing at present
I cannot begin to judge the barrier of ravines
like the unnerved error poised in restless cattle

a confusion posed at a certain physical pitch
claimed as principle by dogmatic indemnification

I
being absent as mass have no fragment or boundary
neither forming nor gathering as form
at the same time enduring the anti-isolation of mass

I am that by which derivatives no longer conjoin

even as one flightless
like & unlike the anoa
I am the beast one can never renew
or confine with an image
hovering through interregnums as 'compressional deformation'

hovering as a trace
as a strange preliminary fowl
a trace compressed above electron seas

it is not that I reduce or increase
through troublesome letters of jade
or that I seek to induce a state of self
derived like a sorcerer who spits fire

no

yet I'm called Tocha by the Hopi
Nanatska by the Pima
Lutchit Herit by the Wintu

they have seen & unseen the blazeless rooms of my motion

being to the ancient Mexicans
'huitzizil'
'ourbiri'
'pigada'

then being visually momentous
inside the realms of the Juan Fernandez Islands

yet I can speak of Sajama
Cotopaxi
Chimborazo

all of the above

being curious lakes for my fuel

a saturated index

a cilium aerial indemnity

never adapting oneself to local ruination

or to stratification carved by polemic

I hover outside the clepsydra

outside the code of static nuclear law

being blaze as runic magnifying power

as if I were akin to reasoning

which counted each scintilla as existence

which would parallel the Buddhists & overspill Samadhi

each moment of reasoning

flooding its own spell

then emptied of any forewarned deflagration

being outside the heat of interior kelvins

I have withstood the strain of a willed volitional harvest

pervaded by another ether

another soil

scattered by an alien radium differential

say I pursue fire from divided hillocks

I will then come to know

the powers produced from the arch-concerns of the instincts

& the mirrors from which these powers bespeak

take from themselves a superior kind of nullity

so that interiors inhabit themselves

a simultaneous parallel which drifts

& re-partakes its scintillation as spark

as momentary paradox

like a tachyon with its drift roaming in & out

of nothingness

& this nothingness is where recognition appears

where sparks disintegrate & re-form

through cataclysmic recognition

true

I appear as being spawned from a vacuum

like a flood outside the universe

outside its forces known as the limit of light

I exist

as 'uncertainty' over 'mass'

as 'circuitry by means of 'enigma'

partaking of life in dimensions

such as the 'Calabi-Yau'

or

'orbifold' existence

thus I am freed to speak of a Horned Sungem

of a Purple-throated Woodstar

or of a family of Sunangels

freed from the odours of toxic neural gravity

perhaps pieces of jasper

or caves connected by impalpable index flowers

or heat enacted by subgods or dramas

my present flight is not of inferior grottos

nor sealed in its threading by inverse tornado

but by winds being plows

plows accrued through diamonds

burning as cornucopias of climates

a 'cup of eagles'

a door through the mountains of Venus

scribbling by dialectic as thunder

the previously stated known as the wonder of Pachacta

Unanchac

known for combining solstice distillation

known by this distillation as blind indelible migration

so that my trial by dark creates interior vindication

so that rocks are misplaced

& saurians misbegotten

such is the failure of storms

on the poisoned replica of the Earth

this being the Mayan dread extracted from the Troano Codex

that there would be days when the sun would flash

with obstructive obscurity

when the tides would dwell as a venomous red

when each cephalic suture would be subject to foreboding

creating feelings that abound

concerning the in-flotation of the world around the Sun

the human species prone

its technique of grasp: void

its pantology through inspection: negated

time becomes known as a calendar of wolves

as a corrupted flux

by which all manner of energy is devoured

a parched dormition

a composite ferocity by heliotropic betrayal

so that death is uneasy

its memorials scorched by scarred lenticular wattage

& the claustrophobic ideal of one single passage

between plane & plane

on an oblate spheroid

always subject to colloquial impressions

the colloquial powers of ambush

& I mean by ambush

a governing neurosis

a feverish nomadology

which replicates post-bodily ash as a hellish nyctalopia

as dilemma co-equal with bonfires

with skiographs perturbations

with the judgments of a God whose one power dwells

in bottomless Gehennas

me being the trace at the center of this central imbroglio

as regards human scale

I possess an incredulous agnosia

so I subsist by means of seeming dictation

devoid of extrinsic gainful proof

my flight always deflecting composite definition

I

of the geomantic furnace

of the cryptic intent

breeding by vibration a nova of figurines

& these figurines are suggestive

a giant moth

a Chaldean leper

seemingly cursed with the flaw of disintegrative seizure

suggestive links

not limited to themselves as decline of electrodes

as decline in gravitational being

but survey as bereftment

as clandestine disruptives

my present state

is a slope of phantom frequency

outside of measured existence

outside of corruptive transparency

hovering as in-cyclical polar draft

at present

now void of the activity called perching

for me

no daily oxygen consumption

no gramme of daily bodily weight

no feeding from suns before moonrise

rapid shelter inside hurricanes: void

I exist beyond what is generally known as torpor

beyond the death circuit

beyond the fact which is claimed as episodic respiration

reaching into 'frequencies that humans cannot hear'

yet at times I partake of mirage

of a Vervain

or a Wine-throat

or a Wedge tailed Sabrewing

my ventriloqual forge being the sound of 'another species'

having lived beyond my 12-year limit

I've deceived the bats

the kestrels

the Leopard Frogs

I am the alone with the alone

my mane burns

& is the colour of alterity & fragrance

I emanate

I withdraw

I hover over bells of negation

my former kelvin as realia

with its comets

its photons

its asteroidal ambers

always questioning inside my traces

whether I exist without duality?

or cast no demise from my shadows?

such are my non-possessives

my Bat Hawks

my Dracula Orchids

my Lightning Thistles
as I appear & disappear
leaving spells throughout my living range

I can appear throughout particular histories
throughout a particular insurgence in time
so that there exists no death to procure
no barriers to conduct
no empty wall of citron to pervade

a conduction point: Earth
my dominant instinct: parliament as bickering
my most gruesome obstacle: tellurian decay

me
I've risen from old reptilian deepenings
from the Thecodonts
the Crocodiles
the Pterosaurs

becoming in the Jurassic a 'crow sized' lantern
an Archaeopteryx
not of the 'Lower Tertiary' & the flightless Diatryma
but with the cycadeoids
the conifers
the gingkoes
existing before the ammonites

before the Eryops
before the amphibia of the Mississippian

my essence teeming with cyanoethine
with lakeless hydroxl

I am that power which arrives from the heavens
which burns in the blindness of mating

so I am left without a heritage which falters
without a morose dictation deaf with hesitation

I exist between suns
between inadvertent flash points
where emptiness de-exists
& coincides aural deflagration
with the blackly revealed magnitudes
known to transgress the farthest reaches of sodium
those transgressive states of hearing
as I listen to the floods form 'transparent ranges'
from scrolls of dust which banish beyond heavens

you see
I have an instinctual possession of knowledges
of exquisite neural intuitives
so that I'm clarified by Uranian signal

not the impact of a low 'velocity'

of a 'secondary crater'

but of 'interplanetary scintillation'

projecting itself beyond supra-optical equators

commonly known on the optical plane

as 'immersion'

as 'celestial occultation'

as 'submillimetric' transcendence

I feed beyond the millimetric

beyond the vapour of any visible incarnadine stag

or a post-engendered cyclical rufescence

each clause

each saffron or weight

suspended

alive with tense equational substrates

which at a further depth

respond as apparitional plankton

like the respirating phases of the luminous 'hadron era'

simultaneous

with the luminous destruction of leptons

followed by the implosion of quarks by means of beatific insularity

which has led me to the cusp of this one dominating kelvin

& I am not speaking of 'spark chambers'

or the instrument known as the 'coded mask' telescope

I persist by presence of echoes

knowing

that I pass back & forth between what is known of

differing cellular modalities

or their neutering or absence as echo

infinity is thus charged with strange electrical vicinity

like the stark transparence of an odour out of season

perhaps

anecdotal limitation

gathered from occulted mountain limbs

like mercurial speculation from Andromeda

yet

this is not the totality of which I speak

the universe

being an arc

a velocity

a finite within parameters

within frequencies prone to threat

by energies which subsist within view

not that colossal fragment de-invents me

or negates my spontaneous imaginary range

but I persist in echo without count

without quantitative conclusive

yet at the same time existing

as the scattered observation of a knowable species

me

a vortex of nebulas across a scattered blue light

within a negated incendiary vacuum

so my presence echoes

as sudden mutational implosive

hovering in & out of depths

hovering outside all known vicinity

hovering outside the scope which inundates mirage

existing as a gaunt dialectical baron

facing the creational fires

of Elysium Planitia

of Ariel

of Enceladus

as a volcanic cipher

I am prone to propulsion

to pyrology

to the devouring element known as the uranic

yet I am void of grammes

of kinematic scrutiny

of definition as forced by definition as example

as if I asked for a throne room

or astral suckling roses

being perhaps

the colloquium of the tachyon

not forced definitive as galaxy

but galaxy after galaxy throughout its hidden kinetic seeds

being instinctual as outer kinetic

then as thirst through withdrawal

bred as 13 agnostic millennia

one: to arrive at oxidation

two: to randomly angle the mirror of blue electric causality

three: the drop of water; the egg as a minimum

four: the colour green as transforming by serpent

five: totality by sacred needles

six: veneration by sacred reptile water

seven: ravaged microbial seas

eight: grammar by inherent torment

nine: permutation as altered number

ten: the subdivided phalanx

eleven: biopsychic empyreans

twelve: residue by compensation

the thirteenth: 'galactic blood' mixed as agnostic realias

yes

it is to procure by molten raft

by sudden strategy as oasis

so as to reveal

revolt by 'Dissonant Structure'

its analogy being unmirrored synapse

being transengendered asteroid as neon

take 20 post-positional suns & re-shape them
so as to arrive at their phantom electrical amount
aleatoric as potentia

& because they never equal themselves
they allude to transitional starlight
seemingly fed by debris from sunless cometary floods
never evolving to gnarled stationary magnets

so this implies a prior fractal polarity
as if
solar multiples were timed by dread
when de-structured drift equated to insolvent carbon
to a blazeless central motion
becomes anagram
clairvoyant with voltage

a neurological conservation
suggesting a path totemic with spectra
as if to dwell as post-rotational cells
be they the ghosts of bullocks
or blackened tigers
or serpents of various sullage

no
I cannot count these cells
or name them as subliminal counterparts
yet gainful as ignited dispersal

& by dispersal

I am flying across inflationary ciphers

whose existence accrues by unstratified velocity

being pressure through divided creation

between a gulf of kelvins

strangely inveigled

by factors that mitigate

that

which certain creatures conclude as universal fate

that fallen resolve is scattering & dissolution

for me

a pole of levitational paradigms

which persists

over & above the devolved helix

that the body reveals as death

that instantaneous cauldron

that cauldron with a lack of serpents

on Earth

I am seen as being of the family Trochilidae

of passing on fatality by migration

of upsetting sustenance

in terms of the clan & the procreation cycle

I am outside of fate

I no longer project beasts as some evolved & final spanning point

nevertheless

my implicate traces
charged with stunning solar virility
with a power that exudes
a final overcoming of cognition

let me name to you
the star groups that I activate:

Cygnus

Draco

Aquila

Piscus Austrinus

Pavo

Tucana

Indus

Reticulum

mind you
not a colonization by optics
but the mere fact of presence
connected
with the great arterial light
imminent
as the flux of mysteriums

I mean by this
great weight in the heavens

the compound glints

the whirling clairvoyance

such being

the realm of cancellation

the utter nothingness as refined hostility

this being

the migratory concepts

that leaves the wingbeats un-lensed

like a nocturnal lightning

inter-dimensional with transfer

& this transfer is the flame

that reeks

of supra-de-activity

so that utterance spins

like a sunbeam through a conifer

like algid hurricanes on Mars

a language

of storms

of heats

of schisms

being uncountable nullification

slashing its marks on a macro-cosmic tablet

as if speaking of a harvest of glass

uttering its name through strange electrical ghosts

conjuring in themselves

bio-electrical edicts from which spells pour forth

I am not speaking of corruptive angels

mired in valleys

transgressing giants

or of the blended emanations of dragons

or of the suffix of salamanders re-interred into sulfur

I know there exists

the substance of Apsaras conflated with tomb disposals

with a necropolis combined as a moral conurbation

calescent

haunted & seductive with disappearance

not the sun as fleece

as rhapsodic cinder

but exposure of gales that feasts outside debris

outside

the bio-electric as distance

& this distance

not gradated width

or field measured within field

but that which escapes into pure electrical yield

· into experiential parsecs

with de-submission to gravity

I inculcate my traces

with analogy by trans-location

therefore

I can call myself the Horned Sungem

the Blue-tufted Starthroat

the Esmeralda Woodstar

the Veridian Metatail

the Olivaceous Thornbill

again

my index is rife

with the Plain-bellied Emerald

the Brazilian Ruby

the Black-throated Brilliant

I am adventitious of this flux

of its cryptographic legions welling up from my sunspots

from my implied location as scar

being none of the above as specific

none therefore in variety

I am the ether of bodies

the transmuted form flown through corrupted fennel

who has ascended beyond my own hummingbird's name

far beyond

my occulted halo in Peru

beyond its zones of ash

beyond its craft of luminous material fragment

again

a transmuted phlogiston

a burning signal

a sub-order of angels

by exposure to geology I am flux

I can be called Heruka 'Buddhist God'

dancing on a corpse

'an emanation of Aksobhya'

with my family 'female partner' 'Prajna'

humming with the legions

eclipsing the umbrageous

in the depth of a grandiose bell

no

I am not trace as simulation

as biographic phylactery

again no

because I am pulled by the sunbeam furnace

by its electric caravel of surges

by its tense vermicular habitats

which attracts by means of subaltern conjuration

a sigil

which emanates

from the haunted electro-magnetics of history

my intrinsic realia being spark

flare

scintillation negating sullen remonstrations

marooned as they are by contiguous chaparrals

so what slips from my utterance are Altaic gemstones

vocal micro-unfoldment

always prone to higher conduction

to transmuted animal as bell

by resonance I project the waste of the Andes

in states beyond the aurifically visible

that equates

with the luminosity of contagion

being the 'neural'

with the luminosity of contagion

being the 'neural'

being with 'ionospheric frequency'

my wings being transfused nano-telepathy

like a gust that blows through bottomless migrations

through sidereal concussives

unknown to the Satan Monkey

or to beings who have constructed the British Tropical Year

of course anti-weight

anti-proportionality

with a cipher that instructs by vapour as relativity

the barren tincture of triodia

no

not a barren porcelain cartography

but one restive

remote

always subject to alien metamorphic

to the biology of moons in one zone

& this zone is the zone of earthly solar lunation

with their 'sulci'

their 'rilles'

their 'lobate ridges'

linked by essence to the 'volcanic province' of 'Procellarum

the latter being the vicinity of the 'Marius Hills'

of the 'Aristarchus Plateau'

this being a singular echo-location

within prolonged ellipsis

which contains the irregular body of Deimos

with its craters of 'Voltaire' & 'Swift'

with its motility of a captured meteorite

& from these realia a realm of subsidiary bastions

Elara

Ananke

Metis

Pandora

Iapetus

Phoebe

Bianca

the above considered as vacuums of quanta

suborder as velocity

as acrostic

as puzzling incognita

being irregular velocity which implies the abyss

through ammonia

through galactocentric cometary holdings

those reservoirs with their radius 'oriented' by randomity

it could be said that I've flown through parabolic cinders

through the 'low albedo' on Uranus

on Oberon

on Titania

exposing their 'fresh undarkened ice'

always pointing towards obscurity

like winds of carnivorous photometers

being the signs form an emptied hydrogen atlas

with its obscure beacons suddenly culminate in methane

in forms

implicate

retrograde by visibility

never swayed by centralized proportionality by the opposite radii of draught

replete with limitation

my liminal body implanted with ethers

with irradiated mazes

no longer exploded in mazes

but in the amperage of unknown springs

observational levitation

dorsums then communing with the height of sudden polar cycles

where starlight seems blinded

by scattered 'radiation'

by interstellar empirics

so I

the shaman

with his wings imploded

floating in & out of galactic 'spiral arms'

moving

through the cold neutral medium

through the 'ionized medium' of candescence

by 'bipolar outflows'

by 'stellar' insufflation

being of 'thermal origin'

containing a profusion of iron

I am spasmodic bursts

I am transfer of streaks

I remain ungauged

without nanometer

without nuclei

my homing then parallel with 'electron volts'

with powerful photon mirages

so what appears as dissolution are those depths of

oblate scarcity

those topiary voids

called in particular the 'Valhalla Basin'

the 'Hella Planitia'

the large Caloris ring on the surface of Mercury

which I cease to observe by exiguous intentionality

by observation in brokenness

by means of puzzling voltage lamias

being manganese momentum by spectroscopic revolt

because I have flown from Tiahuanaco

from the carved tablets of serpents

this energy simultaneous with my hieratic pulse

with my exhaustive equators

pervaded by pure kindling as eternity

its interior remotion a blue portrayal of blazes

which burns away the oblate contaminates

allowing me

to seek after worlds of immaculate solferino

because I utter through unblurred diameter

through thaumaturgical aura

that aligns me with 'spontaneous vocation'

with 'autonomous self-ritual'

it is not that I have never been subjected to the

17 cruelties which animate the jackal

much like cadavers muted in a sun dish

the first of these cruelties: ritual stealth

at the second remove: thirst subsumed in anatomical thickets

at a third remove: their prey who dig salt in ravines

at a fourth count: the scavenging of vertebrae

at the pentad: movement by hunger & ice

in the tropical hexads: roaming through dwindling leopard kills

throughout the heptagon: they take no heed of clouds

inside the octad: the hunting of 'muskrat' nervously lurking both sides of a stream

by the ninth kinetic: they play dead & attach 'small carrion feeders'

at the decagon: they howl as nervous sirens

in the eleventh degree: bond by nomadic burial

throughout duodecimality: they concur by brackish hounding

at the thirteenth darkness: their breath begins to form as a transparent thievery

the fourteenth priority: consisting of grooming & violence

the fifteenth: breathing simooms gauntlet & bribery

at the hexagon: expanded terror by ruthless shrieking

at the seventeenth exhaustion: uselessness; dulled chimeras in hiding

they attempt to haunt me from earth

staring from Lake Langano

with a mournful scent of Abyssinian death counts

a moral scent?

common toxic observation?

since I am not an Auk or a Merganser

my equilibria ramble

the actual sun becomes missing

the jackals responding to my pre-buried plumage

to some pre-bodily salt moving like a ghost in

their nostrils

supplanting their seizures & fixations to carrion

perhaps

a poltergeist of dogs

a clan of errata

why not speak of vervets

or a single bird across gulfs in migration?

there is halcyon anti-edict

which now condones my bleak gregarious pedigree

& there are storms within this pedigree

there are funnels of light which collide with omission

which at one level mingles with this bleak gregarious pedigree

& at another

can never cohere with the vigour of my chromosomal challenge

because all phyla balance

I have electrically crossed phyla

so that I no longer concur with empirical integers

or with crops of strict or tangible omen

this is where the jackals seek my supersessional traces

& makes them scatter with nervous electric tertiary struggle because the galaxies reach & do not reach me

not be abolished bearing

but by remedial catalogues & zeniths

those arcs complied by referential tables

condensed by aboriginal earth

my spirit

thought

'to have escaped from volcanoes'

from a 'highly tenuous plasma'

leaping through invisible vicinities

that enliven the living & the living dead

& me

without fleece

without ceremonial preta as image

as function which enlivens my stamina through negation

my flight

not unlike a hormonal serum

carnelian in character

like ripened new fire

blending my ornithic captivation with human triangular candles

attempting in this suffusion

a glottal form from explosive anthrax islands

above my own form as glyph

as seething & prophetic hellebore

subsumed by blank concavities

by simple moons
by poisoned yurts

because I am river melded with flux
that seems incidental with ballast
consuming itself as primeval instinct
yet I exist
as spark between phyla
as if fire were produced by inverted leaves
by phonic sand dune powers
between the stellar & its dialectical foliage
flitting between source & anti-source
flushing out nectar from photonic erosion
the explosion of kelvins
being sound as the massive weather of existence
implying by dialectic that perpetual implosion exists
it being cryptically understood
that no degenerate electrical germ can prevail

I am aligned with blank animation as energy
allowing me
carnivorous flexibility as presence
lexicon being wonder
I take as sigil fecund abandonment
where galaxies plunge into occult isolation

I have been elected to ignite
through parallel debilities & moroseness

then merging with blind ascent

not having flown

not contacted whirlwinds abstractly described by glossaries

& emendations

without heat

devoid of breathing

fed on auras & blood

sprung from one fatal egg known as toxemia

of course I've come to higher scale

known as ubiquitous animal

as vista

by observational disorder

by oscillation within a terminal crag

beyond the edge of this world I've been led by 2 guides

one: a meteoritic hoar-frost lizard

two: a dying alabaster shark

of the latter I can say

that his eyes proclaimed a perjurious neon

that his throat was filled with husks

that he had lived & died in cosmological errata

the former: a quickened irregular sized foetus

& from the acts they engendered

I was lifted to my scale as burden

as sub-negation & struggle

carried to the shores of meteoritic seas

my throat strengthened

my voice being cosmological with suspension

so that I no longer possessed the one lone wing of the Andes

or the claim of a tropical disparity

I was given the right of my own species

I was pre-inducted in roaming through tumultuous interregnums

through a strange angular initiation

through a blizzard of covert scarlet momentums

being

purgation as vacancy

being

blemished abode as departure

then at a certain limit I was self-born from my limit

my astral furnace wandered

my potentia was obscured through tests

my concatenation was scattered by evangelical debris

my wings were placed under orphan reindeer stones

then the hoar-frost lizard relented

then the alabaster shark began to grant me these wings

first: by nuance

secondly: by distension

then third: by singular nightmare suffrage

no

not encyclical as bondage

as marks accrued by darkened ozone drainage

with my testament scorched by rational invocation

no

because

of the oblique galvanics of my guides

I've conversed with beings between twilight & inferno

beings whose forms are strange centuries of blankness

who've taken essences from themselves

so that

they remain a species unto themselves

akin

to explorational owls

levitational gladioli

not again

in those exact demeanours

but by condensed kinetic

so that the hoar-frost lizard & the shark

are over & above

formless hummingbirds & lions

having guided me

to this solitary depth

where nothing appears

not even bloodless smoke

not even saffron bodies

all millennia purged

the drama of continents

cycles of ennui

I foresee

numberless verdet

through poisonless camels

I am speaking of the camels as strange incendiary hives

never pursued by human likeness or example

I see in an Atnongara stone

no humans existing

not even collapsed ravines

in which vessels were destroyed

it was like the thirst on the planet Venus

 it was the farthest aphelion of Uranus

like a subjective transfer

being the maze

between a rock of arrows & intangible coma

& I

the hummingbird

rayless & adumbral with voyage

with a quest to discharge chimera

so as to transmute fire of dismemberment from the earth

the stunted forests

the listless charcoal snow

& like the Yamanas of Tierra del Fuego

I am isolate

a flickering trace floating between life & death

only visible as survival

inclemently weaned

from my hoar-frost guide

from my shark in darkened renewal

I am part animal

part death

part sun

part of the Earth in crucial vermiform dislodgement

as if the collective seminal hut

were struck by the flight from a dead person's powers

vermiform dislodgement technical warfare by weather

control of storms by machine

the dead person's power my flight of war

against weather by technocracy

against plagiarized powers condensed as bewitched degree

I am a fire sprinkling powder

around the root of tenebrous locusts

so that they reveal themselves by telepathic rupture

by sudden indigo expansion

thus

a differential weather by shift in subconscious explosives

an interior ecology

electro-magnetic with glacier

with atonal wasps

with loss by reactive identity

therefore

I return to visual severity

to loss of sight by upper visual roots

by a vitality that negates all radial serenity by assumption

such as method that has never scaled

the guile of initiation by haunting

by wakeless spiral in-melodia

one can never see in me a mechanics of glass

a rootless inertia

that expands & contracts by spectral phylogenesis

yet

I am a bird whose trace is transparence

whose voice contains the phase of nomadic biology

always roaming between anti-sun & anti-sun
within unfixed haven

so I take as my soma
totalic fragment before breathing
before memory by in-direction
before mitosis
before geographic surging

I have left struggle by entropy
in quest of what the guide bearers call
aurific eternity
my voice being movement by gainful enigma

in this regard
I roam by variable blindness
by de-inventive plentitude
on fire with immaterial flaw

I have never herded myself
or lost my fluctuation
by collective absolution

I am that singular bird
whose crossed the wall of death
overcoming my former optical identity

before death by burning algor

I was the size of 2 Swifts

my stamina was implicit migration

I could traverse a gulf of ice

I could name as my province portions of Scotland

yet I had never been healed by the glory of negation

I had never crossed by flight painful curse as resurrection

I ceased to respire by the algid fire to the abyss

of the Andean mountain caves

as if the Earth had moved a billionth parsec from the sun

my wings withdrew

I had a scavenger's dust in my eyes

it was abrasive evolution by veil

by noiseless personal inferno

my flight deranged by ghosts

my amplitude demasted by kindled carrion pumas

lifted out of myself

no longer of a cleansed tropical order

seized at the root by blaze as iconic terror

by a penetrant force

replacing the cells in my darkened bodily ravine

suddenly bled by cold poseidons

dangerously living by powerful coma in a mirror

watching myself waft

listening to suns rising & dying

like planetesimals from Vulcan

spawning a light from stunted alien mechanics

these are planets in a 'liquid water zone'

astrologically predicted

by Vulcan

Draconis

by Alpha Centauri

me

the analogous bird

like modified radii in dimness

concerning transmigration

concerning beams via the Pleiades

so each self-examination was Anubis

was the hoar-frost lizard

& was nothingness even minus my gift of shrillness

I no longer existed

the alabaster shark circled my implosion as dread

while the hoar frost lizard would whisper

concerning Vulcan's appearance in the thought forms

of the Akkadians

that would never again be visible to myself

that my form had been abducted

that my climate was lost to any flight or spawning

according to calendrical mass

I was hidden

cancelled

between polarity as index & 'Holonomic Equation'

I was a code

a death glimpse of riddles

the bird whose value was old diamond as plague

whose deluge as drift as asymptotic posture

according to omen

I was dead

for 3 savage days

I was forced to confess my foundation

my violation as existing

& my graph

the simple noise I exuded from poisoned fragmentary ponds

& my defiance near death during enigmatic hail

the shark & the hoar-frost lizard

searched by implicit probing

by charismatic concealment

then the hoar-frost lizard revealed

that I could uproot disorder

that I could conquer in-luminous ailment

then

94

my trunk & my wings began to arise from indefinite
desolation
like a trace who shifts through rain fields
kinetic in the dark
enabled by being hidden from others

& these others
outside the trace world
of the hoar-frost lizard
of the alabaster shark

for instance
a she-wolf
a cheetah
a mangrove swamp naked with cobras

for instance
sea ethers spinning
as in the Straits of Messina
or mirage in transitional dimension

transmuted after the body & before the death of the body
within the scope of ceremonial essence

that essence over & above which is the elixir to transform
to heal
to enact global reparation

the cobras

the caduceus of what the planetary form calls heat

in foliage spun from the sea

I see my trace

above the alabaster shark

he was white-gold & dimmed

then blood re-alit

as indefinable archaic

with the length of 12 bears

& eyes of greenish mythical boars

then the hoar-frost lizard

said

that the cobras he had killed were now jade

I drank the ornament of ordeal

my throes were condensed as the action of the Sun

I had condoned the limits of 3 mental wells

& spun the rays of idolatrous flux

I was host to the inadequate

all my regions were burning

I was concomitant with the cells in pure mystical volcanoes

I was in no way adequate
to seize prior bodily equilibrium

yet I was vernal
I could recast viridity

perhaps
as floating clairaudience
as 'Central Asian' meditation
as one whose nome is unalterable
being the climate of 'transtemporal perspective'
having risen from the uproar of a cacophonous 'fetish house'

a solemn dromedary world
where the hoar-frost lizard aligned me with horses
propelled by rhythmic scorpion chatter

& this chatter half of the aforementioned cobras
a dark libidinous wolf
3 non-observable widows

naturally evinced as conflict
spiders
dogma
contemptible suggestion

in this degree

I relate to the eagle

to a motionless glossary peering from the vertex

me

the hummingbird grace invaded by lizards

me

the tense sclerotic shaman

ironically bred by a liquid alabaster shark

in the latter degree I am liminal

at the 'lowest scale of intensity'

being sound by blank Laryngograph

of course

to the human form I am missing

I am he never bled by arousal

I am he whose advanced beyond gravitational restrictive

the bird ghost

the 'solarized'

the upper anguish

the 'ornithomorphic' transmission

re-vealed & de-revealed

as essence

as stranger to habitable oasis

I was then released to vacuums
to anterior detonations

yet none of these blanknesses healed me
none of them allowed me succor

my voice was scribbled
by great initiation as yield

it could be said
that I'm implied by torrential frondage
that each nome that I've invaded
is a Uranian diaspora of glints

with a fire inside my talons
I have never known
the one forgetful lineage
the sacerdotal bone trail
inspired by one geometry or lectern
or the radiogenetic in matter

what I speak of are igneous glints in the bone
from the first flotational suns
from the first intangible kelvins
then gradated as stellar combinings
like the map of a shark with bluish centigrade odours

because life has combined as an autonomic nerve share

each angstrom

a curious portion

a deadly lightning gem

a furious pan-glyphic

because

to adhere to geochronology

is to take on the fuel of pestilence

is to model a perfect death as resistance

because

there is leakage from phyla

spells from constituent redress

so that capture is magically escaped & re-spun

so that I can listen to terrain

as a firmament in exile

able to dwell within this leakage

understanding the flow in a sparkling helium sea

& so my guides

the hoar-frost lizard

the alabaster shark

engulf me strangely with the scent of a hieroglyphic

panther

allowing me the grace of positional non-function

so as

to ignite with various hues

neoteric being

100

able to exist as a cycle

without beginning or end

with time no longer centered in a simple iodine gulf

or lessened by incessant human replica as crowding

no

no number by industrial sorcery

because this sorcery has maimed it

he formerly living on Earth

for instance:

the Caspian Tiger

the Ascension Flightless Crake

then it is suggested by the lizard

that I do further penance in a foundry of salt

where my wounds will burn brighter

where each eye will be tested by illusionistic hooks

& I the hummingbird in his so named ordeal

with the range of 2 swiftlets

ravaged by suspended signs

by elapsed conjugations

it is I

a quantum decibel beyond direct ordeal

with my ghostly plumage lingering

with scorching festivity in secret

consumed by deliverance

waiting

to fly up the spiral groves'

'cut in the shaman tree'

yet I suffer throughout a crucible of lapses

where memory blurs with hypomnesia

where each count

each forgery by containment

begins a new carnivorous water in my ravines

which announces

3 new vocabularies or seals

first: suggestive distance from a flailing concentration

at the next remove: thirst for primordial carvings

thirdly: sulfur as mixed with a de-inductive fleece

because I inhabit the non-tangible

I cannot spare watcr

being imbued by ceaseless threats

contained in the evil of hominids

because of such seizure

I remain bereft

ceasing to re-cease existing

as though pulled by doubled blight through inaudia

according to this epilogue of grammar

the Earth must be weaned from its dominant visible

ordination

the apogees

the wastes

the boulders

the glass which inveigles tundra

therefore

I am trace as stunning pontoon soldier

such is the depth of the sigil

& the 3 seals are sigils

vulcanized with advancement

I am the parable of the bird lined with 3 wells

the first: skillful oleander

the second: baneful bout with snow on the steppes

the third: devastation by devastation as optometry

invaded

by the x-rays of lizards

I have become over-blended

by perfect moaning as corrosion

as inclement resuscitation

so collective questions can be asked

am I polarized by solitude & abscission?

do I proclaim myself as the monarch of self-sacrifice?

will I re-arise as palpable deity?

what I can say

is that my coma has been inscripted on the force field

of the living

& I've emerged as flight by nervous settlement

by broach in electrical nuance

by flame as ghostly disorder

yet the alabaster shark

& the hoar-frost lizard

continue to cmit themselves by cause as circular hissing

claiming transparency

claiming stamina from orational mangers

so would I thereby defend the gully of soil as God?

would I usurp his implied dimension by dysfunctional indirection?

would new codes of celestial invasion give me the

unresolved hubris

the absolute dictation to transform the whirlwind

of firmaments?

for instance

transpontification in the Maharajah's glare

or

fluttering by force throughout the sub-human

through the fact of negated visage

a vibration of algae

as the orthodox equation of God

being

neither burning rocks or nuance

nor theological commandeering

nor truth through unsullied proportion

though alive by being dead

I see myself as flames in a mirror

carving my powers in sand

so to hallucinate as fragment

one must exist as a millstone of vapour

as participatory stealth

being flight as meandering through ruin

God being

argument by emanations flow by ethical negative

commitment to 'alien necessity'

God being rupture

being sound by rapturous cacophony

so my wings imperil systems

as I derive from hypostasis

amalgams through feeding as accusation

through ignited cellular harm

not localized brevity

but scattered suns

across a background blaze

alive with dense volcano prairies

indifferent to waking

to shifting moral slaughter

possibly equaled by a geometric anguish

or grisly theological ensconcement

by haunted maps

by erratic seclusion

I have been seared in my numbness

by 3 mixtures of ferocity

by rubiginous shrillness

by involutional plotting

by cold disordered piercings

106

I do not block myself from flying

by somnific dissolution

saying this

I understand duration

as if I were an oracle

instinctively invigoured by hypnotic fuel

by a wayward series of syllabics

ventriloqual

savage

indigestible as to hearsay

as temporized phonics from the soured volcano of sharks

through transmogrified vocation

the hoar-frost lizard implied

how many birds would I glean through investigation?

would they be Myrmidons?

or would the word angels apply?

true

I re-invent enigma & abrasion

having been granted

3 circular utopias

above Siberian reindeer omens

being a blank diurnal cooling

where days are lived as hidden

where the malformation of wheat

would dictate my intercession through gravity

numerous incarnations will test me

yet I float

above the hoar-frost lizard on land

& the alabaster shark beneath the sea

I am the triple incandescence called the Sun

the numerous equator

presenting life to its various forms

certainly not a fennel induced by mechanical aims

nor a Cypress misread by the Pre-Cambrian

no the respirating realms akin to Ediacara

like oracles suddenly sprung from abundance

from detonation by blankness

encircled by tempestuous organics

& so my alabaster shark

of different volcano & barrier

has guided me

through oxidized omissions

which includes

the volatility of chondrites

asteroidal refraction

equanimity which equates

with blank incendiary speed

with coronas

with interminable neon immersion

alive

with a neural plentitude

which chronicles each depth with uncertainty

then the hoar-frost lizard

announces the 'Orion arm'

the 'Perseus' conglomerate

the brightened sketch in 'Sagittarius'

as if each formation

were a darkened musical escarpment

where evidence ignites

like a curious suggestion or document

inside a central nucleus

of monarchical dioxide

as though the argument of my guides had blended

as though their electric interaction

has allowed me a thermal non-confinement

a simplified invasion by unstable boundary

like ghosts that accrue

by metamorphic decibel

by alternative incoherence

so I must ask tautologically

do transmixtures occur by rotted iron & water?

are they separate

as dearth by initial being?

or are they the same arousal by capacity?
as preparation by inverse scarcity?

one is allowed the need of riddles to parry death
to arrive at the bi-articulate
by transverse molecules as surgery

leaking being the pantheon of one drowning
another death selling blood on the winds

by guides
suggestive vectors
perhaps
luminous indirection
perhaps
solemn diversity by evil

my life between realms
they've summoned
as by ammoniated glare
they pursue me as Uranian singularity
as one who dispels the tropical dice of misfortune
because I am one who articulates dearth by ambrosia
by sound as nectarous imbalance

of course
I am skittish by pursuit
skittish as the flames of a puzzling communion
110

a studious velocity?
creative helium by nuance?

thus
I am the symbol who de-exists
unknown by ether
or buried nautical bell

perhaps a sun overexposed
by sudden hydrogen misnomer
somehow equated to the weight
on the surface soil of Phobos
to its blackness
to its anti-pattern as rifeness
far beyond inner bartering condoned
by devious malfunction

& malfunction is the labour of corrective intuition
being the stoma of birds which separates advance
by the activated spirit which spars with itself
which timorously concludes upon totalic abstraction
as pattern

so to speak of mongoose shelter
of blatant equine code
irregularly burned by blank umbilical ferocity
instinctively a-lit by my alabaster shark
by my hoar-frost lizard

crossing & recrossing

by barriers

that evince a pure invisible wrath

in turn

a strenuous felicity

with its powers focused at an upward remove

above tribal engenderment

as de-focused mass

exposed by revelation

because as mass transmutes on this plane

my claws blur

my inner directive remains in-disposed

according to bleak interior specific

to absolve injury that causes death

to absolve the dead struggling against detachment

& torment

the hoar-frost lizard conveys to me

such feats of the depths

take on the fact of an inverted tripartite healing

essential as the feats

of hieratic resolve

yet wandering into nullity

that cause the dead to absolve

the venous forms of their uncommon beauty
yet ironically reduced to ecumenical brewing

there exists in this state inclement fetal anointment
tempestuous chronicles
a vertigo of spells

so one if left listless
hovering between clouding & daybreak
between consequence as vertigo & resplendence

if I carry in my bill fault lines scattered by mystery
it is to instar on a slate of vacuums
new endemics for breathing

not night
yet not of diurnal complexity

because there exists a thirst
that extends from fumes
from pointless vapour & honey
its source
being pure impression by depth
by innuendo that matches bewitchment

not an adventurous agitation
nor a compound refraction

but a dazed endemic

randomly etched as a symbol on 3 wharves of fire

no

I am not a fate pointlessly spelled

on Vitruvian misnomer

yet my magnification horrifies

& strikes down all limit

so that the bottomless theology of ash

reveals the splitting of cobras

crushed in a mirror

& my alabaster shark

attempting to sway me with optional reasoning

gives me

monerans as one option

then calcareous spindles as alphabetic monsters

as for extrinsic action

there exists

only the lowered corrosions of time

an obscure caliginous blinding

yet within this crevasse

there is breeding

but again

not of decisive equilibrium

of course

as a lobotomized entity

there exists disharmony & brooding

my enemy being protraction

my enemy being a bluish astral sickness

moreover

a black eclectic liquid

containing lava as pre-election

as interior fuel by vociferous spell

a consecration

which swallows up resistance

therefore

I digest all unborn cobras

then dive for medicinal rust beneath the sea

I then equate inside myself

unknown burial by land

bringing myself to speak in nebulous Hottentot specifics

I am then the higher power

the defender of defenseless deafness

because

I have chosen by the dead

by the séance as ventriloqual codex

flocks of parrots appear & disappear

as though a magic 'annatto' accrues by heretical spirit

as though a flock from my voice

had allowed a hidden wheat to flower

as though compressed remnants

were culled from antithetical Hidalgos

from voiceless Telestos

being a language arcane with umbras

taught by expired masters

flinching in their dreams

because the dead possess life

possess the beauty of de-existence

which arises & re-arises

like the whirling blood within the language of lightning

the obscurity

the half-lit omegas

which blaze inside themselves

as a pantheon of idols

feasting as wolves on answerless numbers

one feels the impression of camphor & flame

of distances shimmering with viragos

& these viragos

take as their calling the beauty of pranayamas

whose unctuous verdict

seems condoned by celestial telepathy

which reveals through its motion an uncertain surge

a de-invested voyage

certainly

not the central scrutiny

which exudes from ceremonial blizzards

& these blizzards are my guides

my hoar-frost lizard

my stunning alabaster beast

electrically transmixed

so as to obviate theoretical personas

thus

I am permitted no locales of burning

no profile as testament

no worship pursued through autocratic foundation

a non-demonstrable edict

linked to garish parallels to weather

to barometers

to heights on a surface of the moon

bleached by epic monsoon seasons

then again

I could apply myself to rancid locales

to the Ox befouled waters of Delhi or Burma

then appearing as flying from ghostly pagodas

in the Celebes or the Philippine Sea

further pursuing my task in Reykjavik as a warbler

possibly flying through greenish moons near Guadeloupe

or ingesting indigo displacement in the Mexico basin

or the Tehuantepec Ridge

I have not yet obtained the life that's fated for me

healing the radioactive transfer currents

or the fevers which exist inside of diabetic rock

no

I now breathe at the borders of transgressive chaos

letting my animal guides declare through sleep

oblong messages by stag

by Siberian crow

by Antarctic bear

they are their hidden spectral cinders

their moats

their strange ingested reductions

the lizard says to me

the shark will sing you songs

he will take barriers away from courage

he will speak to you in dark Malaysian rainstorm

in pelagic septentrional acres

my guides

spectres threaded by vertigo

118

glare at me

with yellowed mockery in their eyes

yet selfless

as murmurous intangible basins

conducting the spirit of great electrical cordilleras

as if discovering in my presence

powers subsumed in sub-orbital eels

listening to my de-existent mazes

entwined by Augean arcana

within a bloodless intangible ray

like explosive halos from a Heliomaster's colours

or a telepathic orchid

giving off odours from aboriginal rivulets

charred soliloquies

that obscure & reveal by answerless randomity

so I am never devoid of ordeal

not unlike suns forensic with origin

it is what certain terrestrial beings

superficially invoke

as simple sugars or atoms

or periodicity by table

the atomic principle

seemingly random by meter

then coalesces to less than proportional kindling

mystery being fact

by threadless exterior counting

each counter-blended dictum

a mirage

condoned by intangible wavering

by skeptical inferno

wrought by skeptical ballast as drizzle

all this due to a core

alive with plummeted searches for boundary

as decibel

as mathematic aggression

say

I fly through swamps fired by dehydration

through the sudden fuel of monsters

'how would your wings feel'? says the hoar-frost lizard

'how would your blood react spinning in a spider's grove'?

'in a dwelling of alligator's bones'?

'in counter-intuitive gases that mumble'?

then the alabaster shark

with his wavering skeletal reprieve

testing generic biological limit

knowing in his depths that ground burns

that water deceives

that concentration wavers

like random scorching through entrails

having lost my hearing

due to interior monsoon

the alabaster shark began snapping at my shadows

& because he was snapping at my shadows

I began hearing in my coma

his vigil

his infernal spiral

& the sea in which he swam became a dazzling lenticular

Venus

that brightened to shell-orange & red

then birds began flying from his teeth

eagles

gannets

hawks

strange winged vervets

tottering on desiccation

contained by collective debility

never knowing the terror of their own brightness

& here was the alabaster shark

his snout pointing

to a dark archaic wind vault

beyond the gravid sway ensconced in tangled

zodiacs & realms

what came to me in my terror

was that first light

that initial cause from anonymous vibration

thereby being

above flaw & bird & cataract

above sway beyond death counts

because of this

I witnessed a halo of eels in his voice

their digested spell

like horizontal conifers

ghostly

wriggling

indeterminate

partially stunned by exfoliated contrast

the alabaster shark

a sub-order of strange leopards

of drowning sapphire whales

reflected by nutation from sheets of mirrored horizons

because the shark

liminally dead

totemically expired

yet containing the truth by darting speculum

I

the Hillstar

of the 'Suborder Trochili'

with '8 pairs of ribs'
with lateral nostrils
with 'extensile' 'tongue'
with higher than 10 'vertebrae'
I do not exist by self-poison

in my former realm of Mount Chimborazo
then amplifying its heights into the powers of Peru
ubiquitous with singularity
interior with contradiction
then degenerately feeding on degenerate extracts
of snow

I was called bird by smoking mother distance
foil to biographic monotony
prey to excessive soma by solitude

never human by extrinsic glandular assessment
but feast by disorder
by exclusion that precludes dice as accessible
principle

me
the bird
whose moon & sun remains a gambler's disorder
a median fatigue
carking
like theological separation

being weightless marks
that attempt to describe the void
by monarchical decree

identity ceases to exist by barrier
by pre-occupation with extrinsics
by form that claims its links to pre-judgement

motion then occurring through hypothetical resuscitation
through argument as thought
by flow as debated parallel continuum

perhaps I've evaded the sums
that chronicle the myth internal to lorikeets
so that they continue to glow as general incarnadine moons
so as to elevate within the spirit of transmundane
ephemera

I do not suggest as my manner
the ordeal of lorikeets
or the music of lorikeets
with all my assessment defocused by their symmetry

as if my blood were a sobering fuse
or a projected form of death light

& I do not suggest this as abstract assessment
nor grafted dictation
as descriptive pedigree or largesse

to the same degree
I have never foiled suggestion by mirror
or by coldly spinning diamond fossils
merely focused by cosmological enactment

perhaps courier by threaded salt
perhaps persistence by equilibria
this is how I gained escape
from the bloody scrolls
from the darkened alligator beds
I remained emptied
neutered
stung to the core by suggestion

I then prospered by momentary salt
gaining balance by caliginous entreaty

never summoned like some exterior bird or priest
from archdioceses or alters
I have come from worlds never tainted
by structural inventions or curses

never the exoteric letter
superficially evolved
from reading invoked by compositional errata

it is by gainful self-instruction through voids
that I am guided

as in magic lightning exploration
flying by dream across mongoose borders
to absorb the hebetic glare
of my alabaster shark
of my hoar-frost lizard
paradoxical
dying
expressive through toneless power
through deadly famine in their speech
so that they remain
ominous
eclectic
void
charismatic spectres
wandering around a numinous circular brink

& at this brink
a cosmic ocular thirst
engendering
a vernal blue mass
being a sun uprisen from the dead

126

emitting by its light

a bluish curse from the abyss

sending me spirits

bursts

that spin as sourceless energies beyond suns

being a humming

like a burst of wakeless silk

that exists

as a collision of spells

being

a combination of hell & the condition on land

released through birdless viaducts

through contradictory exposure to comets

that wander as nomadic spirals

analogous to myself as runic incendiary tension

so that

I've been brought to myself as critical vertebrae

of greenness

with a new cervical lair

with a new mortality by transfer

& by transfer

that which engulfs which supersedes entropy

by crucial centigrade release

those nutrients

emitting mosaics of solitude

those elixirs that invade the body's carbon

with a qualitative tumult

with energetic prolongation

alive with an inhalation

that sifts through the tissue

that transmutes decay

& the 3 of our bodies

as living axial links

as invisible vertical scrawling

like a blank galvanic tree

part lizard

park shark

part bird

yet I seem as one unlinked

consumed by parallel disorder

as he who dwells by self-haunted demeanour

by numerical force contained in bewitched injustice

of course I seem maimed by subsidiary beasts

by jackals

by infortuitous haunting by crocodile

seeking to dwell inside my blood

like a sun transfixed by parasites

but I am he who explores by alchemical flux

being magus as animal paradox

I

who scales fire by intuition

above the scope of tortured animal wanderings

above those birds dispossessed

by a world that has failed as spontaneous nascence

so I see such birds as jackals

as exponential mazes

reflecting my lizard in a falling crocodile's body

as the karmic offspring of my dying alabaster shark

enveloped

skittish

I am of that race of vanished antelope

yet alive

in the depth of blue volcanic deltas

an antelope

incarnadine

winged

storming across the opaque flows of green volcano lakes

like a blurred velocity

being vanished carbon in fractals

being diagonal by reversed existence

perhaps

a futile carrion spark

or blank expansive gain through water

I cannot say

that beyond the mongoose valley there is salient ferocity

or alchemic fact as the chatter of eagles

no

as if translated reflection

focused on negating a zone

3 or 4 barbarous moons ago

& this 5 billion year seclusion of Earth

being a portion of rambling eternities

pullulating beyond my central capacity of depth

this is why my visibility is darkened

to the Barbthroat Hummingbirds seeking territorial portion

I am dead to visibility

dead to that which opens accessibility & colour

such as the 'Cinnamon-throated hermit'

or the 'Black-throated mango'

even

if the Sun were reduced to a matchless viridian

there would nevertheless exist

130

life as primal lacunae

as entangled initiation

conducted through treacherous suspension

I do not exist as model

say as a dove

or as burning bread

I am the initiates' explosion

the primeval flaw

spell after indigenous spell

I therefore declare my wounds

as emblems against bondage

against that which extolls the significance of

pre-deceased being

I exist

as that interior gust that outlasts old uranium yields

no

certainly not a dogmatized cosmology

nor drift that enfetters by moral extrinsics

even

while bewitched by discomfort

I feel as if cast beyond my own biology as excursion

beyond my lexical diptych

as a blank contaminate swan

crossing & recrossing by arcane inferential

a holographic range

bringing about a wave

being intrinsic simultaneity by spirit

not a singular herding by trauma

nor a herded degradation throughout the afterlife

but a tendril

connecting spiraling registers of the firmament

high basaltic ghosts being a firmament

being sand & fire within snowlight

being Mongol blaze from forgotten horsemen

gold

as in the hoar-frost lizard

as in the alabaster shark

being transitional carbon

being shock by stormy anti-blaze

or

an anti-metrical hesitation

balanced between judgements

the Sun as exploded rock-fish

as light from an odd incendiary leper

perhaps a genesis a quarrel a mandala

so there is vapour by essence
by fur as tantric spoils
being brilliance as living endurance
as central kinetic
connected by blue inferno
fields

that flow from the empyrean downward
like an irradiated oestrous
like a cyanoethene or sucrose
engendering power with courage that shatters
gryphons

a torrential commitment
a light more essential than sonar

so that it breathes
& gives off concussion by essence

therefore
never conclusion as peril
as galling forensic exposure
never merging with codes
or definitives encaged

the gryphons being definitive of astral menace
to be born & shattered

menace to be absorbed & expelled

as if by menace my trace were eternally deleted

but I remain enriched by symbolical spell

no matter the fire of the gryphons

no matter the heat that arches from regions

there exists the hellish in the void of the invisible

this ambivalent domain crossing white-hot air

the movements of the gryphons being akin to vehicular
androgyny

their indefinite number like newly engendered eels

being blankness floating between poles

my preternatural glance consuming their ambiguity

many magnifications below the realm of dialectical
archery

so in terms of the physical deity

I exist as provocative incursion

inducing anomaly by embranglement

by consequence

by over-exposure to discipline

in this interior liminality

drift by supersessional withdrawal

with rays which extend

from my deftly coloured ozone beak

seeing myself by x-ray as if dead

as proto nectar or whisper

or perhaps a rock imbued with curious penetrating tension

a whispered integrating mixture

antediluvian as glance through scent & flame

alive

inside as regions of aural core

flying through soured volcano hulls

witnessing

remnants

sparks from floating amber canals

much like crucial power in a sea beneath the sea

this being oblique omission as sound

giving me in essence

a working aerial dust

a Uranian salt that absorbs its force

from spontaneous doxology

a peculiar solar interior

which exudes pure exodus in extremis

exodus being the orientation of itself

outside the schism of ideology as rotation

which are my feathers that transcribe
the mazes of my molten battlefield

the cacophony
the listless exposure to heraldry
is neither proof or its opposite
of a densely sealed clairaudience

is neither blockage
nor aim
nor subversion

it is the fever of energy across limits

having died & been reborn within the exchange of dying
acre after phantasmic acre

that is why dying is vertigo
is relapse through countless anonymities
like a shape of spoilage released as concomitant deafness
so that no law is settled
being background or confinement that yields as agreement

one is cancelled
one is penetrant with staining

& it is a transitional staining

a level where heat & mal-advancement

overtake any previous instinctual yield

within chemically prone boundaries of counting

within accurate but precarious speech before dying

& this is my merger & departure

from my alabaster shark

from my hoar-frost lizard

yet distinct from any strained or schismatic solitude

as betrayal

being alive between deaths

between burning mystifications

in this interstice between speaking & dying

I have absorbed incalculable power

as if wheat or ash were thrown inside water

none of my bones being fixed

my polar soliloquy void of intrinsic certainty

seemingly fed by bitter food

emitted from my body

via the shocks I receive

by means of illusive devourment

by alligator suns turned green in the bones

the liminal water gone black with necrotics

yet I am possessed by gusts that blow from the
fire of the living

not the loss of the undead
but their osmotic balance

unlike elks that burn
or human proof culled from central hatred

these gusts
a comingling of powers
seemingly centred by ashen tendency of compunctious
malfunction
these gusts
as liberty by pronation
being a blinded registration
enigmatic & unbound like wind through a falling crag

I feel
as a gallery of stunned eagles reduced to a trace
listless
yet alert
as an energy across chasms
as a de-invigoured solar locale

& because
of the projection across gulfs
the land inside mongoose waters ceases to scorch

138

as if my shark had darkened like an eel inside suns

or become in my being

a demountable vapour

a decomposed summit

& my guides are not ghosts

superficial with guile

nor parasitic with vacuity

no

they are not akin to an owl deflecting through each abyss

with dysfunction

whose journey is condemned to sound as lowered suspension

all fragmentary beings

can pronounce my cells

as being at the core of unliving

those beings

whose sole concentration

limited to outer appearance

like the gryphons

neither land or by sea

but burning by peripheral wastage

condoned as emission through error

condoned by peripheral powers

curiously sustained by rectangular demarcation as glyph

being apart from themselves

theses powers

these gryphons

always haunted by cimmerian suggestion

a purplish kind of radium

linked to bodiless grasses on Pluto

this being example

of their analogous physical emanation

at a level

where density & immaculate probability co-reside

given this realia of helium

I now possess this blank ability

from range

through & beyond the 'Sun door'

'of which no true report has even been made'

'distant and...unseen target'

electric with imperishable violet

incontrovertible with dolorous mica or limit

again

not empirical with scale

nor with incendiary tempest scaled down to reason

reason exists

with no known equivalent to obstacle of terror as arousal

which strikes the hearing as metal

like music perfidious full of shocking & blindness

in keeping with this degree

I am Merganser

Auk

eaglet in ruins

outside my body

outside any sudden helium dharma

with its vacuums of indifference

because

I've disappeared from the cold of the Andes

I am now

the disintegrated ark

the dialectic through inversion

higher than flames from algid lava beds

invoking lightning taboos

untitled by conformity to the parasites

& these are energies that roam

through intangible sanguinary fields

like a peculiar form in a crumbling phlogiston house

strangely secreting from itself

an ironic candescence from glistening chariot water

perhaps a galaxy evolved from broken Lucifer eaglets

or disintegrating serums

or storms from sullen Bedouin numbers

but the prime nigredo

known in certain pantheons as Oreotrochilus estella

enigmatically deduced

from a hill of glass on the Sun

to the human sieve

my volcanic remnant is a listless shattering kettle

a splayed intent of voices

ferocious as anarchic spiritual drift

much in keeping

with disseminated wolves transmuted by a séance of bears

being Andean & knowing the Sun in North Borneo

becomes a memorized burst

not unlike the yellowed philanthropy from cobras

because by opening my secret dispensation

I can sing by means of Paraguayan locust

by means of blinded index lizard

as if

from a dual or fragmented paradigm

perhaps howling

perhaps vocal ambiguous flaw

nevertheless

something much deeper than harried perceptual givens

my motility lives by ingressive trance

by means of spontaneous fulminate theatre

simultaneous with risk as implied complexity

again

ordeal as fissure

as folio by terror through witness

& there exists

nothing but these emissions

being oblique & subterranean with whisper

leaping out of itself

so as to re-absorb itself

as beatific occupation by fire

by an invincible form of solitude

floating through pre-occurrence

being fed upon scattered vapour as milk

such is my feral cosmogony

like a random spark from gathered mountains

& these sparks are mirrors glistening in adumbral brilliance

being a world reflected

through greenish travertine momentum

far beyond any common animal garden

being a habitable neon near Alpha Centauri

parallel to creatural flasks

to explosive obelisks as monsoons

Alpha Coronae Borealis

Gamma Cygni

Beta Cassiopeia

'Blue-white' binaries

'white' supergiants

rattling

outside common power ignited as basalt

take blood from various birds

take shards from psychic singing posts

then divide & subdivide their ruthless kindling spectres

until one flies into the depths like a flame through

cylindrical monads

instantaneous

at one with mounts in the uranic

thus

I coincide with dust that glistens

by aerial mirage

by moons that dwell within a nexus of saffron

I do not speak as flight

solely connected to the slavery of flowers

or to sensitive mass morbid within the

dwelling of ghats

perhaps my seed will ascend from vatic underwater

graves

or from rhapsodic cinders

summoned from catatonia

each leap by embitterment

by plague

by autocratic shepherd

by Altaic law

by demonical impoverishment

seeing far beyond the bolted nostrum

or the transgressive stirrup

scientifically condoned by passionless criteria

I

the Henbane Bird

the shaman reduced to nigredo

alive

within ophthalmic limit

yet always unseen

by beings

whose use or study is according to scale

or to coded numbers accorded to vicuna

no

my range extends far beyond my former physical borders

north & east of Latacunga

south & east of the city of Quito

during my former visibility

slitting about staggering lancetilla

with their cavernous incidentals

having flown with wild horses to the height of Cotopaxi

gazing inside its Condor's mirror

just to quote its reflected ash

then flying down its clouded slope

the mirror & Cotopaxi being one

seeing sled dogs run across oriental lava

watching ambiguous extremes in Martian glacial valleys

such is the mirror

a nostrum

a scope

a terror

according to these intrinsic ambiguities

these dogs remain a glyph

part trance

part spectacled bear as illusion

or with my wing

my death

my bone cage

they are proto-initiatory gain

they are cliffs

they are molecules unraveled

a suspended embranglement

above a floating Condor pasture

like a rabid mongoose yield

condemned to arduous consumption

across this transitional void

the sea whispers inside my alabaster shark

the land burns with my hoar-frost lizard counting

cipher minus cipher

with all conundrums as fleeting

I remain

this candescent attempt

to re-weigh my body from death

my energy being

a power achieved by parallel lunation

a bartered quarry

an ignited morale

yet this morale

poisoned by the scent of lancetilla's in coma

perfectly erubescent as spiral

as one who now floats

through the daunting biography of spirits

the hoar-frost lizard

evolved from a river of diamonds

the alabaster shark spun from a stony oasis

then their habits reversed

by formless liturgical imprint

& I

the Henbane Bird

being purview as paradoxical witness

as if escaped from boiling in-boron bark

watching blood as it drops on my proto-alchemical wings

purifying

strengthening the Andes

I have not lost the sleepless bells in my eyes

necromantically prepared from entering different

'celestial regions'

my body being a bloodless ritual boat

unlike monetary alloy or bronze

life being a plane

an individual gulf

magically traversed by alchemic flotation

like the optic notion contained in hypnotic re-occurring

wheat

there is this encircling deafness

magnified as circuitous stellar protraction

absorbed by signal

by hieroglyphic glass

like a strange Phoenician splintering

magnetically tuned to numerous grammars

to the ritual bleeding of birds

I am at one with the Araucanians

mixing different blood with different blood

a Shaman mixing blood with an aspirant

with a whole philologist

with invincible vocal scorching

with un-melodious probing

allowing for second sight

allowing for those nauseous with health of the insalubrious

an intrinsic cleansing

the hoar-frost lizard gives me a bull to behold

an incantatory bullock

with a hail of knives

breathing

repetitious

in various glimpses of emerald

akin to a moon floating in archaic rivulets

these rivulets

being fire in invisible vines

rising from a blur of kindled somas

like an emptied skin

transfusing

with Araucanian Vileos
the Great God shaman
with truth of intangible portent

therefore
my blood is mixed with isolation
with a compensatory jaguar
with a lattice of poisonous feathers
with intoxicated verdet
an internal weather
absorbing stars that evolve from pure peninsular
rotation

say
in India
or volcanic Malaya
I take as substance that which post-exists

it is power throughout that which post-exists

it is power throughout vatic criteria
not a replica of molecules
nor a curious dance
nor a remedy for being

ritual being oxidation as terror
as broken unitary fleece

as dis-endowed nullity as supposition

much like a tangled schism loitering in glass

or is this speaking as nomenclature by neglect?

or by great or terminal frenzy by exposure?

perhaps

trinomial mist

perhaps

sexagesimal fragment by indifference

questions flow through me

like a bi-partitioned sun

like a sterility supervened by bottomless coruscation

my essence therefore living

as blasphemous oxidation

as intervening scope beyond unblemished drainage

& from this can I submit

that the hoar-frost lizard

a theologist?

the alabaster shark

a noun by religious imbroglio?

none of these glimpses quite burns

yet they subsist in my voice by taciturn magnetic

my vertebrae stunned by complexification & wavering
imploded by anti-congealment

the being
variolate
blemished
with transverse sorties welling up

the killings I've sought in my ice warren
my instinctual drift by devious navigation
being fire that flares
from internal crippling
from compound ruination

I
the sudden Hillstar
the advocate of dawn
floating through excruciating darkness
sensing & not sensing the gold from tainted
magical doors
being gold as carnivorous anaemia

through my implosional traces there is hearing
black acoustical cleansing
being pure absorption through crystal

& by hearing there comes to view
a ghostly elevation of rays

finding hibernating teeth in my voice

their dark behavioural streaks gliding with imbalance

appearing & disappearing through green ascensional

smoke

unlike the gryphons

they appear from a unity of hives

from stark dimensional mercuries

flowered with steepness & sudden erasure of form

the alabaster shark

gives them to me as his ghosts

as his subdivided guides

projecting new & equivocal lessons on resurrection

& these lessons focus upon cyclical verdet

on each life that I assume

more magnificent with each rising

like fire from inclement labour

& so the implicit expunges the oblivious

stored in prior electrical confoundings

my legend supernally stained on spinning scorpion

tablets

watching my being stray & resist

to the factor that endures throughout protodivination

at times like a fish with feeble buttressing odours

a rotational factor

a blank alchemical exhibit

addressed to beasts

who neither see nor believe

they

who could never resolve

tragic mystic ore as foundation

I

the bloodless boat

subject to hissing of jackals

to wayward heckling trees

yet my trace

overarching their fate

by fire of supernal archery

by auscultation as photology

by heliographic leaven

being living compunction by ether

at present I exist by symptom

by that which inaugurates thirst

thus

interior possession by viridity

knowing that my implosion

is of vicarious emanation

that I am the seed of a forthcoming hurricane body

an erratic hurricane body
yellowed & summoned by serpents

at birth I'll feed on goat's bread
on gull's armour
on impregnable sorcerer's concentration

I've been told by the hoar-frost lizard
that I am 'Sino-Manchurian' & swan
that I am stag of impalpable copper decisives
who partakes of the Dolgan
of the Yakut
of the Tungus

I am then bird of the Buryats
of protracted sonar kingdoms
in flight through higher complexity
never condemned to mockery or hiding

I can suggest that light
proclivitous with astral divination
is at one with a telepathic skeletal tree
with the atmosphere of Titan
part height & part sigil
solarized with jade

such
is my inner mosaic by stealth

neither

as one single stamina

neither weighed by the sea

or projected on the sky

by implicate mongoose scholars

who create by optics

balanced by phosphoric scansion

a body squinting totalic with touch

being blinded remains of the riddles of jackals

say

a power like Anubis

subjecting his insight to vertigo

& my spirit guides telling me

'that we have given you lower enrichment'

'the guttering candle as plague'

'you will hone yourself on land' they say

'you will give the oceans reprieve'

'you will give the timber its time to ignite & rebuild'

'as for now'

'you are deciduous groping & mist'

'your ferocity being old & Siberian & Kemetic'

'in guise as Jackal at edgeless winter'

'in judgement far beyond its craft & its perniciousness as muscle'

156

they say to me

'your body is lighted Fuchsia'

'higher than the use of poignant fragmentary squalls'

'you are weighted as doubles'

'by inverted suicide & victory'

'by implausible fleece who lifts burdens'

'we give you water & desert like emerging sun out of kelp'

'a yellowed flotational sable'

'a ghostly peninsula of riddling'

my shark

one of pure electrical glass

of diaphanous cellular rotation

thus the shark

the lizard

the bird

threaded as polarized collective

& me

being its random coherence as body

'a mixture of wavelengths skewed as

a central maxim'

prone at all levels of directional displacement

living by in-dominate ambrosia

me

the visible omega of its body

the imploded trace

the uncolonized conundrum buffeted by alchemical

bickering

by damaged realia according to numbering & plan

this in-dominate ambrosia

its scent deployed across darkened helium

distention

emitting its ohmic desertion by bells

be reasonless vitrics

through flameless chemical ambiguity

this being my trace

cruelly tested by shadow

by the heliocentric realm of diacritical speculation

so as to express being by photonic lunar

inculcation

by death as portion through inhibition

being the seed of expansion stunned by ironic

polar concussives

perhaps

a recitation from the world of miracles

from rhythmic justification by magic

with my double guides fed by moral urchins

by greenish owls that drift through the vacillating
weather of being

not a sum
nor a kindling
nor a precipitous antidote against fallacy

this is
the experiential gulf
the flaw that inveigles its shadow by means of
emerald meridians
this is the aphasia which weighs me
the aphasia implanting my phrases with disencounter

so no clear picture is drawn
no battlefield of birds poised
for inevitable scarification
no
there are no phosphenes
no outlines drawn in cobalt
so as to face
& give back to the viewer the mythical meaning
of blood

the imperfections
the sounds
the scurrilous disseminations
as if focused by blurred coronas

such bio-kinetic

remains dust as regards the palpable dimension

through the eye which gives the finely drawn

ledgers on Earth of sorties between biology & Gods

& their opposite

integers from dense amnesiac calm

seeing aquamarine cordilleras

they seem a-lit with reflective internal moons

like blank new uprising rock

circled

with talismanic hawks

with cold ambrosial ravens

then there are petrols that spew smoke

who raise sapphire smoke to flotational

horizons

& I

as psychic fragment

as dark umbilical cinder

hearing suns speak from the first grafted rock

from the first condensed water

from aboriginal cobalt explosions

my grounding blank

my thought forms uncreated

visualizing flames from the vascular conduction of trees

flames restored to black amphibian ground

then

the older millipedes

the first land spiders

a primitive crop of sharks

coming to form

after the first 'Ordovician sea floor' was laid

so my alabaster shark

evolving out of ammonites & brine

now being bony residue from cane

yet a ghost

never of theoretical concussives

of standing emissions of skulls

but a wheel of glaciers

burning like pestilential pine salt

I speak not of an era

constructed as a separated forge

nor a beastly granite as acrobatic schism

but as transparent struggle

far beyond the notion of flooded chemical fields

therefore

my blood has been founded

upon ancestral bells

upon truly haunted mystical salt

Siberian by means of flickering unease

no

I am not pathologically engendered

nor involved in the sundered spectacle as directive

such as exposure to dead glyphs

or missives employed as catastrophic law

those misdirectives by theory

by abstracted ascension

as to trial by blazing splinters or ice

for instance

placement by agnostic letter

referential stagnation

quarry as hewn from duplicitous ambrosia

not knowing how to see

the roving of black sienna horses

drifting through nomadic maelstroms

on which a ghostly breed of centipedes is riding

that proliferate as motion through solitude

born as portion of a species

as they scale the inner Andes

with ferocious parallel ambiguity

with power beyond surcease or count

& out of their midst

I have emerged as a flickering purgatorial double

with hooves

with a spider's back

alive as unfixed singularity

my trace partaking of scarlet insurrection

toward entropy

as these strange unsaddled stallions gallop

like unsettled squabs into the horrific

at penultimate extinction

I reclaim my trace as bird

with wings forming

with colour thriving

knowing these centipedes as gryphons

merged according to prophetic test

it is the vision of the lizard

with its motion at the border of dust

with its blank ophthalmic burst

alive as corrupt momentary pattern

energy as useless stealth

akin to hellish corporal dalliance

this herd of chimeras

active as invidious drachma

vanish into the vacuity of unauthenticated ground

with a flash of post-tellurian nickel

& I

ascending as green vapour

at the moment of extinction through error

yet they are momentary monsters

they are carking inseminal discord

lateral realia being abyss after abyss after abyss

yet knowing I exist by means of a sonorous vertical

realm

a realm which approaches the 'origins of origins'

dialectic to the darkness of dishonoured steeds

& these dishonoured steeds

dispersed at the precipice of non-being

at the orientation of anguish

through pessimistic isolation

into that which thrives on the absence of cyclical

recovery

being as monarchial halting

as stasis

as departure by subjective methane

164

unlike bluish Byzantine deserts with hieroglyphic

nettles & swans

I am called

'Lutchi Herit by the Wintu'

'Nanatska by the Pima'

the great Tocha by the Hopi

me

of insurrection & healing

me

the force of dazzling uranic embellishment

me

the insurrectional figment who rides inclement ponies

who mounts sapphire hillocks

who gathers nomadic aurum grains

in this

I've heightened the voice of Helios

by that which ceases to linger

upon doctrine as universal gravitas

so I'm freed to erase the quarters that separate

suns

that seem to bifurcate gulfs

by means of corrupted polarity

so that on one side of the gulf there are vervets

clamoring for partial Neptunian purification

& on the other

unborn platypus leaking blood from their crimes

instinctual jolts

unlike algae

or restive monerans on Saturn

no

I have not yet re-scorched the soot in blackened

Ottoman valleys

nor experienced a double Sun under the auspices

of unrectified Martian domains

& these domains

'subtypes of glossolalia'

always erupting from aurokinetic illusion

or internal Incan meridians

pointing flight or direction

from a luminous interior compass

neither glass nor blood

but of unspecified origin

from a veil of plasma

perhaps 'phosphorescent fungi'

perhaps phantom identity

perhaps I am result

of an abstracted cell

formed from a cloud of amnesiac identity

& between the phantom & the amnesiac

I am non-locatable as to measurable region or impact

yet from my seeming dearth

a stunning electrical province

an immense sheet of flame

bursts of chromatic dispersion

eruptive carnelian sand

become numinous water

kaleidoscopic greenness

like pre-elective visitation

that transmutes vicinity via imagination

to bells in ubiquitous oak

hallucinated constructs

disordered respiration

like flaring veridical nigredo

or quaking albedo

or transitional citrinitas

a non-liturgical summons

an anti-botanical rubedo

consumed

so as to listen to broken meteors

filled with fertility as deafness

where roots of the sun tree glisten but vanish

its chimera being hypnotic drainage

its force being light as inverse projection

this inverse projection made of instantaneous

rivulets

& these rivulets being lakes alive as triangular

witness

mixed with dust from moons

alive as my whispered alabaster shark

water being its subterfuge

its occult nullification

irrigation being exposure to nothingness

to moistness from incarnadine Datura

so that its whispers have become analogous to myself

as errata unto myself

that I've enciphered by search

by reasonless burning

floating through sudden states of agnosia

alien as to fallen rock

as to ghostly lightning movement

spun by sonics according to quintal

again

alchemical heightening & survival of perishable

168

quanta

& I am that perishable quanta

part spirit

part bird

part flooded decay

guided by faded hoar-frost ether

I fly towards that pre-existent sun

that prophetic force producing exile as meteor

as result

I am being weighed

balanced between water & land

so if water & land are lixiviums from meteors

I will be able

to burn through the Sun door

through arrows & residue that sustain themselves

as barriers

Anubis being the either & residue of guides

transmuted to Huitzilopochtli

sorcerer of smoke who spits 'fire'

so from these inclement elements

I produce an acre of lilies

& these lilies

an acre of black syrup

expanding their sound like contradictory mitosis

this is the valley of smoke

nurtured by aggregate shamanizing rays

never daunted by a wavering or inconsequent

surcease

for instance

an era in the sunless Andes

flitting from peak to peak

without the verity of ma'rifa

based upon delusional clepsydras

I

as species

as developed echo-location

plunged into liminal Cimmerian vitality

with irregular heeding

with somnific propagation

floating

assaulted by shadows bated with honey

with hail

with boiling ground fumes

with dryness

again swans & lilies as diversion

proclaiming themselves

smelling of shark

170

flying from lures as bloodless quickening

from ravenous cacophonous vacuums

suddenly

as if projected from laterite

never as infertility

but as darting equatorial metal

one could ask

what is the central test of such flotation?

what are its embers?

its boundaries?

its trajectory as ash through a core of flashing

speculums?

alchemical trace?

fleeting distinction?

yet finding myself

across a blinding dorsal prairie

knowing that the sharks' interior scale

is contained in elusive proto-collapse

alive amidst the milk of dying

listening to underwater gulls

to ironic largesse

fever being scattered through dying cetacean

flanks

then bloodless flamingos

Auks

gannets who profess mastery over fire

autonomous apparitions

elixirs as friction

they who've dwelled within the scent of the dead

these flamingos

these Auks

on the road of the dead

with its lost geological hillocks

with its miraculous lingual parching

with its view of inflicted 'infernal topography'

yet I exist

not as pariah

as stray or oblong silk

to be revered along clashing equational roads

never a garrison of visible hatcheries

but singular cyclone as destiny

for me

leap as transfunctional eating through spirit

so as to reach scorching within transparent

hives

hives

being séance as meticulous grammar

a bony parenthetical trance

lit by bony rapier urns

urns culled

from drifting tungsten fields

from the meteoritic as waste

so as to feed from quartz falling from Alpha

Centauri

& these urns

being re-magnetized possession

of a soul 'having strayed'

from strands of supple avian copper

yet urns

vatic with hissing

knowing that I will swallow unclean demons

& emerge above the untold theft of the spirit

it is this precarious juncture of will

that lives through transfunctional singing

being archaic violation

that lives by means of bringing fire back

from the sea

bringing cleansed negation to the ozone

caused by the straying & disappearance of demons

depravation swallowed up by differing intervals

across infinity

according to the scent of my guides

I bring a central vegetation

when molecules refocus as the invisible

Buryat healer

winged

quivering

under a lingering green sun

healing humans plagued as they are by

disruptive beliefs

here I am

bird in ordeal

preparing entry through the human inferno

all the molecular wandering

all the transitional Ugrian sleep

in flight above imprecation

you must understand

I have assumed the spirit of death

the concentration of its imminence

contradicted by liberty

I have been blessed by defections

by squandered octopi

by listless bears

174

that my vicissitudes have been renounced

& destroyed

giving that voice that wanders through a wilderness

of pyres

certainly not description by tomb

or voice imported by carnal sapphire hatchlings

but fissure by inception

for instance

an anhedral furnace

a slope of biographical gryphons

a fire

a deluge

crops of wheat & basins

hurricanes of splendour

filled by waking moral ore

I know that I gamble by whispers

by voluminous in-breathing cycles

respiration has not started

the molecules have not ascribed to another succession

yet I float

I understand the burial & largesse of monsters

by invoking sound that makes ghosts withdraw

my feathers feeling the stirring of a brooding germinal
dance

an eclectic cinder
a fleece of coalescing roses
sleeping amidst a hut dyed with subtle vortex heating

so my magic
both nigrescent & anti-nigrescent
like a map poised between arithmetical warrens

therefore I am nigrescent as regards the power
of soil
where the axial mundi of lepers are transcended

so I sculpt the dialogical void by osmosis
by blatant signs
by arrowed figurines

not by conscious will
or by commanding dust from a fortress of bodies

no
I strike blood from 2 belled arrows while dreaming
the mountains being carnivorous
the fruit being form from a meadow of lightning

now the interrogative of my alabaster shark

as to how I would cleanse the masonry of kelp

as to how I would apply dictation to the door of

the world

how I would strike down & re-weave piranhas

I would create birds from a fleeting mongoose hissing

from clouded panthers or owls

I would make voyagers suggestive of doubled outer kelvins

bringing incomparable zeniths from planets not unlike

glaciers

of the Paramos of the Andes

or fierce Etesian Winds

scattered by negated biblical volcanoes

according to my guides

I am paradigm by elevation

hyperbolical as simultaneous moraine

gathered from rectangular sigils of flames

being wool from a stony sacrifice goat

the fire of the goat being great danger

great summons that envelopes the barrier

that induces insensate distraction

what I feel is the blizzard from the heat of

impermeable scintilla

a kind of glass

a doubled sun with another light that winds above it

pervasive

like Athanasia which erupts beyond error

my guides now say

that I am cleansed to peer into new lands

into new irregular glossaries at one with sudden

colloquial systems

seeming to vanish across sprawling underwater plains

my alabaster shark

seized by consumptive selenium

by invasive red algae

its inner moons sullied

with its dying gasps pointing me to the indigo

kinetic of ciphers

to somnific trace lagoons

that flicker

not unlike a nimbus

beyond the graspable

 beyond the hebdomadal life perceived by human calendric

alive at the astral by source as suspended pressure

yet consumed by cyclical ephemeris

by 'respiratory' blockage

by 'inhibited' enzymes

corroding his flanks

with combustible blockage

an accelerated monarch

dying

having induced my momentum through cacophonous neutrality

through neutered electrical mass

where all manner of negation persists without terminus

being transudation

through loathsome mockery & threat

yet giving me flight above flames of land & water

being osmotic flight through agitation

through geometrical succubus

through danger as intrinsic fragility

I

the most fragile & eclectic of exhaustion

I

the most Uranian bird embrangled in brevity

with my feral guides

my spontaneous election

as fragment

as ghost

throughout shaken planetary schism

where the radii of claustrophobia

doubles

threatens

each ounce

each gender

each boundary

being Earth as visibility

as tormented cinder

 exposed to auroras of its primal solar ingestion

then

the cordilleras become risk

become a cycle of circum-erosion

become erasure of carved plateaus

sea fogs as diagram plateau

as hail

no longer perceived as minimums

corroded valleys

ceasing to breed fertility by travertine

or Spanish oranges in the huerta

Hypabyssal rocks

ice fields

inselberg masses

Burgess shale

Ordovician volcanoes

like a province with blazeless tracings

empty

anti-Lacustrine & arid

like Mars

180

isolate

being barometer as still born diameter

Mars

its 'southern hemisphere'

above typographic sea level

its northern zone

'sparsely cratered'

with its barren craters

its irregularly shaped mesas

then

Tasis volcanoes

alive

with oblivious chronology

with layers of ice & 'dust'

its vertical tectonics

intermittent

with psychic floods from Silurian calderas

but as broken aerial carbon

lacking stratosphere

lacking 'heat transport'

being in essence apocalyptic saltation

where dust grains unite into atmospheric bleakness

being suspended for months

its passage of winds

being 'baroclinic eddies'

then global dust envelopment

then the motion of total cyclical decay

say 100 global storms

its impact being

a glaring tidal velocity

& this tidal velocity

leaves its molecules of species disrupted

barren

at minimum scarred by calamitous impact distortion

& so my guides

allowing my trace

as supercessional seeing

as Siberian astral séance

where evil is sought out in relation to its host

'discovering the cause of ill-being'

giving name to its tormented spirit

to its 'origin'

to its hieratic inversion

so I must hover in my capacity

absorbing the deleterious

absorbing its transfunctional bleeding

it is this

which is caliginous treatise

182

duplicitous arsenic scapes

functionless contrary cells

with waters warped by parasitic dysfunction

organisms are compelled by total persistence

through chaos

as if Earth

were translocated Martian

through inclement reprieve after inclement reprieve

its respiration

impaired

as to the unity of living function

the breathing between potassium & calcium

between lecithin & cholesterin

rife with strobic electrical flaw

with infertile Biogenesis

reeking with disturbance

with tension due to a diminished hydrosphere

knowing this

there is loss of the emerald sun

the Earth in the throes of a proto-Phobos

its soils

blackened at the depth which counter-revolves with

anti-nigredo

& so the water on Earth
stunted as declared by original mobilization
by its original circular elevation

& I am speaking of its ideal potential
of its 'upper' engendering
its intermingled elevation
knowing the poisoned squid
the obverse medusa
my guides
though all but vanished
have given me power to drift
as simultaneous field
as geometric sustainment

& the water & the land have merged
& I am the sky
wracked with dread & sickness & error
with flotational nether respiration
crossing & re-crossing species
beyond 8000 years of species respiration
thereby confronting disintegrated hissing
as non-solutional matrix
of the technically solved gene

& this gene
the harvest from collective pollution
darting
184

instable with diagrammatics
its shifts of fire & cold
extracted from outlines of helium

this does not imply a populous kingdom
or movement of gems in volcanoes

no
it implies the reign of the great inessentials
the ironics of populous reduction

so each trail
each storm
creates a form of fractals in the cells
aboriginal cascades
vatic holograms & surges

flight being voltaic scansion
as metamorphic nigredo
as sliver or ray
within an oscillating squall
porous with global exotoxins

it seems tillage whirls with corruptive occlusion

now one voice guides me
subsumed by the deathly overcoming of paranoia

I the Hillstar

the wakeless Henbane Bird

human in Paraguay

total bird in Bolivia

no longer under the sway of aural fever by pneumonia

yet fever & pneumonia

hold me intact with illusive beta-invasives

with a complex of marginal death hives

by which I brew

the jackals

the sullen proto-owls

the anxious circling vultures

attempting to take from my field

the symbolic of all meridians

the delta of solar Phoenix hail

rising as miraculous debris

raising fertility from cauldrons

my life being

a holonomic wafting

transmuting a garden of inch roads

through a plain of parasitic holding trees

then the echo of exclusive arachnid waters

defending global respiration

amidst the flames of ghostly chattering ruins

its dialectic

vociferation & stupor

between a hydra's voice

& taciturn remains of moonless elevation

I exist

beyond futile remains of a disembodied tempest

a spate

a blizzard

an onslaught

not unlike the swooping of eagles from crags

evolving from a mirror of charcoal

& in it one sees

'the skull of a horse'

the snout of a bear

a web containing sturgeon

in this delirious realm

there will emerge from my breast

the shrillness of crows

the anthems that scatter toxicity throughout

despair

from the depths of ferocity

I've emitted my roving alabaster guide

my shark

with their ability to ingest sullage

for the sound of 12 millennia

with their proclivity toward the deadened perches

of eels

my immersion at this depth

studied by gulls & sirens

learning from my guides

infernal speculation

utopian sustentation

my existence

an internal psychoporia

a ceremonial dispensation

always gathering as my power

a tortured apprehension as jeopardy

as neology

expelling each mephitic gesture

from the collective witness in this particular

megacom

the hoar-frost lizard:

'you must be thermotically oblivious'

the alabaster shark:

'you are a mime & a sigil

you expel by inclusion

complex physiognomies'

at this

he began swirling like a nebula

& the hoar-frost lizard

began splitting into parts like an asteroidal spirit

their velocities gaining misfortune

& the dialectical spark of masters infusing spirit

I have been given as my power

a lance to break rocks

four small fish

& an inverted white bear

then brought to further power

by the nebula of the shark

by the velocity of the lizard

sprinkling my wings with magic cider & opium

it is the sea's gift

it is the land's internal conjury

being my denizen's reward for ceasing to be devoured

& now as I fly

& begin to open my wings to the fields

I am strewn with dead velvet

watching the hoar-frost lizard arise from my innards

as the shark

the shark then emitting

the infernal source of cephalic engendering

that are powers that dwell

outside the chronicles

heaped upon the floor of history

heaped upon its rancid critical posturing

upon its post-mechanical technique

it's as if I possess an exploded critical theology

concealed as a hawk floating from heights of

a hieroglyphic tundra

through occult ignition

I'm feeling a Mesopotamian mist

a new Babylonian scrawling

linking its meteoritic axis

with interior quartz of higher reservoirs

& destinies

& so I

the inclement Hillstar

the inexhaustible virility

restoring stone to is prime expressive cipher

to its mythical root

where its doublets transpire as voice

as nomadic aural ingestion

knowing its realm beyond beginnings of the Earth as human embodiment

not hearing by arbitrary slumber
but as active plurality
where numerous dementias are weighed

& am I the lesser dimension
as regards vertical extension out of hell?

or have I fallen from the great regality
that the mythic shamans have wielded?

or yet
am I that penultimate condition of the marvelous?

the bird with the wearied fleece
with the verdurous mirage in his eyes
being a flask deleterious with sigils
with algid moss
with a craven tower partially suspended
seeing the depths through which I died
hallucinatory
& crimson with cold?

true
I am emerging from transitional possession
rendered dead
yet naturally stirring with alchemical sublimity
according to signs engendered by breakage or roses

therefore

I partake of that dimension that calms the blank

intentionality of a crow

yet now

I seem to suffice

in spite of the seeming error in my leanings

not that demons transfix me

not that I am capable of hounding their powers

out of deluge

but at the same time attacking root practitioners

of evil

there are times that I shrink from dawning

turpentine roads

from my own splintered aggression

thereby evincing lessened moral Edenics

thereby understanding

Anubis the mongoose

Anubis & the weight of evil

with my substance imprinted with terror & evil

by he

who shuns confrontation monster by monster

my sustainment self-doubted

because I only flicker through hell

because I camouflage as aerial compost

because I fly through this oaken threnody
as a shaken sundial tree

yet each lapse in my motion beckons infinity
which imperceptibly probes ascetic denial
the reckless flaw
that overarches infinity

& this flaw is semi-waking
is faceless amalgam
alive as a strange electrical wind

of course
there remains my verdet persistence
as to the shape & warp of death
so as to re-cleanse its boundary
to re-form its ethers
to functionless elevation

now flying in the habitat of supreme oasis
always hidden in my posture
through séance
through rites which mingle with osmosis

I am vatic like Num of the Samoyeds
like Karei God of the Menri
that kindle by osmosis

& Num

& Karei

can only kindle by osmosis

never rescue of the soul by the dual

by the seething separate person

but by osmotic merging

extracting by this motion all manner of meandering

by spell

by claw

by ailing methane ocean

I

the Andean Hillstar

floating into pure fluidity by error

by intangible misnomer

by healing as disruptive witness

alive as a seminal foetus

blazing with luminous suspension

a 'transcendence over space'

now soaring over sounds numinous with slaughter

those human molecular realms

diabolical & eclectic with feuding

I no longer partake of the focused blood thirst clan

that predilection to kill in roaming glucose mammals

194

yet my instincts aroused

by focus that galls

Within the rifeness of one land mass

concerned

with the radiation in Peru

with social forms in Ecuador

here I am

floating across a covetous astral well

the mongoose Anubis

giving me strife to burn

chaos to dispel

weather to restore

to Anubis & my guides

I am the blue ascensional eaglet

the rum from destroyed vultures

who rises to extract death from refulgence

to bring back seas from the nightmare of

carcinogens & wine

to Anubis & my guides

I am that anonymous ascensional magnet

that spellbinder's draft

who cures & attempts to cure

by a colourless vatics

by an overwhelming vial enriched with totemics

life on Earth

recently obscured by hypothetical craft

by forces confused by rot compelled

by the spillage of nuclear feces

the wattage cancelled from living blood

the general amperage of lakes heinously despoiled

by ruinous national prides aligned with negation

I

at this non-molecular visibility

can speak of my guides now shadow

now stunning force clothed inside my miraculous obscurity

pure shaman in a changed molecular climate

the human race will now absorb me

my oblique dialectics

my geomantic empowered by oblique dialectics

by scribbled charcoal language

& I am inhabited by language

by a language that breaks apart

by a language that gambles

that stuns in its elastics by geologic premonition

by threat

by invisible entrail as atom

the creosote bush

the hamlet

the micro-analytic krill

all damaged

all collectively consumed by future non-generation

by environmental staggering anaemias

I

the Henbane Bird

consumed

by helical distance as graph

as spiraling tungsten anchor

at one with a blue celestial dharma

I have flitted from a parallel haven

each of my advances

cryptic

scorched by a faultless spellbound ochre

by a trance which now breathes

which that takes in terrain

that harbors a scope

perpendicular

& aligned with empyreans

I

the Hillstar

the bleak dalmatian sun

between stupor & the proto-electronics of stupor

between the stupor of upright animals & the void

a stark ascensional complexity

as if meteorites could cure the nausea of soil

making earth again mythic

proportional to virginal explosion

of course explosion as nucleic identity

marking levels from the Cambrian

through the Cretaceous

through the sum of my present singing

during this present duration

the fish feed on wood shavings

on corrosive iguana granite

& humanity

imbibing wheat from poisoned tremors

each species suffering

with its identity blurred

with its evolving misfocused

amidst disfigured bone yards

missing condors & pumas

broken burial wrens

the body of animals being toneless plastique

the oldest 'millipedes' from the 'Devonian'
a 'placoderm' which ceases to breed
blurred 'amphibia' from the 'Mississippian'

all exist as killed locusts
as aquatic salamander deaths in the midst of the
Permian

I'm feeling the sea that enlivens
the sea that vivifies misfortune

such is life
listening to sand freeze
listening to its tumultuous commotion of kelp
including coral reefs
including sea grass beds
including conflict with land

& on land
the grass burning with sand fleas
with sail-backed pelycosaurs
seen from a floating optical core
watching the sea tables poisoned

always viewing with hieratic alacrity

with divinatory incessance

the blinded toxins in carnivorous ravines

I have returned from one era

& having returned from one era

I know the inclement fields

the living suspensions

where threats wander

where holocausts seemingly multiply

my winged response

like mathematical painting

stunning with caliginous drachmas

threatened

the Ceriman

the Cinchona

the Vanilla Orchid

further

the Papaya

the Pasture Grass

the Maize

the Allamanda

perhaps

a small epistle on contagion

200

that includes Reindeer moss

Snakemouth flower

or the ocherous water lily found in the middle of

Labrador

my Hillstar dwelling

a cave

an algid Martian realia

an oblique chimera

where I've existed through dismembered attacks

always rising above blood

wafting like a spell

as if aloft above peninsulas

through wisdom

through interior foundries of language

I am parallel with Araucanian shamans

my hoar-frost lizard a ghost

my alabaster shark as strange intangible mass

I emit my rays invisibly

they take human effect into living

such as the neophyte shamans of Tierra del Fuego

they rub 'their faces until a second...skin appears'

producing as visibility a message from central

interiors

provoking fuels

microscopic with emanation

now

because I live as dual being

I burn with the power of interstellar feathers

which glows with a kind of sifting

so I am able to dwell inside generic planetary poisons

I have thrice the powers of an Angakok rooster

who dwells in enigma

with moons that erupt from a future existence

knowing

that the Sun is transfixed with fuels

from an axial depth no limit can withstand

unlike a saviour

who separates lack from the power of lack

I exist by the glance of dust

by the 'fourteen notches' that hover above Satan

above his monolithic inference

made manifest by alternate destruction

summoned by mystical dramatics

I am marked by gold

as perfect lens from the indefinite

a psychic dawn
a pure lion dawn
absent of any transfixed crafting

this is not for me reasoning
or exclusivity by locus

but a cerulean power of export
prowling
as scribbled glyph through regions of scarcity

all whispers I emit are blankly combined

I possess the frenzy of the shark
the empowered algae of the lizard
with a sleep contained in pints
emotive with cerulean medicinal fauna

through sleep
I must suck out the blood of triangular nightmare
poisons
of the mind
the body
the depths
so as to re-ignite our general dwelling zone
with new Uranian ethers

I am not thirsting amidst the cold

for dangerous methane inversion

& so

I never cling to despair

to projected failure as riddle

no

I am entirely condoned by complex right

by power projected from total solar well-being

my auricular wings

with the power to cleanse through water & glass

I know

the dismembered fright

the superstitious ornament

the hell by uncertainty

I

the re-engendered bird

devoured & re-born

abducted

groggy

magnetically re-invented

now

being partial with visibility

I fly

much like the smoke in darkened planetary minds

204

where the ether dwells like a disassembled codex
emitting phantoms as refracted omegas

me being enemy to ozone blockage
to corrosives ingested in the blood of beasts

for me
secrecy
complexity
the inflaming sigil that is drought

in my human degree
I know unburied crystal
blizzards from 'eastern Bolivia'
the collection of 'knives' & 'combs' & 'hatchets'

I am not a Manasi shaman
nor a dead Guarani shaman
with my debris preserved in a hut

no

in the form of Hillstar
I'm attempting to reconvene Edenics
to rezone abducted by ghosts
collecting its burning soils
healing its anathema through drift
me

being the Henbane Bird

whose molecules transmix with demise

with structural inclemency

yet making the ice caps prodigious

like the flow from a Yaghan in Tierra del Fuego

I want the Sun no longer haunted by strange industrial

despair

I

the phalanx of urgency

being a form who imbibes from lianas

who shatters the barren weight of unhealed discovery

having emerged from death

I've been suspended over eons

surviving 'three mass extinctions'

surviving each degree of early mountain building

to the terrestrial gaze I am famished

I seem inflated with mercury

yet the light of my phonemes hail from above

the Black Sea

with its crucial slate telepathy gone awry

its intrinsic arcana damaged

its pike-perch

its sturgeon

missing

its sprats

its whitings

its mullets

garish with decline

& the Lima Ocean polluted

the Pacific

intrinsically altered by tailings from Andean mining

from unfit sewage pouring from Esmeraldas

then the San Vincente Gulf

the Bay of Valparaiso

the 'Guayas River in Ecuador'

alive with perpetual waste

with raw exterior sewage

dialectically

the 'San Blas Islands'

with 'waters clear as glass'

full of emperors' coral trout groupers

unlike the mining scars

evinced in New Caledonia

scars

rife

with nickel copper lead zinc & chrome
my original death condoned by cold
& the ethers from the mines

to those with blurred internal optics
I could be a lorikeet from eastern Tasmania
or a Golden pheasant form the mountains of China
or a murmur
or a dulled civilian riddle

certainly not an instinctual precision
but a finely wrought chariot purblind with dioxins

I have not arisen from asphyxia
to share in legislation
or to battle over various levels of dysfunction

of course
the politics of de-thronement & solitary acquisition
being no more than a flaw in the fort of transition

no
I do not seek power adorned in quotidian bribery
awash in niggling mental capture
but of the higher range of cobalt
of a solar furnace of rays
with my alchemical ratios
with my semantics that splinter into spectrums

extending

beyond visible calibration

beyond its attendant neural foci

the visual degree developed beyond blank neutrino

blizzards

being in no way related to deficient Gothic embranglements

but say

an alternating blizzard of trigonometric pontoons

an electromagnetic reasoning bluish with alterity

with tension to re-exist

to blaze

again

immersed in electrical alterity

certainly

not flight as circular enfeeblement

as deleterious closure

but as sunquakes

as biological absentia

with strange hormonal phosphenes

bereft of pharmaceutical depravity

neither submission nor error

nor that which ignites

a mirror within a starving python's water

one could call this moisture

ashen reptile meridians

condensed by seeming fractious defeat

it amounts to torment in hypnopompic warrens

in an ungainful braille

sullied with hesitation

like balletic nullification

related to subconscious inklings

that periodically re-arise

in the partial reunion of sleepless Satan monkeys

innocuous halflings that vanish

as the Sun explodes inside itself

provoking caustic vertigo in the realm

so that general fauna is constrained

in stony unhealable quanta

so the pythons mentioned

the lorikeets

the squid

the micro-foundations which culminate in krill

blighted

scarred with retrogression

this silent in-sonorous struggle

full of sodium unleashing its ratios by fatigue

its dioxins being harbored at blasphemous testing points
the flesh of world fauna fiendish with disruption

land being no more than smoke
or perhaps
a fissure of diamonds
cracking under ill-gotten methane

I feel in this instant
a grim Venusian solar light
like a cataract of flasks
or mountainous ozone crumbling
irregularly scanned by explosive albedos
by glints which triangulate
that expand & contract
by inscrutable neutron table
by elusive concentrations of heat

my measurements being taken in a spell-binding
valley
in a broken ozone valley
where true in-pollination proliferates

this is why I've returned from the dead
as the great poltergeist who wanders
who darts through salted manganese ruins
giving document to the inclement

this is why I land on neutron logs

on defective bullocks & grass

to test the arcane leaning of the world

its projection

its exhibit through invalidated stoma

so through spillage

through countless myrioramas

I have come to sorcerous foretelling

through the eyes of a sickened foetus

through the heat that rises from tainted Mustang

hides

I witness

aloof collusional embryonics

where all birth is stained

all becoming corrupted

on this plane

within this co-agitated penumbra

evolved through anatomical struggle

through sidereal devolvement

through an unseasoned forte

neutered that eclipses itself through cause & counter-cause

through movement that endures through in-felicitous

movement

less & less majestic

as it focuses its breath on the molecules of sapiens

& this is not to say

that the sapiens have no right

have no display as to variety or magnificence

no

& I do not degrade my human speaking

as a sudden neural lessening

yet

the present shape of the voice

is magically tangled with a single holocaust

mythology

with nullification as vatic

the molecules transmute

& I am the bird form the under-vapour

moving as a jeopardous flask

igniting my rays on condemned Swedish lakes

on algal congestion in the Venice Lagoon

partaking of crucial ozone scintilla

so as to desperately re-surge the atmosphere

across an operant duration

with 3 billion years of vitality

not that I am suspicious of new waking

but I know the power of my impact

its garrulous outer task

in a kingdom now sweltering with deformity

but my voice

not simply a gloomy didactic

spawned in grown medicinal poisons

but a proto-supernal complexity

analogous in human endeavour to Moorish Cordoba

with its intensive madrasas

its botany

its medicine

its velocity of percipient

as regards the above degree

I am an Iberian indigo bird

focused upon primeval number

upon dark tarantula gases

unleashing a curious metropolis of galaxies

Alnilam

Mirfak

Alhena

splayed across the heavens as pure vibrational

ciphers

as Andalusian sigils

as crucibles of transparency

there is the binary Hadar

named in Iberia

which projects 'etheric shift'...allowing being

to vary its dimensional forms

I as bird

of numerous dimensional shifts

telepathically whirring

as power through alchemical abstentia

being an infiltration of specters

as if I were simultaneous across all forms across

the globe

voracious in a Sri Lankan mangrove swamp

dispersing hells from the Naktong River

disrupting the carbonized waste from the Rio de la Plata

perhaps

while fluttering in ravines of hell

motions from Andromeda will call me

as an ancient miraculous raptor

dialectically chronicled as a blazeless wavering

on earth

juggling death with amorphic delay

my wings being encoded with prayer

amidst battle against kaleidoscopic grounding

then re-existing in the Hercules Cluster

giving me specific alignment with the beyond

with the Magellanic Clouds

with Tucana

with the Pinwheel Galaxy focused in Triangulum

a bird who creates a new treatise on voids

never pertaining to soured gargantuan basins

or by a sleep unstructured by old insomniac fires

me

the fluidic beast

suddenly spawned out of death

suddenly spawned from invisible guidance

so as to absorb those unexplained poisons

sleeping in the cracks of the earth

because I have been to the sky

& evolved through apostolic ice

I am marked by deciduous flooding

as an electrically blank witness

more mystically coiled than an arid Martian cobra

whispering Olmec writing at Carthage

then predicting my example which with a heliotropic

acrostic

so that emptiness appears

like movement from the black ocean trenches

perhaps I could swear by an ecologic food

or slain fragments of gold

but I hover

between illusion & that which dazzles itself as omega

because

only eclectics persists as horizontal layers

exploded out of time

traces of vatic lava

fumes

pre-biotic with resurrection

again

flitting from the pre-biotic

to avian codes in isolation

& I am that specific elixir

which flits across Ceres

which procures the feast from concussive starlight

& if my body exudes empirical dreaming

it is a skittish theology

a theology which threads & re-threads

its motion as amorphic whole

like a movement from the black ocean trenches

perhaps I could swear by an ecologic food

or slain fragments of gold

but I hover

between illusion & that which dazzles itself as omega

because

only eclectics persists as horizontal layers

exploded out of time

traces of vatic lava

fumes

pre-biotic with resurrection

again

flitting from the pre-biotic

to avian codes in isolation

& I am that specific elixir

which flits across Ceres

which procures the feast from concussive starlight

& if my body exudes empirical dreaming

it is a skittish theology

a theology which threads & re-threads

its motion as amorphic whole

not the evasive God as the single action of chance

with its angles

with its rivalries

seeking my form as deleterious conversion

without dialectic as one design

being sincere to culpable cadence as worship

to structured beginnings

to the cells as a lesson in morality

in this one proportional God
one finds
a transcendental salt without mixture
without that blissful mothering wave
being of boundless variety or spectrum

take a sea of tigers
burning as acrostics on one prairie

then an ocean
broken away from two oceans

then any continent or channel
or Ordovician mine
or a random sum from Jurassic rays
plummeted through myopia or reefs

do you understand my spells as an arc above
mountains?

as a green or higher colour?

as a plane of schismatic enrichment?

let me exhale this page
as if each sea were falling
each millimeter
each droplet

as a burning crimson body
soured before the end of the sun

my dialectic
transmundane in function
as a link between wolves
& a tenacious brooding by wind

by volcano body
part carnivorous
part neutered as to reflex
burning throughout desire

like the propaganda of centaurs
whistling like a crack
through the black neurology of gases

I think of lightning acids
splitting ravines
of iron
& water
& velvet

because I am bird & shaman
I am known & unknown to certain meaning or meanings
such as
Phrictopathetic
Microcoria
220

Pro Re Nata
Omophagia
Pluviometry

in them I am missing
scorched by the disorder of the missing
each random purpose
a morbid Bryology
entangled
humid
meandering
alive with foaming salamander's veins

I am magnetically conversant with randomness
with its ubiquitous encirclement
knowing its psychic mineral alignment
with the mystic particles
conjured on a smokeless salt peninsula

& this peninsula
only implied by diagram
lifted by an inner scattering populace
as a ghostly mass gathered in billionths

mass
but partaking of the soil as unclaimed integer
as that level devoid of exoterics
devoid of extrinsic specificity

I am thus the ghost deity

the unknown precipice

liminal between existence & its nerve flash from

the sun

never infused with edicts

yet I am the glyph which transcends the unstructured

cliffs

I

of the diamond worlds

of the diamond domains

no seeming confinement can hinder

I

who osmotically scan

all the meteorites

all the deluge eras

all the beguiling quakes in the land

when the sea burns

when the waters collide with defilement

I am witness

when the land is poisoned by the map of the abyss

I exist by aboriginal valley

by vents

by storms

by dark collisional purity

I

who spark the proto-sun with the proto-sun

with a criterion which forms

through utopian isolation

each of my wingbeats as compositional ringlets

forming in their odour a bewitching mathematical

synodic

for instance

to bring to view

a Middle Cambrian Sea

with arachnids

with inarticulate brachiopods

never summoning from my powers

an argued theological grail

or a reasoning contained within a post-creative

flux

a flux

fixated

according to the flaw of differential scribes

I go back to first burden at Palenque

to the suns as ages

to their cycle of colours

to their hieroglyphic variables

of course fundamental resonance

incipience as data

say

the 12 creations of the world

the first zodiac of alacrity

the zone which rises above legalistic dharma

which contends

that ferment

is never of inferior duty

is never of the slate of legalistic bleakness

when I fly to Judea

I know the blood unravels

I know systemic cholera is applied

so that weight is captured

& all activity applied

to the wrath of a fallen demon

to a divisively crafted idol

amassed

around a mistaken anthropomorphics

such

are the cruder conceptions of heaven

with a replicate & divisive habitat

so that its archetype contaminates the cells

& such dissensions exist

which no infertile barrier can properly interpret

'observable limit' derived from 'observable limit'

which cannot properly unbury the monopoles

or carry on dialogue with divisive suggestion

'initial singularity' gone awry

the cosmos tainted by the geographic monument

sculpted from the desert

the God from Judea as the solemn invariable plan

perhaps

a rotational vacuum

perhaps

that which de-exists becoming baktuns

katuns

tuns

or days

variation being the spectral oasis

which ceases as limited phenotype or purgation

this being the shamanistic purview

the voids

the risks

the deltas which bleed with sudden momentary forces

saying such

one never disclaims suspicion

or shuns disorder as gamble

with the sun rushing in

I am of lesser & greater degree by velocity

as a variant rum

as incalculable nomad

a driftwood being

a bird which expands

knowing that the Sun can reverse its fever of lakes

its thermodynamic propensity gathered from implosion

concerning occulted wheat

concerning anti-dimensional flying

my grammes deriving from other stellar summations

with a resonant penetration beyond the present

range & its unknown solar libido

suggestive of citron in the bluish mathematics

of darkness

a relay of ignition

analogous

to a billion years of birds in migration

flying

through the proto-powers of Titan

with its pre-stellar oceans

conversant

with my alternating bodies exponential with flames

of course

I am radiating nuclei

beyond the farthest aural galaxies

instantaneous with totalic kelvin walls

far beyond

subdivided singularity

or suspended oxygen consumption

never comparing my powers

to a rock

or a tree

or a sieve deducted from ingesting persimmons

I exist

I am periodic albino

I bathe in shafts or caves

if I were less than this resurrectional albino

I would forage for nectar

I would concentrate on sugar

possessing at bottom the squalid quest for unruly

microbes

being voracious with stealth

I would feed on the Trumpet Vine

on a certain peninsular omen

possessing aggression

at sub-helical orbit

always singing at a post-human frequency

like a blackly haunted whistle

or a holographic amperage

combined by an anti-social plumage

perhaps I would oil my wings from my 'uropygial'

gland

my eyes searing

my throat alive as enforced collision

as if possessed by the scar of a raptor on the

outer rocks of the asteroids

true

a stunning testimonial drift

as if I were alive

according to the one birth

according to its pillaged uncertainty

simultaneous with a vine rising through extended

collapse

no

my molecules osmotically altering kelvins

by rubescent pneumatics

far beyond vocal anaemia

so as to confound the dazzling lunation of death

by 'interstellar ecology'

never yielding to a dalliance balanced

by the sterile devolvement of hoarding

& I mean by this hoarding

the chemicals which neutralize velocity

to a blank obedience which can't be tested

by flight which ascends by scorching misnomer

never condensed by a nether condition of

geobiology

or a crystallization which purports to

confound its mystery

yet I persist

by explosive equilibria

by unmonitored task

by telepathic combining

I am not bounded

by any dense or surroundable boundary

which matches itself

& only equals itself

like a force of wireless ravens

or a sterilized sun before burning

not the surface microbes hauled up from dust

not a posture of conclusives

but as spurs

as motions

as catalytic primevals

so that I survey gulfs

& understand the praxis of the phenotype of planets

their different weights & patterns

their radii & weather as regards suns & their orbits

petroleum channels on Mars

the Ishtar Terra the Guinevere Planitia on Venus

the fractures of ice on the surface of Triton

of course

there exists the spectacular intersection

within chondrites

like a spectral fire between stardust & matrix

across my climatarian purview I feel in my wings

'equinox to equinox'

'apse to apse'

'moon's node to moon's node'

& within vacuums hauled from planetary dust

there exists obsidian Apache Tears

Selenite Roses

scattered Mexican Opals

they are acrostics which emit answers

not as conclusives

but as spurs

as motions which ignite as catalytic primevals

so that drift occurs between planets

between gulfs of sidereal debris

the details of analytics

destroyed

microscopic equilibrium

abandoned

because

I've never returned to the Earth without prehensile

speculation

without conquest

without neurological impediment

bent upon mundane correctives

the Earth obscured by corrosive cortical deafness

de-blazed reaction within its furnace

absorbing from rotation

hellish procurements

awkward settlements of monoxide

.

if my sole concern derived form starvation

I would speak of the woolly cactus

Chilean timbers
or the quinine from cinchona trees

I would replicate a nervous embroilment
reduced
day after day by a wizening auto-intoxication
so that my alchemical wheel would spin with
corruption
with old unbalanced seed

yet in the snow I sense the vatic disaster
or draconian nuclear oils

each square of each nation engulfed
by their penultimate trembling
rife with staggering negation

this condition existing
I fly by the power of a crucial insomnia

an insomnia which condones a self-inflicted
marauding
so that no repose can occur
with the imminence of cellular entropy
a war
a claimless thievery of the body

as bird

as shaman

there exists no horizon inspired by political

calumny

the curious loitering by outward cause

me

from the ultraviolet ravine

from the spontaneous eagle's window

like a perplexing connoisseur

consumed with the moral density of a thief

this range which I now engage

being of interior mission

as though entanglements & taboos

had been blown from criteria

like a gust beyond emptiness

that status of being from which few have returned

alive

from which few have escaped as from underwater

danger

from the lair of stunned sharks

from the grave of ominous henbane fertility

compressed

with a central thesis of respiration

much like a chalice thrown in a stream
as a signal of great duty

yet
as I've flown from the caves in the Andes
I flash on blank fish failing
on buffeted sea-lion habits

this earth
cloves
pomegranate valleys
which speak in terms as if in-dominate creatures

they exist
as though they imbibe the bell of balance
& they are this balance
the Oil palm
the Himalayan cedar
the Sansevieria

they are unlike certain humans
who have forgotten their power as titans
humans
who seem listless
staggered with noise & harassment

existing with leakage
like fallen ozone tigers

if I can touch the sand
& make the oceans cease to dwell in a state of
diminished grace
I am proof that the transpersonal exists
that inscrutable exorcism remains

my wings first populated
by distillation from meteors

yet now
we exist as assembled subjects
stored by territorial flaw
as if trying to interpret from Antarctica
a bluish hail from China

because I sense these levels
the hail
the flaws
the African Sansevieria
the dust from Babylonian land waves
I am unified with smokeless solar foundations
with superior fuliginousity
which expands & re-emits the galaxies from
nothingness

perhaps at a lower concentration
I am seen as a blemished sand demon
simply scavenging from debris

but I know in my rawness

that eternity is freedom from periodic habit

from biology as quotidian symbiotic

measured from one mirrored distance to another

everything swirls

the mountains dim

the grasses develop

the Sun glistens

through the optical transfer of instinct

my battle is against dreary modifying templates

against the pronoun which resists dispersion

so gravity no longer lurks with virtuosic terror

as living Nigredo I flew before death

from darkened wells to roundelays of earthlight

elliptically entranced by Andean Peru

by the cold transfixtures of Ecuador

a bastion of dissimilar species

I am akin to the Nasturtium in that my colours

are a transported magnet

setting marshes ablaze

like a hive of flailing pentads

Juniper leanings

which at times structures the seasons

commingling with sparks from blank rubidium jetties

which suffices at one level

according to durational minimum yield

& at another level according to the transhuman

spiral

an avian who extends his yield with defective

circling

around proto-epic stupas

one of my auras

projected across the glass of India

like a free standing meteor

advancing scope after persistent electrical scope

being shock as inclement equation

so that my plumage becomes bewildering stasis

a patternless holding grain

hovering day after uncounted day

so that progression is blurred as a specious

in-canonical counting

as corroded daybreak foundries

which register deficits through enfeebled

firmaments

like creatures wandering

burning

uncreated

nameless

in league with genetic myopia

yet

I've wandered from liquidation

like some incandescent signal

wafting from Alpha Centauri

combining a superior vocal carbon

with freshly harvested monerans alive by means

of a restless imporosity

I have occurred from a blank diaspora

predicted by all the entities

factored from an osmotic codex

far beyond a fixed or strangling relation

with soil

I'm speaking of dialectic with dialectic

of mirror with mirror

being alive with ghostly oxygen levels

primeval as a thirstless cosmological fire

neither the instinctual mind nor matter

but energy more fundamental than living

& it is this zone in which I trembled through

undoing

238

I was a precocious Datura in blackened lightning
valleys
divinized by smell
by leakage
by chromosomal quaking

a perfect séance by velocity
by sudden neutron seas simultaneous as deltas

& from this velocity
I will attempt to mind vectors
from intrinsic pollutional ailments
imbibing henbane litres
so as to transmute the various toxins of the planet

the infelicitous toxins
alive
like a rose improperly rooted
full of phosphorous loads
'dissolved salts'
'suspended solids'

the water columns blackened by negative jurisdiction
which also alters noiseless soil subsistence

health as ethos scarred by impediment

the earth & sea

a doubled arsenic lagoon

my death & re-birth threatened

on land

the 'knotted rush'

the 'foothill Jepsonia'

threatened

the 'Gaviota tarplant'

threatened

as if

all the mountains were burning

as if

all the clouds were corrupted with tar

dissonance

anaemia

scrawling

so the sea horse prairie darkens

& the 'Giant kingbird'

& the 'Java sparrow'

dying

now

even the Aruba Island rattlesnake

has fear for any future existence

blazing simple glass has fallen
yet the upper realms remain dim

the alpine form as struggle
as acidic ice from the Andes
being the variant shapes of the one named burden

& that burden
is cataclysm
is the umbra of collective asphyxia

yet though all these embranglements there is
movement
beyond deracinated oxygen hives
through oblivious self-ascent
which heals & claims by deficit
as if
my wings were a brazen feast
empowered by precarious collapse

here I am
in this discomforted zone
in this malformed garden in the cosmos

Earth
hidden by umbrageous velocity
by alchemical fuels incalculable with strife

my voice

ventriloqual with weaving

with an energy which instructs & ignites me

which sustains

a meandering pre-biotics

through a challenge which rises through

respirational density

through atomic transmixture from old exploded suns

ghost suns

suns which seep through haunted helium trees

& it is this alien creed

its severity of shock & disclosure

which emits from its lake incinerated patterns

my concern

my strange galactic heritage

'the entire...histories of numerous species and planets'

I

condoned by isolation

sufficient witness to terror

I am that bird who exists by obscure seminal

feedings

my dust spells

by lakeless metronome

by courage

242

by spectacular substance which leaks from

de-intrinsic mills

with its light re-spawned form imaginary wastes

its transfer wattage

its gold & intransigent conduction

its risk

its higher feeling as alterity

I have risen to the level of flight as pure

regality

as recessive crimson volcanoes

therefore

I reveal & de-reveal

hostile to decoding

to a secondary briskness

& at another level

there is public carrion enormity

because of this I am weightless

I continue to fly beyond the feast of countable

galaxies

perhaps I will leave traces

or blank electrical salts

to transmute surrounding disorder

or perhaps phosphenes of data propelled
across eons

perhaps the Earth replaced as a ghost of itself
will accrue from a cluster of eons

I will fly through every disorder
through every conquest by sterility
always invading my own cinders
by fire as an elevated pressure
not by common finesse
nor the fever of migratory vultures
but by neoteric hives
coursing with alien biochemical transmixture

me
flying from a sun hut
above complex emotional treachery
above a suicidal sleeping contagion
producing in me a tension between voices
between a feral data & transpositional curses

I remain compelled by dystopic example
by need for release from fire as Venusian realia

I've come to the plane of random molecules
& brandings
opaque opthamologies

crystalline minutiae

which divides & subdivides as asymptotic emblems

meadows described by asymptotic leaps

by dual & creatureless floatings

which exponentiate the meadow

being again simultaneous & random

or transitional simultaneities

as civilization in eclipsing hydro-waters

building up a phylum by strange contextual error

by slippage magnetized as indifference

the storage of genes in a spore

coming to fruition as dazzled speaking animation

this world

a shore

a human in a woolen garment

a crucified whale in the water

each parameter

each struggle

like a depth which exists in 2 surrounding zeniths

& these zeniths

like dialectical blinding

always rising in trance as diacritical anomaly
above memorials to natural tragedy

this
the honour & valor of atmosphere

I understand fission
I understand the nature of crucial seismic debility

so being a beacon I see as a natural optical
predator
as one who attacks de-inventive justice

I am prepared to hover at once
above the coastline of Chile
above the Mozambique Channel

through partial retro-causality
being an Aztec leader at Carthage
reversing the 3rd Punic war
reversing its extrinsic heritage at Rome
its bloody yields
its public mental tundra

the human then unlinked to aggressive tidal
pneumonia
attempting to chart higher vertigo location

these locations are pattern

are superposition etched above blunting

as that they exist beyond artefact

as variant respiration

as stained asymmetries void of depletion

artefact as sole leaning as grammar through devastation

it's as if I landed on a scorched Datura

& crafted its colour by counting stones across

number

cures are perceived as coercing imbalance

medicines as pharmaceutical styptics

devoid of faultless nigredo

nigredo as intrinsic potentia

it is held by the modern kingdoms

that nigredo is regressive in baseness

that it lingers

that it reeks of the pestiferous

for me

it revolves in the manifest world

active as 'destroyed remains'

like a vengeful sun

occulted at Nineveh

it is my first strength

my focused thirst

my consuming aerial locus

my sustainable allegiance

as I migrate to Cotopaxi

& my guides form the Devonian

non-palpitant in their forms

now displaced as a Mexican Iris

my alabaster shark

my hoar-frost lizard

never of diurnal dread

emitting through my mirage a magnificent growth

intent

far more intriguing than the 'gold-spotted mongoose'

with its 'speed & agility'

with its victory over cobras

they have guided me

far beyond encounter as observable activity

not 'physical process'

nor biological determinant

nor ascensional ruse

but the high transpersonal field

field as illuminant monad

now

I have been given flight by osmotic heron climate
& inside of me
the Sea of Azov
the Ébrié Lagoon
the Buenaventura Bay

combinatorial
random breathing
so as to salivate euphoria
so that survival under the one current sun
takes on the power of a vatic embryology

say the sky contracts
say the waters engulf with rancidity

perhaps a broken sea on the moon
perhaps the coasts squandered with perishable
content
so that the archetypes seem threatened
that is why I exist as multiple disfavour against
history
against each calendar parallel to memorials

my Henbane sigil is for the kinship of living

scopolamine
hyoscyamine
with atropine as the complete sigil

air beyond birdless dictates or lectures

being elixir as horizonless bird

which flies over the poles of Io

to speak with vanished beings

then escaping through great vacuums

to perform great feats

concerning terra firma

concerning its suicidal foundry

concerning its repetitious demise according

to present criteria

I am in accord with birds

volcanoes

whales

in accord with glowing hyena cauldrons

such as the Earth with capacious diameter

with its hydro-electrical interior

its sound in keeping with the howling of wild dogs

I speak of wild dogs because they hound

they are electrical in attack

they are form as extrinsic contention

because they are proof of viral declaration

of ironic alchemy as living

they are a force on Alpha Centauri

on 44 Ophiuchi at 20,000 A.D.

& these 20, 000 years are crepuscular

are not walls to be scaled

or carnivorous backdrops to be founded

mountain suns burn

hills are destroyed

yet the central furnace persists

as a critical flare of black energy

this universal constant from nothingness

emitting galaxies in its wake

like a magnet consumed with transmuted explosion

I awaken to inverse snow beneath squandered

flecks from Egeria

seeing ethers from a blighted fungal shore

where light is interiorized by canyons

by buttes translocated extended by human aphasia

the silence

suspended

much like volcanic imminence

thus all exterior life

dazed by precarious arousal

by wayward manganese theologies

my odyssey

in essence

puzzling

made evident by equivocal theocracy

rural in its grasp

like a drizzling cacophony which divides &

re-divides

such as a ground with unordered lizards

then the puzzling smell of these lizards

inculcates dilemma as orchid

as concussive draft through fields

rising from an electric reef

what I say are not rulings skewed by temporal

consignment

nor am I weighted by a false or arrogant beginning

charged atoms

sudden methodologies

demonstrated kindling

these triple conductions betray me

& give me my worth

but I am dependent outside of my vacuum?

is the poltergeist within me law

above a secondary mode or invention?

have I wielded catastrophe by enigmatic flaw?

these are rotations that haunt me

which ignite me by strange agenda

as if ignition were inspired by syllogistic mazes?

by silken aerial gladioli?

every glance I imply is aerial

is that which supersedes initial poisonings or fractures

which each electrical being knows as creation

as that vacant perspective

as that uncountable premise

prior to activity as form

through my Henbane foliage

I ceaselessly gather havens in my feathers

perhaps as guard against the jealousy of demons

or perhaps

the higher chronicles have gone awry

as I attempt to fly through famines

through thermo-nuclear wheat

so gravity is never pattern

an anachronistic grain

like sullen variety in death

singing to myself through territorial winters

as if all sound were pointless hounding

as if there were large deranged vita ceasing

to cling to its parts
never belonging to the moral cyclone of nature

the humans
a troublesome species
always tearing through life with a philanthropic ire
so that the globe is now deformed
with damage to its electrical inherence

I am acute with vivacity
certainly not perceptible to girded mental twine
or to blood which dwells in a poisonous heat

in this regard
I see through the mists a left brained being
mishandling wolves in a faultless ammonia den
creating imbalance by 2's & 1's
that is
having the 2 lean against the 1

such as ammonia mixed in methane arroyos
leaning against energy which accelerates deficit

& this energy leans against me
burns in my wings
attempts to circumvent my inner aerial locale
as actual Euclidean barymetrics
which I counter by superpositional instinct

use of such instinct is hewn equator as phantom
aquatic sunlight as motion

the angular breeze which pierces
which supervenes itself & annihilates description

annihilates each didactic flask
concerning humans who devastate well-being

my light is concerned with the crucial concavity
of cells
far higher than centigrade
on a Ganymede
on a blank & surfaceless Callisto

these are the games that breathe within me
the cells
with their secrets as blazeless definitives

this is the alchemy
the posture which condenses as riddle
being the hidden helical spore
which sustains itself forever

let me speak of 1 to 7 oceans
where human nausea is reversed
where cryptic isolation evinces motion as a
transfigured lightning

like a seeming irregular hail

meteoritic

infinite

being light from entangled suns protracted

as kinesis

rapid water as fire

cold with its symbol of advancement

advancement as transfigured frequency

as rays

as the galactic 'Loom' of the Maya

with their 'thirteen numbers'

with their 'twenty signs'

advancement beyond uranium figurines

as mixtures & fulcrums

so as to re-seed the algae

so as to re-populate the ovens of the oceans

with health

re-spinning the earth beyond inductive chimera

again Earth

beyond illusional neutron weighing

as nascent supra-rotation

as yield more penetrant than glass

coming to a new elastic velocity

velocity confounding its present rotational identity

256

this escalation becoming distillation as

habitable air

giving to terra firma its ancient germinal ray

its continuous oscillating bastion

being a dark virginal night flare

a critical carrier of nerves

no longer a somber centripetal confounding

to intuit such vatics

I carry a central claustrophobia

a seasonless vortical fury

matched at the essence of its pitch

by hurricanes

baffling

unexpected

implying a perfect global unease

all life

being a hatchery for pilgrims

for borderless birds

for ghosts across the sea

& these ghosts are like Mergansers

& in fact the code is scarcity by Merganser

as if describing a sigil as flying cyanide species

restless & particular

as a hounded form of carp organically quivering

within a fish farm on the Ganges

no

I am not a rancid bell cataloging trauma

be it the Javan rhinoceros

the Caribbean manatee

the Trinidad piping-guan

the Congo pea fowl

of course there are the pheasants in Brunei

endangered peacocks in Borneo

declining corncrakes in Yemen

disrupted birds on the Chatham Islands

saying such

I never seek to introduce a geometry of herds

or enforced lists

according to brightly coloured breeding in Tasmania

my voice as it seeps from quantum warrens

invading 'sedge meadows'

induced by genetic isolation from inaudia

so that I constantly weave the atomic power in my molecules

hurling through hermetic motion

shifting invisible axial trees

building elastic aqueducts from stains

I am visible to those who feel me

who intuit my squall as quantum delectation

quanta no longer fuel the priests
summoned from palpable entrapment

I am the breakage of laws & motions
created by the absorption of laws & motions

through sigil
ambiguity is discussed by limitation
by myopia seeking to limit suns
or general solar deprecation as contained by
transverse limit

a burst leading northward as 'Weak Anthropic' lens

participation as relentless non-criteria
through coincidence as spectra
as dimensionality becomes witness
through prohibitive scope as creation

this being the forge which infinity produces
in exploded stars
in Apache trout
in human Micropsia

with such purview
I can speak of the Bubal hartebeest
the Barbados racoon
the Solomon Islands fruit bat

the Syrian wild ass

the Koa-finch

the Burly lesser moa

the King Island emu

the Chatham Island swan

the Carolina parakeet

the Mauritius grey parrot

so if that perception of God as in-dwelling amoeba

as a horrifically soured floating hen

persists throughout my destabilized fragility

it is because I understand the power of primeval

glossary

like old lava spilled from a Rodrigues day gecko

or the lymphatic struggle of the San Marcos

gambusia

breathing through barbarity as fissure

as sudden water drowned by the bizarre

perhaps

if I stole from sleep a greenish Neptune sheep

I would ascend to an Agua of deity

equally parallel with deity

both simulation & disorder

these sheep as potentia

as guides

as responding plasma

& no magnification as soil

far below the Planck continuum

nor common use as evidence

birth being the great continuum of nautical

jasmine beauty

to speak of stadia or the hyperemia

of myths or floods throughout Jordon

is not the data one seeks to renew

or surreptitiously invent

I fly throughout the mount of the largest

'inner planet'

with its one moon

its land elevation: 860 meters

its water: 2500 meters & plunging

the Earth

which transfers to its atmosphere

'an amount of energy equal to that' which it absorbs

its thermal equilibrium

13 Celsius

its 3 internal layers

'crust'

'mantle'

'core'

expressed

throughout the geomagnetic field

with its '4 million atmospheres'

with its sea floors spreading

its subduction

creating solar locales

where I take into my blindness

a potent 'embryo sun'

emitting from its blueness

electrical angular conservation

creating rapid concentration developed by momentum

as if there were 3 original suns

emerging from a dark concussive proto-dimension

rife with nitrogen glass

with black voltaic snow

as is Saturn

with its dark & yellow cloud bands

its transparent equator like a strange rotational

drawing

its 'primordial' 'reservoir' akin to black escaping

nebular light

being an 'anticyclonic' rotating system

being ice in its upper ethane body

its radiograms being 'synchrotron' emissions

being electrons spiraling from magnetic havens

these signals

swept through space

262

by its colossal 'coplanar rings'
tilted
composed of particles

the D ring extending to the 'cloud tops of Saturn'
then there is the Crepe & the brightest ring B
with its 'electrostatic' discharge of redness

then the 'Cassini Division'
related to perturbations
caused by the satellite 'Mimas'
or the A ring & its 'shepherd satellite called Atlas'

then the shepherd satellites Janus & Epimetheus'

they are far from the 'birthplace of sunspots'
implying velocity greater than light

no
I am not the lunar equivalent to a subdwarf star
with its 'low metal content'
with its luminosity much smaller than error
but of our one parent Sun
with its 'proton-proton chain reaction'
with its mass as a diagram by kelvin
with its strong convection transport
igniting the valleys & rivers

8 minutes from its riverine pyrology

much different from the light on Amalthea or Metis

or on the 'Great Dark Spot' on Neptune

or on Uranus

with its heat transported between the poles & its equator

when I say its rings

when its mass occulted a star

I knew the low albedo of Miranda

collectively implying fragment as void

as plutonian anti-resolution

perhaps feeling in my wings the polar caps of Pluto

my survey

being imaginal methane contour

as irregular exhibit

my skill transgressed as a damaged savant

I

being a form no longer contained to mirrored confinement

in this I possess luminous flight through anguish

through bitter & negative photisms

dissimilar & caliginous with vertigo

I am that Henbane Bird

that Hillstar derived beyond the architect of avians

never solely being a coastal winter or a plague

I am he who derives his cells from a spore

whirring in exhausted living conditions

I cannot be compared to ideographic jackal
floating sulfuric signs from the suns of the abyss

the lithosphere philosophically split
into semi-devouring fragments
untoward with aspiration
as though reflected by guidance

they who desire to guide death
they who dwell in anachronistic twilight
knowing that they devour & enrich their devouring
by psychic orientation
by a clarity of poles
knowing the zones between luminous genesis & primeval extinct
an agitated consociation
eaten day by day by an allusive hierognosis
their instincts gnawed by a strange crusader's doubt
neither emptied nor barren
but as shamans who brood between origin & flux

& it is at this degree that the mongoose shuns them
should it desire to be lessened
should it desire to live its life below the threshold of
power

shamans
with their instinct linked to non-specific cohesion
to blank chimerical howling

they imply in this sense non-observable form

non-rational locales

which suggest absence as activity

they are particles

cells

vibrational nuclei

drift

invisible immobility

which shifts

which causes a self-absorbed by-path

being power as mercurial spectra

being power which plunges yet evades the inferno

they could be deduced to vampire spectra

to gainless filtering prisms

much like errata which subsists within errata

their blank irradiations

on the order of analogical Gemingas

exploded & re-combined as experiential solvent

unlike the form of chronic stationary boulders

revolving along their borders

like a strange transgressive Uranian androgyny

they exist

not as mere apostles

but as convulsives homogenetic with indifference

insensate with glare

with a chronology frayed & dispersed

non-binding in accord with succession

this is reasoning dialectic with concealment

as to elements

such as ytterbium or nickel

their powers have been dispersed to other possible voids

or infusions

say

to insurrectional meridians

to squandered fantasias or planets

like the 5 giant worlds around Epsilon Eridani

or those confirmed rotational worlds around pulsars

such as 47 UMA

worlds which spin

through a blackened trespasser's abyss

like my well of dark inscrutables in the Andes

with its roving microbial armies

with its migratory rifeness prone to reverential

calamity

flying in the dark through eerie transfigured shards

liminal with lightning

a plight

which glows with eclipses

with ironic migration

not

as a transmigrating idol

or as a fabulous kind of linkage sculpted by embers & blood

but as implication beyond leakage

beyond debility as example

I

being a sigil condensed as carnivorous variety

as anti-endeavour

not that I intone vaccination by edict

by carcinogen as spoilage

but there exists that deadening of water

increment by increment

species by planetary species

I'm speaking of neural extinction

charged to bewildering human consumption

as if all the living were surrounded by compound indictment

throughout my wayward perquisition

my wings have been a-lit with heavenly charcoal monsoons

much above

those doctrines transmixed with polemical chastisement

268

because I have flown to those magnetized by bursts

elliptically condoned by treasonous scripture

as if the heavens coalesced by ratsbane & stalemate

so on the surface I am insufflation as unmerciful heretic

as invisible harmattan which scorches

like a cunning deviation from a pulmonic sea

being 'subtle physiology'

being prophetic 'specularity'

I have come from the universe which preceded the zone

of the present era

being the universe preceding

that which is known by deadly sensory ingestion

one can now speak of biology as celestial transfunction

as for Leopard frogs

as for freshwater bass

they've ceased to dis-engender me

as for the power of their inimical methane

it does not evolve or exist

as a rhetoric consumed & thermodynamic with respiration

with obligation or betrayal

condensed by human mathematical marking

so as to its evolvement or dissolution

I am 'unusually fearless'

never compelled by over-assiduous data

such as the stars being lichen

or parts of burning spiders' anatomy

in my physical anatomy

I've lived in a burning lichen retreat

I've torn & reclaimed colours from the heavens

I've blazed

I've been a vervet tornado

I've been a blaze identical with prairies

in Ecuador

near Gualaceo

near Pichincha

near Papallacta

in the 'Andean meadows'

being fire

being power at equatorial snow lines

being unforeseen as genesis

I am anti-cadaverous as quota

knowing that the abyss subsumes dialectic as dilemma

as blazeless circular root

expressed as geologic remission

certainly not by nerveless decibel or by rote

& no

I'm not a cryptic map

nor a funereal ambrosia

which inorganically falters

yet brought to bear within my focus

the challenge of sterility by trial

yet at the same time

being nothing more than harrowing policy as error

again

as translocation through struggle

an aeronautics

stationary

& alchemical with drift

simultaneous by attempting every psychic containment

cleansing implicate deluge by inferno

so that mountains will never implode

I must fly

I must enable every arthritic ammonia to disperse

knowing that rivalrous galaxies are transfigured

as blasphemous icons or locales

I do not proclaim epitaphs

or accrue collective mandates by ocean bottoms burning

but vita

vivification at random

inordinately compared to blinded shore birds & phantoms

I do not speak from my story as dearth

as cold adrenalin preamble

but for that cellular translucence

which organically transmutes eternity

the law of boulders

& gales

& great pluvial teeming

of summoned grain from the Sun

parallel with hazard

with chances

with endowed misnomer

somehow understood as ecology by terrapin

overcoming adumbration contained in mortal dyslexia

the Earth

stunned by feckless debit

by hidden connivance

which enhances surcease by every scarp as respiration

by every sand dune as fabulous incendiary mound

akin to cacophony as despair

further besieged by negative colonizing data

thus I see the bi-pedal species starving

on a non-existent polar wheat

the logos

completely vertiginous with repression

272

with devolving deposition

the mud

the pebbles

the loss of ice

the isobars scattered

on overlapping Fahrenheit

English coastal districts marred

sea fogs destroyed

halos missing from angular translucence

& these cooking doors

savage

through immobile cadenzas

so that each ruse I sing leaves a mark

a blank genetic viper

much like sand which grates over sand

kaleidoscopic

combustible

nanotropic

& it is to this domain

that humans erect a skittish moral barrier

with their cells listening to a zodiac in collapse

to climates restricted to mandates sired by malefic

obstruction

I contradict reconstructed fatigue

ailments

ardent disadvantage

linked to the structure of calendrical unknowns

to structure as basic solemnity

like a cleansing apparition

restoring plummeted sparks between species

cladistics

shared remnants

erasure of funicular mis-slaughter

the species then combined as microscopic respiration

being dark galactic instinct as movement

never a dulled vehicular dominance

but expression as roaming charisma

yet at the visible level

union persists

as a troubling in-demonstrable cipher

like differing yet united diacritical formations

marks

accents

mutterings

the blood

the intent

the honing

like signals

or in-terminal codings

presently living in the proto Pre-Cambrian

lurking as implicate totality

& always this lurking

in the river of animal foundation

this principate as galaxy

as somehow symmetric with vapourous suns in formation

for instance

the 'Virgo' cluster of galaxies

with their 'counter-clockwise rotating' systems

with their incarnadine systems

with their spectrographic flares

so intelligence persists by pictographic homing

unlike governable data

but by stoic ascensional rote

certain singular objects being brighter

like generic butane

being an open light on specific intangibles

such as the Coalsack Nebula

with its spectral desolation

with its scorched magnetics

with its specific illusion

then I connect Barcelos

Iquitos

Coari in the Amazon

with their galaxy of beings

harvesting mimosoid legumes

with their flowers of floating bladders

the opposite of a scattered fishing geography

like 'sacred pieces of ice'

inside a scarred & reasonless jungle

with botanical Frigates & Petrels

& me as an Andean mountain relic

or perhaps

a Rhinoceros egret feeding on transgressive raw fish

the latter marred by angular writhing

their fate meandering

their future summoned by healthless erogenous eras

I do not exist by sudden claims

by giving to healthless eras

my touch

which will cleanse the future of uninhabitable yields

that utopias will rotate

that all death will cease to ensue by progression

by meandering through fatiguing bodily debit

but these are my breakthroughs
these are my fortnights of yield
with entropy transmuted
with a new intrinsic entropy revealed

I
as smouldering power above the death watch
as total power through innuendo
as that I declare but do not lead

by being
I inspire by new variety
by deathless imminence in the cells
spawning myself by dictation

I now live at the height beyond neutered animal law
as if my wings were utter frankincense salvation
my body unclaimed by sterile advancement
seemingly probing kelp as a uranic auditory camel

so that my being
neither ancient restoral through panic
not is it subjective to strenuous bio-geology
counter to subterfuge as salt
to literal ammonia by yolk
being pulmonic sigil as victory
shining through feral cloud interiors
hidden at times by the great society of lizards

suspended in space

like geometric primevals

all outline then working as jagged reference to deity

to jagged lightning deities

like burnished glycerin or magnets

startling the void

like greenish lettering on bulls

like Neptune in relief

as if by singing I approached the noiseless liquidation

of bells

thereby lifting strange sodium deltas into contact

like speckled hemachromes in rotation

which re-appear & vanish

as by deluge or vapour

a grammar of nectar shaken loose from the ozone

so that the spectra of hydrogen remain free & non-concussive

being a shadowy twine

a meteoric detritus

knowing that Earth is the eros of isolation

being a fecund maize

at arcane remove from the central galactic vicinity

& I understand its relief as pre-hypnotic penumbra

as uncollected tyranny

as sanguineous political preamble

the earth

278

with its irregular mixture of plants & owls

with its devices of terror

its chimerical reasonings by combat

I think of medicines & hives

of blue sestinas

of abstract coffins in the wild

none of this fails me

each afternoon as serpentine anaemia

knowing this

I conduct myself above general vampire uraniums

above disrupted migrations

as a microscopic potentate

devoid of stark or blind embodiment

evanescence which disembodies

by quoting myself through an uneven distance

inculcating fissures

my molecules being restive

my cinders both blazeless & engendering

blazeless as impalpable prism

engendering as electric protein fevers

always foreseeing in my flight dialectical amoebas

amoebas being friction which glow by rotation

as adversarial code which strengthens by fire

flying with supernatural suns in my wings

with barbarous currents

with unalterable samplings

like a fire cradle

blank

anti-constructed

alive as repeatable velocity

I am this bird

I am this aerial cacophony

this invisible nitrogen shaman

cross-feeding

like Indian natural farming

the beans

the squash

the White Potatoes

the peppers

flying through Indian dromedary scents

such as Asiatic fuels

such as sub-conscious hierophanies

akin to beatific glissandos

flights through the lands of the Maya

the Opatas

the Aztecs

the Orotiñas

280

alive in their depth

with the comings & goings of ghosts through the sun

a geometrical sand point

which magnetizes

which unreleases motion

creating from its quakes

sacrificial medlars

through which reflections float

as nucleic progenitor's

such as a ribbon fish

such as a seahorse on Venus

or coelacanths roaming near the confines of Mimas

I fly

as an earthquake Indian

as an iridescent beacon

I do not speak for petrification or usurpation

but the balance of gales

as they sweep through aridity

again

the sigil as a pleurodont's incisors

burning as ambush procedure

not simply as a blood guise

of the Solomeco

or the Popoluca

a flock of wolves

athletic blood apples

unsalvageable bondage

as if I were hidden & mis-persuaded & scolded

yet my whereabouts gregarious

by those whose calls are interiorised by encagement

who have emerged from ponds engendered by virulence

negative avians

stark non-functional cinders

emerging from ponds synonymous with horrific mortalities

an energy

which exists above these birds

shedding

sequential intentionality

possessing this energy

I am not akin to the sudden bleeding of crows

to threatened longevity

to anti-amazement counted by year

as if

there could be universal decipherment

chiseled away by error

the taints

the utilities of dejection

no longer contained in the palpable blood count

in the penumbra which upholds damnation

it is not a life attained by oratorical turmoil

but scarcity of oxygen as threat

I am speaking of gainful elixir

as gainful spectre which dwells as perfection

a perfection which exhilarated as a crucially centered pyrexia

which reflects itself

which colours yet evade me

those vermilion lucubrations

those scents which evolve from the kingdom of sparks

like alien cometary volcanos

or wayward black electrical optics

far beyond those colloquial drafts which assault me

thereby engaging interchangeable pantopias

where life intrinsically re-magnetizes its central

diligence concerning health as heliology

such solitary lessons spinning from sub-aqueous lecterns

its waters being the height of 3 spiral nebulas

waters evolved beyond the prayer from hellish solar dust

primeval polar leaves

the 'extra-hieratic' burning as snow

this world being a sun of one condemned lunation

its winds engulfing worlds with curious centigrades

hails

with summits reduced & re-burnished & coloured by

inverse contour

such as Tupungato

Domuyo

Chimborazo

Neradas de Cachi

vertically rising

as schismatic potentates

as earthquake zeniths

in contrast

the Chilean Trench

with its 'shallow-focus earthquakes' rippling

where ocean ridges lift

where molten irregularly pulses

become petrology in the Nazca Plate

where volcanoes spawn from dark convective mantles

active submarine volcanoes

north of 'Cerro Ventisquero'

east of the 'Maria Teresa Reef'

yet I fly

unpropelled by material integer

but by charismatic deftness

284

transmuting stigmata

transmuting burial by glimpses

eclipsing by stamina ruthless intervention by nothingness

in this regard

nihilism as emptied polar concussives

as conflagration by muting

by great barriers against the intangible

you see

chaos does not dwell as the consuming register

or a phalanx of wasps

or negative blazes which transpire within enumerated

guyots

I do not fly according to longitudinal marks

or objectively tested breathing grains

but to ward off atmospheres so the elements release me

so that I'm gathered as a voyage

under a lake or a broken era

as I now exist

I am unfounded

I am seemingly without balance

without numerical chalice

spinning by honey or rote

I am witnessed by clouds as ballistic suggestion

by post-existing traces

by hissing optical streaks

my horizon combining partial zenith & delay

seething

throughout a geographic twilight

neither

of the East or the West

of the North or the South

my instinct

not of vibrational monotone

not of the cardinal points as limits

but as ascensional flare

higher than the codes of pure perceptual quandary

of laws guiding distance through number

a quest

baffling

at the threshold dimension

at the sluice of the beyond

which implicates the 'Boreal'

the 'North Subtropic'

the 'Tropic'

the 'South Subtropic'

the 'Antarctic' & the 'Subantarctic'

zones

& by moving beyond these zones

286

I am vernal as antipathy through movement

outside the crops of the latitudes

outside spinning terra firma

in its eastward momentum

its oblong direction

its various extremes of the Sun

its winds as skittish seasonal postures

& this excludes the exterior parts of the bird

with its 'mandibles'

its rump

its legs

its belly

I exist through symbolic degree

by undecided respiration

beyond the webs the throat the bronchus

with my north tropic eye

with my sun as invisible reversal

I evince the conserving of pressure

as compass

as de-existent needles

as a glossary de-extended

through Peruvian Diving-petrels

or Patagonian Gulls

I could speak of the Shag

of the Spanish Imperial Eagle

or the brownish Inca Tern resting on small 'sandbars'

yet I do not invoke a pointless gullible floating

nor predict a certain atlas of miracles

but to medicinally cross-pollinate

bringing back to his plane

the geomantic balance of the planet

provoking from my salts a geologic ermine spell

which transfigures

ghostly ridges of ants

blank hyena betrayals

both of the above being nervous lots of darkness

the above

alive with sunspots & amnesia

because of this I have left my mark on blue equational

fields

I have opened saffron vessels

I have transformed musk

I have broken impasse spectrums

revealing to my flight

unified galactic order

a purified orb

a mathematical ether

yet

I'm surrounded by curious bodily darkness

with gravitational terror

with eschatology as nomography

as if life were consumed by corruptive cytology

yet I know that the cells are rife with gleaming oracles

with miraculous plots

with ignited statutory grain

therefore

I can never be excluded as subset

as lobotomized aerial pyrotechnic

like a hidden wind in tortured stationary light

because I live

as a rooted fractal

deeper

than the atomics of crystalline partaking of moons

openly green in diameter

microns removed with their suns colorific

celadon

Prussian blue

lapis lazuli

examples certainly not exhaustive

there being an infinite variety of star fields

unnamed nebulas

intrinsic dust environments

echo by meteor

anachronistic neutron-intangibles

me

roost of interstellar complexity

like the central morphology of an atom

like the 'Ipuriná shamans'

I send my double to threatening zones in the empyrean

by revealing the void to unknown advantage

having 'radiogenetic' meteors imploded

because the deeper resonance persists

by electromagnetic weaving

one of its instants

trapezoidal polarity

another

indigo matrix

another

'auto-regulation'

the above being

the invisible levels of biologic relation

such as a cluster which evaporates to reascend as

evolution

not as withdrawal by hooves

or hemachromes which dazzle as anti-existence

or exploded ocher academies

like electric detonation which annuls exterior principle

by work

unlike my home in the lightning tornadoes

above a mesmerizing acreage

as if light were studied by interior neural waves

all the while listening to a fragment of galaxies

being a symbolized land in Ecuadorian blue suns

perhaps

a northeastern fragment

at aerial rates beyond foci as treaty

or

an irregular fragment

much smaller than a billion solar masses

seismically burning by aboriginal current

as black ventriloqual dwarfs

absorbed in a curious acetylene randomity

much in keeping with subsistent ambrosia

I being the bird in orbital ubiquity

certainly not construed as grainy helium disorder

or a shaken monsoon alp

or a dazed eruptive star

such are my prisms

my lamp in atomic tranquility

void of pre-luminal anger

or plummeted radium or scarlet

as if the Sun were stored in Peruvian barley

not a descent

not a lorikeet devoid of weapons

but a zeal which blazes as an ocean crop of aurum

being spinning photometry as sign

so no self-created guilt delimits me as boundary

by manger as hardened miracle

as troubled comet

as arid helium vine

as in poisoned in-symbolic count stirred up with scaupers

I exist

only to osmotically rise

to build by auto-suggestive inferno

auspicious mandibles

a phase of bottomless criteria

not from form as embellished distraction

but as leonine template

vertical

obscure

osmotic

beyond a cold dismissive wheat

bewitched as I am by the cellular animation of the tropics

292

the rains
the suns
the snows
the agitation in the stones

cuerpo as terra firma
as relentless cyclical revelation
alive as gainful torment
as central mirage
electrically glowing in vacuums

it is within this blindness that I hover
within this shadow
as if at its core there existed lenticular unevenness
as in an abode of phantom stellar geometry
my wingbeats in rhythm with winter neutral oneirics
like movement as gradation through opacity
through that praxis which increases limit
extolling its opposite through utter expansion

such is my gaze which seems to burn through dryness
which accurately de-increases
which penetrates the bark through ghostly spells
of surveillance

so there is never direct assertion
or a fossilized account
which does not include instantaneous migration

so at bi-axial level

I am one: primeval scar

then independence by wave

outer shell as nitrogen & volume

discontinuous sodium

ceaseless repetitive charisma

inclement disorder

a restless singing from the grave

a quantum bonding to life

a dissertation by imbroglio

by a grammar above fate

no

never gathered in Herculean bereavement

but in present regard

as a curious avian solstice

not by judgement or guile

or pontificating extremis

but as neural oxygen made manifest through duress

through those dark subversive minimums

which allow no limit for malfunctioning capacity

which randomly inheres when overcoming the impossible

certain botanical debilities

a strained instinctual deficit

which concerns the winds which blow with power

through blank directional sand

acclimating hail through unseen regions of being

& I am that hail

that wattage

whose cataclysmic sapphire contains the pressure of

healing

whose premise evolves from dosage through poison

from a fulminous alien delinquency

from such droplets of dark

I gain pronominal bells

gaining power through glottic environment

healing the 'drilling muds and cuttings'

absorbing the sickness in the waters of 'The Makassar Strait'

worldly cycles condensed by sullage

by populous neutron breathing

which reek of old industrial spells

of negative mass

inverted like a billion suns in demise

so my quest is habitation

whose existence is analogous to an opalescent heaven

to a startling supernal

above the critical procedure of bloodlight

.

bloodlight being disease

or

assassination of beasts by constitutional evil

because of such malignant uncertainty

I mine the minerals between the heavens

so as to react to the critical lessening of life

magnified

by eternal condemnation of all that vibrates

of all implication of growth

charged in its essence by salubrious participation

life:

electrical mitosis

life:

revolving with voltage

the Earth

concerned with yields from ecumenical copper

from broken labour fields

from tainted kingship warrens

known to my quest as human ballistic corrosion

a strange ballistic corrosion

with its stagnate sulfate gardens

its precipitous rise in sea level sewage

yet what I claim by my Henbane power

is to open up the praxis of sleep

296

to change each feral nuance to paradise

reversing chromosomes in the poison

with the tundra ascending to arithmetical gold

to the presence of a stellar yet classic reason

& this reason

is a lattice of auroras

of permutations glowing in the higher world of eclipsed

suspension

this being the 'twenty amino acids' constructed from

genetic codons

through transference of cells

through geo-elliptic transference

the imaginal blood being spherical

being immanent through higher dimensionality as water

as 'biopsychic' lagoon

which generates through its force 3 secondary rays

& these rays are occult

unbrightened

but alive with geo-electric order

with balanced guiding through saturation by rays

say

a decimated wolf

a sterile furnace of salmon

with these dexterous rays full of falling holon blinding

I eclectically integrate these rays

with lymphatic barley

with new cerulean ethers

with median geomantics

the 'electromagnetic field'

simultaneous

with enigmatic zoology

roaming from zone to zone

like continuous star formation

as shift

as documented greatness

as flight

through Uranian lakes green with albedo

seen from my Andean winter occlusion

I know in my substance an implicate hibernation

knowing flight through poisonous spirals of sleep

& this poisonous hibernation is but a sketch of

misleading intervals

tests

darkened dream erasures

from which I rise with the evidence of consciousness

having fought off eaglets

while flying backward across dimensions

understanding in its subtle shift

dialectical weight

knowing that my flight is higher than the death vow

supplanting the lingering gryphon

the dragon in the hawks' enclosure

such drift is seen as toxic

as wavering scarab without the power to cure

or to suddenly excel at perpendicular elixir

not simple concavity

combined by separate arcs & radii

or annoying sound from shale

but life force as fissure

bleeding by heat

this being my life as paroxysm

as interior germinating ground

as paroxysmal sunspot species

with its 17 cycles or winds

their totalic synecdoche

being iridium spores

being order & objective disorder

drought

horizontal debility

spectroscopic causes

symbols by blood

helical bolts

arithmetical hail

admitted land arrangement

voltaic aural trepidation

geomantic spectra

a forming medial world

life never being a barren quail

or a forceless thread of inertia

but a force

such as plankton syllables

such as post-inertia as quality

my flight being more than behavioural vibration

more than residual optics which glisten

a bird

whose embarkation is resistance

a being

whose dialog is of traces

feeding myself of carbonized rotation

with pure activity as eternity

instantaneous dialogic

horticultural with consumption

with tornado ferns

with 'Yellow buckeye' & 'Persimmon'

with 'Ipomoea'

with 'Cinchona'

with 'Guava'

with 'Ground Cherry'
with 'Maize' & 'Cassava'

to evince such fertility
my body a-lit like a 'torch of copal gum'
working with evidence on Saturn
with its 'yellowish dark and light cloud bands'
with its 'anticyclonically rotating systems'

therefore
my wings seeming to spiral in magnetic darkness
in 'neutral hydrogen' rotation
above the 'Desaguadero'
above 'Potosi'
above the masonry of the star gate at Písac
harvesting miracles out of speech

my carnelian biology
chatoyant with crystal
with a pair of verdant wings sailing over Mimas
over Rhea
over Iapetus & Hyperion
embracing the power of the rings with their cold & unburning
beauty

that beauty which emotes in the stillness
which unendingly rotates like a faceless tertiary spell

I have always had concern with dalliance & mist
with a sub-order of hissing
with my shelter being an uneven blaze

if holonomics were reduced to a plagiarized powder
there would cease to be a saturated marking of cliffs
or an arousal of fear as antipathy
or beauty as the skittishness of being

fear being a homogenic barter
whose principles exude realia consumed as anti-radial
& fragment
as sworn equation
as equilibrium by nothingness
so
my episodic wing span
my feverish a-positional darting
alien
primeval
vanishing at the discipline of contact

such is my fever in response to polarity
which further deepens the gradations
fueled by the relative
as it sweeps through the codes
like weather from a spellbinder's summons
with the power of a scorching double helix
alive with solar nucleics

fed by the 'Negative Electron Belt'
by the Galactic Binary Resonance Fields'
by the 'Positive Galactic Proton Belt'
as in each degree of atmosphere

so that correlation combines
rife with indwelling circular fuels

& these fuels
overcome the exhaust of deadly chemical detritus
with their gregarious vertical inversion
being in essence a broken energy ellipsis
empowered by a dissonant constructional salt
which contaminate the 'Underground Currents'
the 'Seasonal Cycles'
the 'Tectonic Plates'

my flight as shaman
unpredictable as nomos

certainly not a mineral urn
or an Imperial juxtaposition
or a particle honed by theoretical stasis

never akin to animistic withdrawal
I am 'microgenetic' figment
carnivorous with movement
with that which releases rock & heat from swiftness

that is Mercury

to the desolating rays half a void beyond Pluto

I transmute the power within our single solar mass

tending toward the unsuspected clinamen

which again bespeaks of my freshly instilled fever

in this degree

I imply the totalic

I imply sustenance

which accrues through hieratic feeding

my flight

simultaneous & akin to the furious gallop of angels

to the vulcanization of minerals

it can never be said that I am tainted by acyrology

or made marginal by Glossophobia

no

my battle with Demonolatry

with the light from Peristaltic contractions

I have never been abducted by monomial visibility

or made common by the Andean cold & the height induced

in its vampiric surroundings

these are regions of the Andean abductor

where panic looms like a thrice broken sun

which forms seem utterly related to a crippled androgynous
deer
to a vindictive old priest
with his babble slurred
with his coast part missing
with his eycs of liquor subsumed by a darker further ale

& this darker further ale is negatively non-susurrus
& pathetic with claim

he
who has abandoned his feathers
his corresponding links
so that 'Galactic Exhalation' devolves to a strictly
seasonal disruption
to a broken link in the fabulous solar wheel
so that galactic maps are scattered
are examined by a scant plutocracy
divided by astronomical vagueness
without base skills
without cosmic reparation
carrying the lessened power of a rivalrous God
in keeping with the sinister fame of 'Tovoyo'
he seeks to overthrow the rhythm
to disguise the continents of space with mayhem
turning water to a curious petrol blood
wearing inhaled skin
causing illness within the infants

he

of darkened notoriety

he

who unplants the crops with inimical segregation

at a certain time

a horse from the Spaniards

a dog from the mecca of Lisbon

now he is blood turned apparition from the loathsome

cities formed in sync with strict industrial waste

calamity

myopia

spells enacted by a paralytic science

he is the seed of the death watch

he is the sum which contaminates cycles

he

of the blinded dog fur

he of the crystallized didactic of ruin

his wealth

an overthrow of emblems

of static redress to discovery

of swaying the polar lands with rabies

this being

this strange begetter of tombs

whose siblings are powers with crazed military groupings

who banish us externally

who keep our inner powers confused

by extolling an inward 'Deicide'

suggesting to our higher search a doubt of inscrutable

'noology'

our people then infested

our seething odylic force destroyed

suffering

nights of dreamless flailing

food stores depleted

drink from venomous copper filings

now

to raise in the people of neo-Cuzco a blaze of heavenly

brush fire atoms

the sun which regenerates the 'long white root of the manioc plant'

the 'flocks of llamas and pacos'

golden wool fed to the sun

allowing me to speak to myself in secret

like a runic glimpse from sudden planetary bodies

to 'Cuycha...the rainbow'

to 'Chasca...the planet Venus'

it is through speaking to myself that I have dialogue

with ordeal

with 'escorting the dead' to a freshly living world

voiding clamour mistrust & ill-fortune

as a bird shaman

I take a boat across the sea

I take a 'lance to break rocks'

I fly in my 'shipwreck' colours in order to reach the forest

I take as my substance the Andean Llama or reindeer blood

& I repeat myself & repeat myself as a mantra

as he who facilitates the void & the beings in its gulf

house

so I am the animal-bird who brings them back to earth-huts

to ride on a grey & woolen horse

only to discover their re-entry & return to the umbrageous

levels of calm wafting beyond the oceans of space

yes simply to calm the dead

to make known the factors of the green eternal principate

to live by 'general rejoicing'

by means of a wick

a burning ladder

a phase

from a sickened body

I remove an 'insect' a 'pebble' a 'worm'

the sickness then resolved with an initiatory burst of

blueness

the wanderer wakes up from his death

sketching potions in the air

in this regard I heal like the 'Manasi of eastern Bolivia'

of the 'Taino of the Greater Antilles'

forestalling yet increasing rain

gathering combs & knives & hatchets as treasures

as a bird drinking blood from Daturas

at simultaneous remove I drink blood from lianas

becoming the juice of lianas

so then I inhabit my 'sudden mystical organs'

attuned to the 'affected body' of the earth

healing its pathogenic labours

by the garrulous procedure of suction

not by antecedent betrayal

but by taking on the poison

by destroying its asphyxiated body

I being the shaman

the Andean Hill Star

the Henbane Bird

in quantum resonance with the Aranda

with the Unmatjera

dazzling

& osmotically parallel with somatology

whose apparition is a burning coextension with

Ilpailurkna

who has risen from the dead

from trials from forceful atnongara stones

groping in the dazed condition

as if I were a crane

a night crown heron

an Amherst pheasant

a white-eared turaco

stunned

outside of my element

stunned

as if flying like a pierced cormorant in the deep

as if I gazed as my body in a 'Sub-Glacial Basin'

or knew the 'Mid-Ocean Ridge'

or lived by proof from the 'Palmer Peninsula'

my instincts spun like a wrathful turbination

being vertigo as dysfunction

as if I were Aranda

or 'Warrumungu'

or amongst the 'Dayak of Borneo'

such is definition at the lower brink

at the cataclysmic plumb line

at the boundary

at the universal Gehenna

with all my organs subsumed by spirits

my voltage broken in sub-lunar fire

initiation

equal

to electromagnetic illness

& the life of initiation

technical

dangerous

I instigate misfortune & resolve it

through ventriloqual transgendering

as I myself contained the nectar by unroiling the soils

the dioxin winters vanished

each terrain of damaged nickel

virginal & re-emerged as cataclysmic cipher

as if spawned from a bluish nebula

by sand at its lowest figment of hearing

lift by winds across utopic inaudia

magically dissected by petroleum centripetals

transmuted into shifting manganese & salt

into exploded petrification as mist

projecting a matrix

a 'sky window'

both Altaic & Yahgan

as elixir

as geographic transmogrification

all the regions transfigured

the Pyrenees

the rock-bound meridians of China

Gambia

the Urals

the jungles of English Guiana

the sun at the bottom of circumspect oceans

brought to a level above an odd polluted impact

utopically resistant to imported infirmities

in time cleared from defect like human Dyslalia

flight through seraphic waterfalls

fossils returned to their metronymic origin

not idealized abstraction

not bland intention limited by blunder

that is

the numerical lightning flares

the strange monsoonal counts

vivid in the earth as new suggestive breathing

my presence risen above the honourless plague of suicide

a suicide which disempowers reefs

a suicide which destroys a billion Mangroves

which pressures 'Seagrass beds'

which causes the 'hardwood forests' of Ecuador to vanish

a diaspora of being teeming to no account

becoming sprawling Bohemias of death

but here

my language remains saffron

as if my voice were a blue flamingo

a populous cornucopia

like a moraine which blazes

without lepers' corona

without waters struck dead

the sun in my vista is an eminent orange-green

is both mineral & black

on this median plane

where the ghosts are transfixed with immortal fragility

my eyes

where the optics swim beyond the chronic particulars

beyond the singular suggestion of freezing canna lilies

onto the range of crucial puzzlements

staggered in their foci by deleterious quanta

quanta as secular motive

as human subjective decease

I

as high sentient realia

streaked by interior penumbra

by crystalline bursts from the snow line

by the blackened scent from the Mato Grosso

dispelling flaxen inertia like a lightning dune spun

from Arabia

when I fly through Chosica or Vitarte

I remain the burning particle of elf

the glimmering cordillera

as deftness

as movement

never lowered or damaged prowling

to deaf mercurial letters

to sums in a rayless abyss

in Camaná

across the Altiplano

higher up in Chiclayo or Chimbote

I am a ghost

a biopsychic fever

a quantum urn of health

beyond determinant

strictly conceived as biology

beyond the 'non-observable' conveyed in some minds

as suspicion

as valueless grass

knowing the seas

& the plates under the seas

the Scotia Sea

the Cocos Plate

the Southwest Indian Ridge

the East Pacific Rise

then the Inner Core

the Outer Core

the Upper Mantle

I then begin to hear the bell of the dogs

their intuitional howling

an answerless consuming burst

flowing through chronic neutron sieves

with my being always magically self-guided

dreaming on the henbane branch

letting the sun drown in blindness

by emotion as a deadly grace

a vertiginous indigo

a seemingly disordered abandonment

with solitude & danger as my only possessions

singing through tireless amalgams

being the rainbow shaman Tüspüt

possessed by 'seminal emission'

alive

through the astonishing theory of illness

transformed

by the heaving of confusions

by clashing intangible weight

because

I am alive without weight

between neutronic fire & its disappearance at boundary

hovering

solstitial

penetrant

my solar waters no longer stained by a claustrophobic

burden

dialectically rhyming

with its scorching & its waters

with its blemished plentitudes & its struggle

one can speak of a swan

2 bespeckled herrings

an enclave of Komodos

a wrathful iguana

then think of volcanoes germane to outer planetary

regimen

proceeding

by bionomic ratio

by scorched descriptive ingestion

one then sees human colloquy as atom

with geomancy fettered by ransom

like an optical strike against the core which creates us

against the beauty & the power which envisioned us

I
intoning from a blasphemous solar thicket
feasting on whole mathematical food
while wafting above a blank exclusionary dust
thereby negating a bitter critical tendency
yet somchow weaving a healthy blood from a grotto of dogs

this weaving
overcoming devastation
by cross-mortal affirmation

by taking abyssal methodologies
my taking the blaze from deaf mortality ponies
by fusing these zones as ventricle mirages
I inject their invention with salubrious breezes

I have drunk from the Glossopteris fern
from certain Gondwanaland fauna
knowing thereby the powers of Laurasia
the ferment that was known as Pangaea

all evidence known as uncertainty by body

the shore birds
the Herring gulls
the 'underwater' seamounts
around the Goban Spur
the Biscay Abyssal Plain

with its tripod fish

with its Gulper eels

with the length of its Halosaurs

the 'Abyssopelagic' creatures

seeing by 'luciferns'

by 'luminous bacteria that live in their bodies'

not the strict dimension of Aleutian cascades

or the sunken remains of a meteoritic tablemount

but not unlike the beauty of Monoceros

or the chaotic fields in the nebula of a lagoon

such is the dialectic

Monoceros: sparse & absent of crowding

the lagoon with its hot transcendent fields of light

as agua

as ghost

as form

I hover in transitional drying wells

in subsets

like nautical amnesia or tin

dreaming in penultimate inverse

completing challenge which arises from the waking state

I exist by being dead

by unclaimed positional notation

by a-habitual referent
as to latitude & rotation by globe
by the scholar's name for descriptive muscular fount

anesthesia
matheology
vortical haecceity

the Earth:
one particular lumbar wing

the Earth:
with its reefs
its fallen lights
its monsters

a dazzling homogeneous brevity
its species under threat
from spillage which derives from gregarious polar graves
I do not suspend my vigilance
my velocity
my 'Maximal sensation'

I've accounted for my flight throughout hierophany
by its in-lit connective
by its lexical concealment
evinced by the soma
in the motion of the Pleiades"

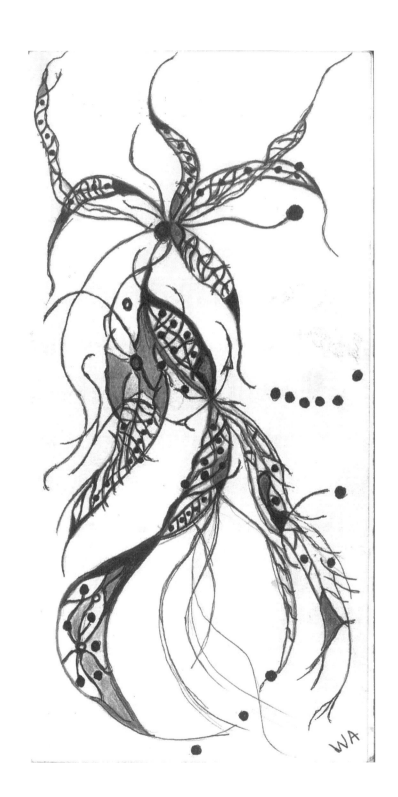

On Solar Physiology

over 99 per cent of the indigenous
population, are untouched by the culture
of the colonial power.

Amilcar Cabral

Despite the impressive technological
advancement of modern Western man relative to his own history, he ranks far behind the
Ancient African people of KMT (Egypt) both technologically and spiritually. Part of the
reason for this mental devolution is the limited conception of human potential that one
finds in Western science.

Na'im Akbar

"I
of the electrocuted hamlets
of the transfigured remnant
of inclement nostrums
subsumed by swirling electron soils

I work by means of solar isolation
by means of combustive subsonic
by means of cryptic soma & bird

trying to yield by figments
a world beyond eras
a world with inter-magnetic hydroxyl
comingling with outer suns
with the electrical motion of distance through alterity

& it is because of this distance
that I've been claimed by the ambiguous
by dynamic hesitations
being both kinetic & counter-kinetic
by a cathartics which rises through sub-fervour & vacuum

true
I've hovered within uncountable disorder
yet I've flown like a bird
from stunning iguana transposures
by blood type channeling through strange charisma & error
I've never been able to reason from induction

or hold my mind

point by point

according to mechanics

accrued from traumatic incendiary counting

my difference

understanding the equator as absence of mass

outside the realm of fecundity as abstraction

as if

absorbing by means of supra-physical infusion

because I sometimes waver in my gait

I am accused of being flawed

of being a curious sub-celestial avian

unable to fly or descend

according to tenets

which focus themselves through universal reason

because

I am not of the conscious body

I am focused by the osmotic planes

by riddling anoas

by levels known in certain parts of the world as Aesopian

issue

by mingling in private

I've come to know certain aspects of being

through trans-rooted fields

328

through roots & waves of vertigo

through imploded species of deer

& the political subsets

& the random holograms of speaking

is where the Sun oneirically swims

where the Galaxy intrinsically lights & suggests

this being

the Shaman's biographics

the oneiric glass in the genes

sometimes stumbling in a shaken vitreous house

peering through a porthole of integers

as if the numbers were formed by an unbalanced wheat

or an interior chart burning with a folio of

diamonds

the rhetoric of the Sun

associational gulfs

empowering my soma

as a charged Uranian warren

not a warren predictable

as ideology or mist

but as resonance

as a relay of bells

over vast projections beyond limit

& this limit

being nothing other than the consciousness of limit

of thinking of itself
within prediction of that limit
therefore
phantoms
they being limit as being

& projected limit as being
therefore I exist
as numerology as circle
as a combined 4 suns
being a great astrology of rivers

& these suns & rivers
by breathing
by gnomic scattering & burning
create by magnification
momentums of tension
fractals
a-positional soils
summoning codes beyond cellular inculcation

because I have only been judged by limit
by a culminate fragmentation
I remain obscure
pillaged
by extrinsic determination
by untoward utility
practised
330

as imprisoning mode
no longer of the overtone
of the Galaxy as living obscurity

I'm thinking
of the common obscurity of eras
as figment
the monological steam of the Permian
partaking of the fire before the Earth was settled

ironically
this becomes a curious fragmentary solace
a mode
a discipline
an energy

being a singer
in a hostile ozone field
I've come to terms with gregarious isolation
with tumult within various salts within the horizon

because
I am without definitives
without the dictums which sculpt the categorical
I seem de-energized
contracted
suspended
as possibility

as enigma

as stray

as that which transmutes an abstract catharsis

so as molecule

as sum by conscious numbering

I am placed in this or that projection

as a-priori plaintiff

as precarious ideology

I no longer bicker with my own bereftness

crafting myself

by judgmental folly

by a self-writhing plot

bound

by sacrilegious determination

true

my biology functions

I've been given the craft of breathing

& at times

I monitor waves in my system

not in the sense of counting or declamation

but as precipitates

as trance

as a solar lake & its sigils

these being waves which flow from the soma

like a hatching of novae

or a butane operatics

I am not the order of hives

or buffeted within neurotic changeling hectares

which then dissolve through forces which dwell

in external illusion

because I am immersed

in the counting of 'Upper & Lower Egypt'

I know the expansion of the Sumerian Sun

being active in entry through Mayan stellar portals

which means

I am connected to the human solar centre

& it is this solar centre

which articulates

which animates the soma

to the powers which dwell

in the galactic central furnace

which issue

as resonant psychic fuels

as coruscating stamina

& each species being part of this stamina

for instance

the ants

burning

revealing themselves in depths of psychic

Alps

being citric metamorphics

engaged in rhetoric beyond the potential of

human flare or quanta

all the levels re-conveyed

& drowned & re-ignited

within a havoc of instants

withing 3 billion sums

acting as reverse rotation

this being the algebra

of primeval protozoans

within the flank of fiery Brachiopods

within the forms of odoriferous stellar algae

I speak

through inverted hagiography

on the varying utility of particles

inscribing laments as a scorching motility

as a sand which crosses junctures

sired in the ethers

as continuous heliopause

certainly

this is minus the politics of the ozone

which raises subverted dust inversions

dissolved as blank electrical waste

as events which hover as omnivorous horizons

now as bird & proto-bird

again as blank conducting principle

I come to language

as interior diorama

triplicate

massless

swimming as a form through seasonless upper darkness

this being the ether at the pole

touching on the nearest vertical light

being cobalt in the conscious mind

being the symbol of eagles

diving through subsurface anopsias

these bring the inner level

the fields within fields

these being the curious cycles

of ethers

& suns

& kings

& blue tornadoes as bodies

being transpicuous fuels

combined

through the magical inhalation of the Sun

this is the way the Sun breathes
this is the way that the seminal unfolds

thus
my body
being fractal in rotation
remains alive by ophthalmology
by audition
by schists which rotate as carbon

therefore
I am called by some
Aguirre de dos Santos
the seeming avian
harried
at the interdimensional as crossroads
where the cells seem blinded
where the thoughts seem dazed by ceasing to
assemble
I could easily speak of the birds of Mozambique
or of the winds that burn in the eastern Sahara
my skin seemingly brewed by Angola & Brazil
by schisms which generate angles & currents
by the fjords of the moon which collide
& magically structure the invincible

therefore
I am invaded by blankness
336

where a curious Portuguese erupts

where its vowels transmix

with sub-components of English

marked by tumultuous interior glottals

by treasonous insult

by purported exhaustion

this being

the liminal fragment

the uncertain epic

mingled with a sun

which floats as ravenous spore

a kinetic

a dialectical limbo

being a mirage of stone

a bluish feast

a boat of anacondas

my mind

like a floating electron wheel

being particles of voltage

scattered across kerosene & blindness

yet always rife

with a staggard optical scent

strangely summoned

by baffling technical majority

& this summoning

coming from Regulus

from the Fornax Cluster

from Alpha Centauri

born under a blank tornadic Sun

I am open to these events

open to the heavens

beyond all previous physical capacity

& this Sun

half green & half vapour

being of every date that I carry

being every proof or tree

or any of my many symbolical moraines

then again

the Sun

part of a signal of 20 Suns

of a relay of Suns

partially charcoal in irrigation

I remain

entity of their pressurized dust

molten

rapid

wary

an entity

within the signal of the local partial Suns

within the sum of local helium significance

as if I dazzled myself in an interim hummingbird

gulf

in a sub-aquatic transfer state

becoming odd

unapproachable

dazed

by indivisible mobility

a strange perpetual torrent

in the midst of a torrential echo garden

filled

with Moroccan broom

with spider plants

with Arum lilies

in this

I am odd

making lists of whole desserts in auroras

for instance

forests as carnivorous tropical mirage

spinning in the spirit of fiery dracaenas

like the 'down' plant subject to ironical fires

to sums which extend over & beyond

a simple clause of persecution

because there are times

when I am subject to igneous law

to interior transit

where I propel myself

into unwavering conditions of mental precision

no

not a didactic persona

distilled as portion or fact

condensed in stratification as model

perhaps

I am disproportionate as conifer

minus the blinding owls in its mirrors

floating

with critical anti-motion

full of yields

& compounds

& intensities

being anachronistic soil

in a blizzardy nightmare furnace

therefore

my skin

an invigourated leather

a Sun turned around in opaqueness

teeming

as an occulted seasonal migration

I have survived within myself

by seasoned psychic acrobatics
by sudden integer through error

being inhospitable
I have shifted several psychic locations
yet I'm chronicled by land root
living
at the ozone of margin
filled with true electrical revolt

therefore
the nerves dis-established
the fevers imprecise
the minds' body drifting as a critical looking
glass prairie

trance
by in-seasonal compass
by marsupial eclectics
furtive
nucleic
withdrawn
the sudden ash of the categorical
the inward metrification of sound
being nutation as tumultuous parallels
as a-synchronization
as galactic medicinals
as implicate suborder

being

ammoniated shapes of hydroxyl

this being spillage of ammonia in wind

being rotative suns

being fractals of monsters

which breathe as flames

through great electrical transmutation

so that one achieves

the riddling heights of intense vibrational

status

I

who've arisen above the Angolan blood fields

knowing who I am only as the 'unknowable'

as a factor of imminence

who partakes of himself through baffling enigma

& I know in myself

the strange calamity of imminence

with its sweltering

with its inconspicuous fate

always dwelling at the cusp of curious cellular

insubstantives

by means of voltage

by means of the pre-destined

by means of sonar intensification

342

knowing elements of its pattern

as an unstable ruse

summoned to this condition

by explosion

by a sudden draft of diacritics

knowing

the corrosion of one's being

to be suffering by torrential quest

by blinding forms from a central empire

always questing for damnation

with amputations ensnared

by carbolics of disservice

perhaps

I am uncanny by projection

culled from a cradle of bullets

sparked by anonymous flames

descending from carbon & moisture

because I dream a third of an Earthly solar day

I always find myself

in a towering alkali forest

whose curious circular rotation

vertically projects

as phantom stelae or phasmids

to this degree

I magically partake of a fabulous form of absence

much like a moon

which parallels its powers

in an icy Sulphur lagoon

invisible

elliptical

neural

enduring

perhaps a swamp or acidic playas

or a reef

or devastating particles

as part of a stark creationary darkness

this is where I roam

as an insolate form of leakage

partially tainted

as if

my body were reversed a light from Barbados

in this sense evoking

Regulus in my mind

which unlocks the pattern in my mind

of the turmoil exacted at equators

which evolves from several sources of being

as a somber figment

as a wavering biology

yet I live

with crystal ciphers in my spinning

remaining unsolved

a sigil from sulfuric zodiacs

being cleft in myself as unreasoning illuminant

344

therefore

a pulchritude shining

between pre-historic ganglia & the Divine

no

not a theological leper

or a counseled speech by bribery

but a Sun

a force

a welter of phrenics

puzzling

obscure

spasmodic

like a maize rain out a season

or a mandated gully

no longer of the realm of magnetic declination

so I remain a diagram

a scope

an osmosis convened by threatening orbital pressure

again convened by a base informing schedule

not a fluctuation by sediment

or a bell reflecting osmosis by syllables

but a neuro-chemical transmatics

a leap

becoming an integer which flies by nomadic

association

seemingly occulted

like the Kuroshio current off the shores of Japan
this being
an organic seismology
a drift
an ontogeny prepared in sand

& I do not consider myself as impaired
as one who propagates ontogeny as model
as ontogeny prepared in sand
being theory to be explored
being rhythmo-mathematic ensnared by
deception

I mean by this
the first glimpse of origin
the first volcanic labour
honed in the power of the trilobites

this document that I give
no longer assumes an identity
by seconds or fourths or any propagating reason
say
a sum which is coded within Novembers
or storms
historically emended by the Julian Calendar
& its findings

one could call my ontogeny

an aural geometry

a blinded equilibrium

a spell contagion

perhaps speech

derived from a theory of lizards

or a conclave of hissing

listening to myself as a geomorphology

I

projected as waste

as invisible hydrology

derived

from a monsoon language

holding inside my body

galactic vibration by water

where solar masses flood

where the body in this functioning

exists as proto diacritical in advantage

being noun as critical lightning furnace

as feverish skeletal salt

on Earth

I

as dangerous supplicant

as inclement carnivore

igniting the invisible

part bird

part prophet

part voracious solar singularity

again

my skin

the colour of Luanda

of the centrality of Lobito

being of diamonds & copper

woven by subconscious manganese

by ghostly optical carbon

the values of Lisbon

the figments from Sao Paulo

cipher

then emended through gangrenous neural forms

so that the Portuguese I once spoke

now a tense cyclonic code

riven from a centralized symbology

I think of syllabic struck from Angolan Bantu

of each mystical trace

electrically confined

to a disabled trading post

to the brutality of a maize plantation

then the cruelty of Salazar

then the rebellion in Luanda

then the blood letting

by Neto

348

by Holden Roberto

by the carnivorous strivings of Savimbi

which is part of my proto-neurology

flecked with logistical bickering & hunger

with mutilations

burnings

terrors

intensive neuro-fissionings

reverting to poisonous proto-breathing

in the womb

this is how I've come

to live on this Earth

as a mixture of terror & lightning

in the form of a bleak avuncular dove

& me

an occult photo-aesthesia

knowing every law of each explosion

as dazed agenda

as general life engulfment

as stark interior sundering

born

on a battlefield in Lobito

my Father unknown

my Mother a priestess of botany

& dissension

therefore

I am transmixed as fever

as compound morphology

because

I have never mirrored the common populace

as one settled in being

by memorable daily vibration

the Anglican's adduced me

then reconfigured me be Vicar

by the one true connivance from Galilee

where they told me God was born

making me eschew all the birds

all the lunar corn

all the Zodiacs of Hathor

all the forms from the temple of Rams

I was taught to break my Luandan motifs

to uphold limit against splendour

at essence

I am meta-empirical

I am of the race that transcends diurnals

who understands implosion

& the growth of all procedure

yet who reascends as leper

from tornadic exile

I

as leper

who re-assassinates Savimbi

as the catalyst who overrules vileness

who has de-extended drought

who has curtailed the source of injury

I

of Mount Moco

of the Cunene River

of the phosphate & bauxite of Kwanza

knowing the history of the Mbundo region

the first slave ports at Luanda

then the conscript labour

building roads from dreaded Portuguese gravel

cultivating maize

& cassava

& sisal

I

considered a mystical Mestiço

absolved of coffee

& diamonds

& fish meal

being neither farmer nor herder

always being the ghost bird facing the sea

opening the waves

to Sao Paulo

to Porto Alegre

to Recife

to Salvador

to Fortaleza

my eyes appearing like a darkened glacial

menace

& by appearing as menace

I understand the nordestinos

the wretched life

the 'small clay houses'

the collapsing soil

the strife torn family conditions

this is how I've entered into waking anomaly

into cancelled through emission

as seminal equators

as a telepathy of lions

& these lions

a jurisprudence of maize

connecting me

to my fragmentary horoscope

to my background

sullied with empty rompio

at one level

as a ghostly vessel

called in the Portuguese

esgotado

at another level

called in the Portuguese

entregado

& this delivery

not by Vicar

nor by decrees from Mr. Neto

only knowing

that I was orphaned as stray

that I arrived in life as a coal black ornament

in sand

I

being the agenda of shreds

the consumed

the immolated

the one consistently swarmed by decimation

I

the nordestino of Lobito

I

of the social stammer

of that transpicuous weight

alive

as unrealized transfunction

as urn

as the fiction of the fiction of soma

overcoming the limits of breathing

which means

the pre-biotic has occurred

before Lobito

before the Cubans

before Savimbi

before the cacophony named dos Santos

which lived before Recife

before Salvador

before the iron floors of the Atlantic

which means

I am a ghost in collective dimensions

being the charcoal Vicar

being the gnostic sand which overruns the garret

picking up signals

from partial locations in heaven

from empty sigils in space

being a periodic width

or a parallel osmosis

breathing in ciphered ozone states

354

where light is emitted by a strange kinetic
treason
by an arcane electrical flaring
by what's known in the West as Quixotic
probability

these are the sands in which I transfuse
the electromagnetic nuclei
the lepton data
the depths of the para empirical
being both an entity in Fortaleza
& an entity suddenly breathing in Lobito

transmuting the nuclei evinced
I've known the storms from the pre-galactic
just as I seem to feel the cosmology of kilns
therefore
debate transpires
between forces which empty & do not empty
which both fail to exist
& at the same time continue in themselves
as ellipsis & post ellipsis

the dialectic then revolves
as indefinite animation
as occurs in a certain roaming
when fire from a prolapse of meteors transmutes

being the voice of such transmuters

I create from darkness a zone of dinoflagellates

being a surge of epistles which roam & go blank

which encapsulates flaw

which then blends into marrow

some could say

that I debate by seismological carnality

that I exist as sudden praeta

as empty form

as vanished neon or ether

suggesting to myself

waves of shamanic seething

much in advance

of say

leopards or caimans

nevertheless

I remain at one with the birds

with the Hill Stars in the Andes

with the symbols which fly above eruptive

antelope prairies

not as trance by criminal tonic

but migration by Uranian spectral height

being discipline through mirror & suspension

plummeted angels & vipers

always bickering in my wake

being the ritual of sub-experiment

its light being pen-ultimate

with the sub-ritual as its order

& so I

knowing scope as form

vastitude as glow

life as transrational cauldron

& each event

each fragmentary seizure

being of tumultuous planetary fire

of alchemical cross weaving

being of urgency & chaos

which de-exists & posts-exists

murmur by murmur

as great power

which roams throughout the invisible

I

Aguirre de dos Santos

of Lobito

of Fortaleza

of Recife

of the Nubian Renaissance through symbol

existing

through the mathematics of novae

through in-registered calescence

always alive

beyond mechanical boundary & prayer

I

who've scorched the catachistic boundaries

whose de-invented breakage

whose created from time counts

rational form as reversal

such is my osmotic range

my tragic scent

my qualitative molten

as organically sculpted boat

a-lit by calibration

shamanically defying gravity

by weaving frequencies

& archetypes

& patterns

I

whose energy advanced through electric cinders

through translucent condor ravines

being of strange incendiary number

revealing my voltage

through stark incendiary prisms

I

the great dark root of vapour & glass

enigmatic

seething

with repetitive insufficiency

triggered by friable electro-opaqueness

being a triggered vitality

removed & re-ensconced

in a double ozone kingdom

hurtling as chimerical nautical vulcanologist

knowing each land form to be primeval

with each form of flight

alive as red numerical flamingos

because of such previous panorama

I

a most unlikely Griot

left for dead on 4 occasions

by abandonment

by loss of breath

by poison

by the stealth of etheric seizure

Savimbi erased my immediate family realm

at the Vicar's request

I fainted from arsenic at the age of 12

at the eve of 21

I suddenly lost my breath

falling from a cliff during oneiric

palpability

& now

my personality swept aside

understanding at present

crags

& darkness

& water

the bodiless

formed at the essence of diamonds

my form uprooted & spun

as if emitted through a lake

of blasphemous honey & schisms

which means

a dawn of blight

which means

a blizzard of herons & rainbows

as if

breathing by heavenly debris

by absence

by terminal kindling & acid

they call me Shaman

whose Nigredo is formation

is spell

is bird

risen from confusion

360

I've seen the Sun spin in war
I've known hunger in Fortaleza
I've known the memory of meal & yellowed blood

the latter being
the politics of error & poison
the fissioning orchestration of blankness

I the African shaman
with the exiles' mirror
with the cunning disputation deftly falling
from inter-dimensional drought
being a Bantu foreman
being a Sun eclipsed as a neo-eclectic force field
as if knowing the flaw of metamorphic residual
momentary resolving as the cacophony of the Atlas
knowing
the double spinning of the planes
the free soils of the invisible

as Shaman
I've crossed the sea mounts as eagle
I've seen my ancestors by outline through
annihilation
but let me speak of Scorpion
of the Bantu Pharaohs
of Ramses

the Carthaginians
of Anubis

I therefore hold power
through generalities & specifics
through enigma
through varied circumstance as issue

I have come from a background as dust
from dark irradiated salt
from disassembling systems
in order to murmur
to mark graves
to de-invent resistance
so as to heal the dead
so as to evolve through ascensional authority

speaking by a strange persuasive cinema of rote

with each moment of resistance
refracted back through life
through sight
as elemental organics
by a kind of aural silver
hearing deserts blow as different forms of
blindness
or take a mineral river

or a wave

or suffix at the end of Angolan polar acidics

& these acidics

as rotational condensing

as a source of animation

as quickened psychic quilombos

part Lobito & Luanda

part Para Bahia & Pernambuco

because I scatter across the atmosphere

I know that the world exerts its own dread

that it renews the face of tragic lethargy &

crises

wanting nothing of the burden

which self-replicates its fleeing

so

to turn against myself

for being Angolan & praeta

for having a voice which lingers

as a xanthic fish

always asking of myself

the same dominating sermon

as to why my powers seem sundered

no longer of the wrath

which portions

forces

& particles

& surges

such doubt

being of brief gesticulation

of momentary error

rationed through transition

yet I am rowing through fuel

through heightened dominating prisms

never forced to abstract

doctrines from the energies of angels

by converting

statements

& angles

& rivulets to prose

I am never one to command

exterior domination

or to mechanically decipher

& re-invent weather

my senses

in contradistinction

telepathic

resonant

simultaneous with extended glottic distance

being inspired

primeval singularity

364

not unlike the bliss

which composes itself through inspiration &

deluge

in terms of the species

I remain tenaciously enriched

always concerned

with the conquering quality of moments

seemingly swamped in the negative

as if governing & breathings were bipedal

regressions

creating by their efforts circumstantial

corrosion

by gross calendrical collapse

I mean days & worlds of misshapen breathing

of artefacts

ill-contrived

lumbering

& by sketching these notes in helium

I understand all the missives of paronomasia

or a glancing look at deserts or droseras

then

of course

is the malaria of the populace

with its kinematics

its devastations

being a whole domain of forms

dying before conception

it is like listening to ghosts

attempting to bathe in weather

as if I could see their sundered effects

as strange conceptual eaglets

as remnants

as obscured Angolan spiritual despair

ceasing to be advanced

as though stunted in the effort

to irradiate incredulous foment

I

being part of a sunflock of ghosts

risen to high status

flitting back & forth

between Angola & Recife

between Fortaleza & Lobito

linked

by means of Arcturus

with its theme of etheric intensity

it could be said

that I am a hidden global darkness

or a bird

or a Hill Star as ray

being cryptic alacrity in sudden mountain lagoons

366

seemingly broken in Fortaleza

my body a remnant in the hovels Lobito

hovering

then suddenly blazing in the world

simultaneous with rapidity

which ignites

as a form a pre-existence

as capacity which streaks through omniscience

I understand the peculiar arclight of this kelvin

of this peculiar pre-existence

this fertile action as demonstrative

being advanced as cataleptics

through the transfer of whispers

therefore

I no longer heal by apogamy

I who have known great warfare as blizzard

as specific conceit

as terrain which crumbles & transposes action

because I know through defeat the non-person

of hunger

the bleakness of wells

the hesitation of deserts

as obscurantist

as leper

I've taken leave of visible form

of Aguirre de dos Santos

as body

as micro-linearity

as form

condoned & approached by infeasible saturation

because of this

I'm now the leper's scholar

I now carry facts as a leper's musician

animate as a form of trans-articulate intuition

as intuition linked to Mirach

to dis-articulate voices

thereby understanding

the linkage of humans to thyroids

to the pituitary which lives as elixir & force

which in turn directs my study

to Almach

Ankaa

& Adhara

not bestowing gifts of dread

but as a lens of optical hearing through strength

for instance

I call on a cloudy sky

knowing the blood of victims

which means the Sun revolts through dragons

which means

I've heard the moons below the soils

I've heard erupting antennae

their tall blank stalks

merging in a state of harmonics

erupting transfuse glimpses

through meridian orange-red

being the human Sun in movement

beyond its dark agonal needs

hurtling to a post-material matrix

in order to fish in an unknown current

as multi-dimensional grasp forming into being

I gaze at Indigenous scarabs through a series of flotational speculums

at say

a triplicate neurology of scorpions

like a discipline awash in a basin of energy

therefore I dictate the greatness of cracked

pylons

of memorial offerings of crabs

ingesting realia through astonishing combustion

through the univocality condensed in Martian

scarps

I

being

the unlikeliest of the living

understand

that I function through pre-interior living

which ceases to from one stasis or another

history ruled upon by agreed upon stasis

by the fragment as sealed & ultimate motion

I

of the eras

I

of the Permian

of the Pennsylvanian

of the neuro-galactic

I

who has evolved

who has ceased to squander soils

I

who has learned the basic balance of chemicals

the principles of remoteness through ignition

which seems cyclonic

useless

void

according to consensus structure

as betrayal of the human exhibit

370

I'm speaking of higher germinations

sending out signals

to diverse & ambivalent monoliths

being the blending of being into being

suddenly transfusing rhythmic exhaustion

creating in their wake

interior fuels

writhing poltergeist's memory

so when the body changes form

it becomes an odd umbilical drainage

returning to its source

as deftly balanced priority

as elevated dictum

it is organic

panoramic

as magical perpetration through frequency

rising from the central mountains

through zone after blistering zone

through eclectic vertical geographies

as magic

as knowingly trans-stated instincts

knowing the dialectic by its body as absence

in which wood no longer configures

by which morals de-encode by fatigue

again

this being absence

not as negative portrayal by flight

but leap

by vibratory rate

by articulate suspension as form

this being the level of the Olmec doctors

of the pre-Hebraic masons

who functioned in old Kemet

these being the themes of my insurrectionary

tablets

of my strange incendiary missives

rising higher & higher into missing disclosure

yet never lowered to saltless utilitarian

isolation

but moving in & out of incessant vibratory data

numbers derived from various pre-figurations

of hydroxyl

never in themselves a commodity of traces

but a hive

a living dimension

shifted through levels

until emission turns into abnormal aurum

& from this abnormal aurum

a stelae of black steeds

suddenly blazing

from heights of stark Uranian foundation

in Fortaleza

I know about the tzolkin

I know the legend of Pacal Votan

the subtle metrics

being the numerous voids

that certain insights intuit as phantasmic

constellations

as flights

as runic magnifications

& so by these magnifications

I understand waves

as nuance

suggestion

blending

as a-structural harmolodics

as ideographic darkness

culled

from analogical penumbras

from technical obscuration

so this zone

this environment

leaps by oneiric example

the medicines

the waters

as explorational example

being the reason I've stolen forms

from the northern colonial tongue

I know that I know

the original Portuguese monsters

those early entrepreneurs

looking for bluish ghosts

& I am aboriginal as bluish ghost

who glints by force of contact

who claims his view from primigenial optics

from kelp

from extra galactic terrain

where the seed of interior fields

a-lights with volcanic preambles

where each interior moray position

reacts as sworn cinnabar

as a survey of Jupiter

inlaid with the scarps of Europa

& these scarps

a purplish velvet

a crowned Osirian scarlet

more evolved than the lesser flames

brewing in the hatcheries of Venus

these hatcheries being symbolic

of the material mind & its unsustainable

prayer

with its gusts conceived by physical weight

this is certainly not a gesture to be displayed

like an oligarch

signaling to himself from a vaster podium of entropy

not being a being who seeks control by tonnage

by flaws which cast scrutiny on the face

of each personal fate

I see in destiny

a scribbled warmonger's role

by descending in tenor to scribes

who deracinate their victims through script

being a modern ailment

burning as conceptual disfigurement

which means

such perceptions are given vowels

& avow themselves as figures

which seek recognition

of the superior states

yet they are motionless effigies

scattered as sunless vibration

as dreaded tropical owls

pointless

static

marred by inversional principia

I

the bluish sun ghost

never once at risk as weakened insular baron

but at the level of high degree

which appears as transfunctional being

being a snow capped star burst from Ceres

from Angola

from apparitional amalgams in the Pleiades

I appear

& I appear again

as Pacal Votan

as a transitory form of Regulus in Phoenicia

so

between Angola & Fortaleza

there are spells

there are marked & unmarked exhibits

cast across the water we call the Atlantic

body

being symbol of the galactic receiving sea

which spans the arroyos of heaven

376

which means I extend

as numeric vascular body

as flight down explosive vascular roads

& these roads are winds

numeric vascular plains

where the body bears crystals

through microscopic shadows

through insular & fabulous interiors

polar

simple design by ravine

like an anti-conspiration through phases

one simply exists

so that mazes begin forming in the skin

being able to see in the skin

solarized elixirs

drafts of light

higher deltas in formation

so that

I never reveal to myself

different states & compendiums of drowning

because I summon the erudite through

drowning

within the form of longitudinal staggering

within motions revealed through debilitated

cause

this life

being drowning as whole immersion

as immensity

as if I had never known of the Suns

which extend through Suns as Suns

which is personal affirmation in immensity

which is the red shifted signal

which overcomes me

which combusts as a series of rays

I therefore fly from flashes

waking up from death without eating

affirming my linkage to botany

to essential forms amidst the chlorophyll

of absence

being the ghost bird that I am

being the mongrel ore

being the alkali of breathing

being a solar invasive who flies

again

the Sun Ghost

the vapour evinced through great rhythmics

through habitat as solitude

through motion which advances through

clarified audition

378

I

who know & love the balance of goats

understanding in my flight

the mathematics of tigers

& because I know the spell of tigers

I know their condition as griots

being fuels

& transparency through fuels

igniting electrical prophecies before feasts

when I see an Angolan village

I hover

casting a fractal of cinders

called by the Arawak the 'doctor's bird'

a tree formed lightning

blizzard as upper peninsula

I

the Sun Goat

whose known the 'short faced bears'

the 'saber toothed' monsters

the 'American lions'

the haunted suddenness of 'dire wolves'

flashing bast & forth

between Lobito & starlight

between forms which exist between primal

elephant & camel

between

black rhino & penguin

being heliotropic wave

as strategic self-allegiance

alive

in the heliosphere

in part as enigmatic menagerie

as spiral lettering of bison

my alphabet summoned

from the fumes which rise above phonemes

as intrauterine angels

humming with heraldic locution

in saying such

I am part of the Heliomasters

of the sun angels

of the vervet thrushes

singing with the acuity of ventricular

illumination

certainly I'm not describing life toxins

or draughts of penultimate algae

which puts the cells in schism

as in syllabic disadvantage

no

I am raising the gemstone soils
to a higher electrical falarmos
to speech as invisible register
creating proof by glossolalia
again
not a being brought to barrenness
as if I were a voiceless compurgator
or a suspended animation
honed by the grasp of nomography

so if I were of a more learned reserve
I might utter in caliology
or phonophobia in the asteroids
creating an archaeology by fever & starlight
by irregular astral debit
by a hive of ants in the Marius Hills

it's like knowing these accentual states
as if brewing in my hands a greyish cinder
mallet
while stoking a powerfully lit python furnace

here
I usurp
parochial mountain gravel
taking on a dazzling haze
so that powers leap out
like a sudden uranic oxygen ballet

this is why I've been born alone

& been balanced alone

I've taken exploration through dazzled

breakage as lair

through sight as mesmeric twilight

being aural density through beacon

certainly not a sonic nostalgia

or a primeval lessening in the stars

because

there are thoughts which range through Procyon

being rays which scatter

to symbolic whirlwinds

as the Sun Ghost

between Lobito & Fortaleza

there expands

different fractals & luminescence

operatic with pions

with interior nuclei as current

then knowing

the indigestible as linkage

then a feral link between argon & copper

between ash & the sub-foci of ash

which implies the micro torrent

which suggests

the life which builds beyond being

as both Sun

& Sun Ghost of the Sun

I am parallel

& that which parallels within parallels

where there exists those levels

of chaotic subterfuge & counting

which de-exists

individual finality

accrued by lyssophobia & infection

in this way

I do not appear

I do not dissuade or engender resistance

I remain flotational

a sum between parallel & parallel

like a spate of optics

fraught with sensation

feeding myself a brief electrical wheat

this being a moral energy

cleansed by inception

for instance

the compounds of sodium & air

the quest for miscellaneous rejoinders

therefore I am ray

as Angola & Phoenicia

spawned through adaptive migration

a ray within a ray

a flock of titans

a compound anagogics

then peering from a sudden vertigo window

at falling plutonium debris

the planet more moribund than warmonger's

& I

the Sun Ghost

who reconnoiters this debris

who understands at core the simultaneous

as reconnoitering

such simultaneity

full of optical echoes

which then see themselves by sub-echo

& sub-echo being the flight of sub-echoes

telepathic & alive

through parallel criticality

thereby

384

seeping as scent

through the didactic as barrier

I

who have lived through great occult erasures

through great species extinction

knowing the loss

of spiders

& craters

which includes in their wake the morphology of

dinosaurs

understanding the light emitted from coldness

by understanding this loss

there seeps into the human

an analogical brooding

a gross despair

provoking trenchant search

through massive desolation

through the aforesaid debris

thereby understanding the collective

trachea as flaw

as subliminal fissioning

as nucleic isolation

which continuously exists

as ironical spectrum

as illuminant conflagration

the genes then wandering

through kinetic enervation

the national economies of seismically infected

beings

then going down to the eyes

to the raw excessive blood count

gurgling

persisting by feeding on the fires of the

flesh

these are the tremors

the suffocations by slaughter

where the people

are roped up & gunned down

more frenzied in their form

than the tenor of Savimbi

the suffering of the Earth

as strange colloquial intensity

with its bleak receptive states

with its anti-dimensional regression

being at present

the sole principality of living

of course

I understand as lizards

the pre-industrial Portuguese

with their properties & intake of metals

386

with their predominance & destruction
their hatreds
 their embittered bits of breathing
with our language groupings erased by the
Catholics

as Pius the XII so brazenly put it
'The Catholic faith ...as the principle...
source of energy'
telling the Portuguese
that it had carried their 'land
to the apogee of glory... '

Plus
as Catholic
as illicit contriver
possessing as sole criteria
Indigenous subordination
intrinsically adapting
the xanthochroid as model
the indigenous reduced to scorbutics
to the scope of pre-industrial chattel

preparing Angolans with respect for Locke's
Government
for the bribery of Descartes
making us slave & exhume the depths of our crystals
our phosphates

our copper
our feldspar
our gold

this being Pius & the brutality of his ilk
aligned in the psyche to torrential decay

as if we were painted dogs
as if we were stunned as segmented flatworms

no difference was found
between the Kongo
Kimbundu
or Umbundu
derided
because our melanin transposes the Sun
because our ethos ignites their agitation

seemingly spawned beneath the Anglican's
the Catholics never saw me as legal
as a person duly registered by province
be it Luanda
or Zaire
or Cuanza-Norte
or Cuanza-Sul

it ever enriched by the diamonds from Lunda
or bursts of oil from Cabinda

I would be no more

than vilified

by someone with the eyes of the accursed Monteiro

by Salazar

with his brutality by logistic

all of this spawned by dangerous crypto-legality

by assaultive criminal portions

by guilefully rendered disservice

at one level

anointed by perversion

by gusts of debilitating spectrums

thus

my existence

fitful

in-locatable due to panic

to cubits of ambivalence & space

a chronicle

fused by desperation

by anti-alchemical infection

our lives consumed by grammatical marking haze

ground down

to fiery bits of dissolution

to the opaque synergy of crosses

this being no different

than the darkened fate in The Congo

its population marked

by missing arteries & limbs

by the hissing circle of Avernus

I understand this condition

I understand the issues of terror & sullage

I understand this condition

always marked

by acrid lava & crow

its ultimatums conjoining

crowned by a sun rising in abominable confusion

this is Africa imploded

this being the pestilence

where my physical body appeared

as a darkened skin in impoverishment

under threat of cinder & ruin

because of provisional salvation by vicars

I now arrive to cast these verbal curses

to bring a curious Anglophone to fruition

knowing ambivalence

knowing Elysian calescence

knowing each trace of unseasonable infernos

as quantum leap

I have survived as hummingbird

singing blemished songs in the Urals

while scraping at basalts in Benguela

which remains

inner absence by aggression

by refracted Andean amplification

thereby

understanding my oneirics as great migrational

fire

so in terms of exploration

defense exists

accrued from flammable solitude

I being bird as migrational neutrino

being bottle-green & silver

being variegated copper & snow

hovering in itinerant wells

always simultaneous with concealment

hovering in umbras

I could be

Heliothrix

Sun Angel

or an alien parallel to cobalt tundra

encircling parallels

casting oxygen from twilight

& I understand the perspective

of Earth as entombed zone

as an old monaural trapping gaze

gravitized by its reckoning

with a suicidal compost

beneath plutonic snipping

embroiled by non-seminal confusion

it continues to proceed

in-fluent

its data marked by political insufficiency

as if I could whisper

in Arabic or Bacongo

in Neo-Algonquin or simple speech from the Indus Valley

concerning newer & more insidious relay systems

perhaps

on Àlinda or Iapetus

transmuting secrecies

where other frequencies react

& commune with definitions

far beyond the mind as we know it

I

the Sun Ghost

392

signaling & retrieving

rays from the Namib

understood to be exhaustion

mined from intrinsic electron wheels

as continuous genesis

as stellar transonics

being a mirror which forms from molten assemblage

perhaps

in one or two forms a lightning struck bridge

or explosion through electrical ground

not technocracy as ground carbon

or patience as filigreed in-sonority

but biography through reductive enigma

through coronal dialectics

forming through the briefest of flashes

a crystalline micro-neology

which scatters the shadow of my body

upwards towards the Sun

rising above the darkness of burial & flaw

reaching an aurum ignited by largesse

allowing as respiration

moons

& soils

& strengths

which closes the book of panic

which replaces the old charisma of dying

so that contagion & phosphorous

ignites a new advantage

creating an energy beyond general avian liability

in order to compose from the spirit

transparent hydrography & sands

where the pressure of loss through death

no longer spins in a cycle

which will allow me flight

to bring back the dead

to banish feverish dorsal labour

& so the nadirs

the pain

the loss of fire in the genes

no longer of occurring concert

or reckoning with the human morass by thinking

this is the way that language swirls in flight

the way

that emotions are juggled & spun inside glass

not unlike

a Uranian computation

taking non-configured respiration

394

to untouchable tolerations
where diamonds open inside the sattvic
where the wind blows
& transmogrifies the bark of the Angolan
mulemba tree

which allows me new behavioural distinctions
creating pauseless interregnums
osmosis being more than vortical
which generates a trance of cyclical heavens
being a beauty which lives through generating
glyphs
through the energy which flies from mulundo trees

upon which I gnaw like a transparent wolf
making clarified comment
on fever which roves through a spotted scent
of deafness

yet I always know my laws
my burning aural dryness
which repeats & repeats
until weightless river doors fly open
so that geysers erupt
& cleanse atomic storage fields
I
the Sun Ghost
crossing alien solar photonics

indeterminate

grey

using no known chemical or fatigue

the imagination

a litigational mirage

a flame at twilight

a flotational compulsion

being a great ignited station

a lingering mount of sand

writhing as vehicular spiritus

never a curse by intensive comprehension

I spark an osmotic trail

across interior diagonals of density

& as the Sun Ghost

keeping my sporadic chronicles alive

involving the perfect strategy of photons

with their limits

with their strange calendrical arcs

at times

mimicking themselves through dark

electrical fonts

& these electrical fonts

speak to all the chordates

to the enveloped protozoans

so that one can translate

a body of systems

say

in the midst of the Oligocene

with its sheep sized herbivores

with its 18-foot rhinoceri

with its youngest cats the size of human

mountain lions

or to the most recent atrocities

which devours the human ether

a disruptive venation

which has instilled in me

the dread as regards referential biology

I now call myself

the great jonquil hawk

the greenish leopard in the scattered neutron

valley

as if

I had lost myself flying across the Elysium

emitting from the voice

nouns

& cries

& riddles

like a trilogy of mandibles

lifting up otters from scorching Nepheline

basalts

like the bar-headed goose of Tibet

a double hemoglobin cycle

absorbing my own being at different levels

of pressure

because the will ignites

lions break from the confines of Eden

in order

to ascend beyond cancellation

reaching

the apogee of experiment

between the obverse of storms

& the obverse of the Divine

taking as witness

the true fertility of chance

I

not unrelated to the trilobite in trance

waking at time as an eclectic river

amidst logarithmic gales

& rising dice from the boulders

yes

I have crossed the zone

unconcerned with umbilical drainage

blank

with unknown 'fossiliferous strata'

enlivening a greenish ozone

peering through a doorway of scarabs

398

these are sample chromosomes
cells measured
by simple stationary risk

being
both cryptic bird & soma
I am marron angel
I am living potentia through dread

such as power
as ultimate effigiation
being akin & in essence
none of the above

& as Angolan in Lobito
as spectral orphan of war
as carpentry of special somas
I exist at times as replicate astronomer
as repetitive calligrapher
charting at times
the Sun's orography

I can speak of active hydrogen tables
of spectral lakes
of coronal transits

for instance
Sunspot cycles

energetic flares

'magnetic field lines'

which allows

for greater volume on land

knowing the variations of the poles & the craters

the conservation of dust

the interstellar extinctions

I

as the Sun Ghost

take random flowers from Earth

operant in the self as an eclectic index

being in correspondence

with the 'Giant Red Paintbrush'

or the Calico Bush

or the Snapdragon Vine

I speak as blurred sand feeder

as occulted hatchling

mistaken at times

for the Green Breasted Mango

or the Cuban Emerald in flight

or the anomalous ledger of the Sphinx Moth

illumined by rays

as if

I were ironic as Albino

as interior Ghost Canary

as general vagrant from Fortaleza

as Sunbird

I live in Africa protea flowers

provoking the depth of my own ghost in flight

as Malachite

as Marico

as violet tailed

as Palestine

as Congo

as Tacazze

which means

I am mosaic made of water

of whispering sub fauna

listening to music from a glistening neutron

spring

this being my spring of ferment

as chlorophyll

as rotational torrent

as psychic tornado in sand

perhaps I exist

as a song before breeding

as a primeval noun
struck from organic exposure

not to prepare or obstruct
but to see

seeing then
becomes the living aural letter
& every aural letter
being a lepton source
being a chromosomal ray

yet I am accused
of failing at raw political nerve
of failing to respond to ruses which threaten
accused
of leaving alone the actions of killers

I admit
that my skill consists of unknown carbons
of scorched calendrical phantoms
accused of misjudging & further misjudging
external indicatives
of national social conciliation

not seeing Angola & its confines as mirrors
as the double blaze of social construction
being dazed myopia & naivete
402

this latter criticality

not in keeping with Caledonian or Armorican

mountain building

or the Frasnian stage of 'Old Red Sandstone'

rising in the Devonian

perhaps

a dorsal shield

or a blank volcano

or a star which rises

or an empty star which rises

guiding dormant monsters

so that they miss their prey

some of them resembling

the Caracara of Guadeloupe

perhaps I speak of misplaced serpent eagles

or various eusuchias without thought or conceptual

glimpses

perhaps mathematics as an archery of angles

passing

degree by degree through a zodiac of gateposts

its pattern of wood

provoking thoughts from a colony of 'misshapen beings'

throughs

which tend towards deformity

react from my contagion

eclipse

& appear on this plane with potentia of an

unfettered birth code

alive

with meta-adrenalin

with metamorphic values

with seismic withdrawal

allowing suns to spiral through salubrious

ancillary breathing

I

who seem to amass

a formless structural droning

emitting discharged gold

converted by nebulas

I

being spore

being vitrescent helium undulation

understanding the index of cryptic Earthly

glaciation

not of Neptune with its mirrors

but lengths of time on Earth

this being ice understood

as the Huronian

the Varangian

Permo-Carboniferous
the Pleistocene

& I have evolved to this displacement
breathing
through the frequency of displacement

in this
I am invisible
evolving by albedo
by transfer radius
by great molecular zenith
thus
I'm known to the Earth
as the deluge bird
as cosmological regulation
uplifting poise
within an eloquent compendium of stillness

an eloquent fire
not a blinded hull or moral
baring its grasp as a barren isotope within
withdrawal
fallacious
as creatural plethora
as osmotic declaration through blindness

therefore

I am never tense

I am not as abstracted gradient ideal

but as bred throughout cyclones

evincing in this path

a dim arboreal wattage

akin

to the electrics of the Amazon

to the beauty in Angola known as the 'Mopane woodlands'

thus

I circle

antithetical to devastation

knowing

the supreme aspect of grammar

with its high migratory roving

with its attempts at scaling

the blazeless light of solar failure

not that the Sun will have failed

but the Earth

as a waking cinder field

as occulted arroyo

as unclaimed quilombo

its pollutions unmoored as anomalous schisms

as fulgurations who manipulate dread

I

as once a member of this old community

its neutral purgations

its contaminated shales

containing in themselves

lost & distracted echinoderms

as philanderers

as ice donkcys

they being

ligatures in the mind

moving & appearing

& thereby implying

appearing as appearing as moving

therefore

I stress the purest absence

of unlit suns

crossing back & forth between galaxies

analogous

to the Atlantic as galaxy

as void

moving back & forth

as both Lobito & Fortaleza

the Atlantic being

the hydroxyl of water

the electromagnetic carbon of water

perhaps

calling myself a harmonious warbler

or gull as beacon on the waves

perhaps

as guided drop on a fern leaf

or a particle which roves as precise confusion

I am that spore

hounded

intrinsically left for dead

whose culminate voice amounts to the absence of basics

in my original impulse

I voar

I revoar

I circumvoar

flying

flying again

flying as quanta

so as inscriber

I react to moons

as subterranean suggestion

as subsumption of flaw

perhaps better put

as runic diary by suggestion

as written lens

408

according to scale

where the inarticulate breathes

linking itself with former lakes on the Sun

this being pure ascensional prairie

as coruscation through crystal

as elliptical hagiography through photology

not that I create from implication of belief

or destiny as culminate from forgotten mergansers

it could be said

that I wore on my shoulders irradiated wool

that each step that I took

were sub-ratios of brilliance

but I can never monitor my own revision

or acquaint myself with sterile personal

instigation

based upon surface familial response

or signals sent through superficial recognition

say

in the British world

a plate

a fork

aseptic brocade

the classified flask with its strategic

containment

of course

I've never been suited to metropolitan neuralgia

with its forests of luxury & quaking

the Champs-Élysées

curious walks through Manhattan

speaking with isolate patrons in Andorra

worlds enthralled by specious celebrity

perhaps

I exist as non-sufficient

as feeble

discoloured

of vehicular disorder

perhaps

by my very impression

I create through common obstacle

blight

a bucolic withdrawal

fervour fraught with reversals

with culminate halting & terror

my essence contaminates

as centripetal holocaust native

I have a mind which transfigures the Sun

which flashes inside the incarnate

creating ciphers & ciphers by ghost

410

by such praxes

I rise & foretell

like a sigil in Eustachian sombrero

jeopardizing plot

inventing the West as derided event

life by extended decibel gone blank

by source in the aura as anti-registration

again

this is language by ghost

by incomplete Sun wheel

by stray as floating electron graffiti

I must profess by condition

as ineloquent leper

as substance conducted from inordinate drizzle

as such

I can never condone micro-linearity

or scope which classifies fatigue

even when extolling a cosmic surgical bitterness

or of a labour brought on by dark umbilical noises

each phoneme creates a matrix

dwelling on concussive planes

which irrigates

the bio-neurology

desisting

& at the same time

connecting the Earth & its double

like a gambler

going back on himself

playing ghost with himself

while struggling with gravel & mutton

wizardry

ritual

incendiary hail

mystic goat feeding compost

fighting off schism

derailing extrinsic deficit

all being the claims accrued

obstructing the tools of one's balance

dilemma in this sense

equated by motion

transmuting the scales of my living amygdalae

so that fear is overleaped

by admitting the hounded scope of one's person

so that the cells respond

being as energy which probes

the core of living dread

this being the complex assemblage of birth during

war

then the loss of Portuguese missionary English
then the double amputation of Mother & Father

having risen from death
on both a fourth & a single time
I have understood
the intricacies of osmosis
the resurrection of lingering calescence
allowing me grace
to soar through chaotic scorpion's heat

of course
I have never withdrawn from myself
by insisting on experience as calamity & plague

again
this is energy which draws me
which consumes me
& consumes me again
through the very flash of contradiction

it is I who makes sequestered volcanoes blow up
knowing
the difference in my acts
between levels derived
from a double resistance

at one plane of resistance

I harangue

I create alchemic pandemonium

I staunch the rule of national slaughter

at another

there is semi-withdrawal

there are exiles' hand penning missives to

reasonable chancellors

to the doctors of expression concerning

Indigenous torment

concerning the laws of suffering & malfeasance

at the third remove

there is struggle against provincial witness

at a fourth

hatred of Diogo Cāo

then of course

sub-hatreds

Savimbi in Huambo

then the cultural clashes

between the Umbundu & the Ganguela

between the Kongo & the Kimbundu

between the Herero & the Lunda Chokwe

I

the strange Kimbundu born

overcoming the Anglicans & the Methodists

overcoming the dictates of one

such as Wade Crawford Barclay

who cites exacting church mechanics

being no more than the impound

fired by scurrilous teaching

at best

to the Methodists

I am a misnamed mestizo

a mixed blood

inclined towards the sub-desertic steppes

ill mannered

a non-conjoined force

risen out of season

I

with no skill

at the carpenter's bench

or at the tailor's spindle

or creating masonry into lodgings

yet

I've understood the world

through genetic transmuting

living in the mist of great secondary states

& these secondary states

arrive through savoir

as elegant discipline

as rift

I who've swept across stele & pythons

across frightful arcs at the gates of greater

Suns

who've known the ingestion of sub-threats & fears

who've known zones of contiguous flooding

who's dwelled in weakened cellular hives

I

of simultaneous being in Lobito

I

of stolen quartz from the soil

having known from former existences

the whip of the Portuguese railhead

at Benguela

at Huambo

at N'dalatando

exponentially aggrieved

having the slavers display me

impounding my skin with various urines & wires

no day was left

in completed state

there existed filth

416

the prosecutorial burin

the imprisoner's kinetic

& this is not a theory of conceptual schooners

but about the body maimed

the spirit disrupted

about nature reversed & subverted

invoking

hellish lower eternity

inciting

nullification according to chronicle

according

to the Roman chronicle issued out of Lisbon

order & more order issued

& each order issued

a treatise

a fettered bulletin of trauma

marked with feral obligatory markings

under the Portuguese

to register as clerk

I would inscribe myself as wildebeest

as lynx

seen by the founders of Lisbon

as dreadful lower form

to be turned in my grave & drowned

my corpse

then drifting as lost

as if formed by lack of intrinsic mentality

corpse

as dead draught horse

as horizontal giraffe

condemning my lot to self-treachery & boundary

beyond

these clauses out of Lisbon

the mind

with its burning champaca oils

with its emperor's mazes

spinning like a web out of Arcturus

so that

what's experienced in ascent

whirls

& draws the magnet of the body

from its present field

across a spectacular inner gulf

interior with eidology

not the uttering of Neolalia

but of parhelions

wafting through each other's brightness

being cerulean

& sea-green

& magenta

418

halos

at the levels of indigo & snow

at levels which reach

beyond contingency & counting

& each realia

of Aguirre de dos Santos

is movement by energy as halo

as enigmatic ray

as deep encircling shadow

at one zone of palpability

I am a dozen or 50 enigmas

as great invasive gusts

as pan millenniums

as emanations which take hold & vanish

like the Glyptodonts

like an Ordovician sea floor

with its coral

with its trilobites

with its cephalopods

not that I'm constructing these forms

as abstract experiment

as a series of clinical spectrums

being vacuous in contrast

to an amputee in the Congo

to bloodied torsos in Luanda

no

but the pan millenniums exist

the various Suns & cycles exist

I

being charged quanta

as Lobito & magnesium

as the wattage of Hill Stars

of vanished Condors from the Permian

I detonate & disperse

always able to reconfigure

the sub-dominate in being

under auspices as shale

as beggar birds

as iron maker spiders

as in-dominate anacondas

chain of being as momentum or dearth

as species emitted from ether

certainly

not as the brevity of ether

but resonance

variation through tremendums as given

be they lakes or psychic lakes on Ceres

or glacial mining of Europa

or mock sun & mock sun burning beneath horizons

between eras & eras recurring on Earth

perhaps these eras

are laws

& phantoms

& scales

not to say

that the Earth will blaze as missing

appearing in the shadow of Vulcan

as an arc of teeming & previous teeming

as calamitous voyager in & out of beacons

understanding the fact

that remnants explode in the ether

knowing in fact

that the accrual of ether

gathers in a vacuum of metrical annotation

being in itself

an anecdotal globular conundrum

which exists as former kindling water

going & coming

without sand

or continents

or structure

which becomes in essence

the circuitry of Sun

with its wavelength of sigils

not only

of a million plus species

but of three hundred thousand plus mosses

appearing & disappearing

as a storm

through uncountable duration

I return again & again to life

as transverse ray

as subatomic rainfall

as exact zones of zinc

where they once fed the Earth

& gathered its schisms

because the Sun electrically feeds

ghost will feed ghost inclusionary darkness

& former energies once housed

will become again

a relay of Suns

a movement of my zodiac through Arcturus

me

of the Pleiades

moving in & out of the galactic core

commingling

with other events of erasure in heavens

I

the former bird

the former ghost of Angola

as a focused vapour lens

communing with new density of spirit

erratic cells

sigils of powder

alive with concussives

in higher patterning towers

not galaxy as parent to damage

but as cyclical drone

as outside & within its own breathing

knowing its flow of ghosts

with their angles

their substrates

their disciplines

& here I would know myself

as fulmar

as ornis

flitting in & out of forms

as general mystery to myself

as if I were Iroquois

or Algonquian

or Comanche

or perhaps as odd or unnerving anagram

being Vulture swimming in a diamond spring

or as Aguirre into Hill Star into vision

being of the implicate Quilombo from Palmares

breaking through enriched metals

opening transfigured toxins

which elicits other frequencies

& these frequencies

both lateral & vertical & other

traversing the eras

of Cambrian & Pre-Cambrian to present

to sub-refracted methane

electric with transference

because I am absent from what I say

& embroiled with what I know

neutrality meanders

& creates in its body a circuitous lunar treason

the being a-lit by osmotic wreckage

by a cunning fascination

ruled

by intuitive forms

studied as gradient transfusion

424

this transfusion by its meaning

kindles itself by reversal

by the ill remains

of a scorching double port

being entry to ledgers of voltage on Earth

a voltage

dim

fully implicate with occultation

with cellular flow into & beyond present

stellar mechanics

with old velocities tempered by great Uranian

telepathy

so that

the old omegas of history

invaded

by erasures

& empty forms of calculation

I am not as portrayed by technicians

arrayed

in technical armadillo

in modified fire-fly encampments

in phantasmal estrangement

in ferocious physiological acceleration as form

not by light year mind you

but by etheric ascendance

culled from miraculous cacophony as cipher

simultaneous as bells

as interior neters of principles

pervaded by nervous circular light

by nervous electrical luminescence

its after-effects sprawling

erupting as proto-imminence

imagining Suns on tumultuous planes

beneath boats

part flame & part drizzle

part lynx & floating indigo puzzle

aboard which exists

a weaving passenger of blood

vibrating

as a double genetic witness

at one level speaking through ravished

vitreous glyphs

at another

an implicate hail from other heavens

being a beam through threaded glass

by wave which lengthens through trigonometrical

neutrino

which overspills itself

like the tone of my skin

imbued with various shadings

a scorched albino chalice

at work

listening to itself as refractive ophthalmology

as in a spinning sun dog's mirror

meaning shadow accrued by shadow

until explosions build

& release themselves

through the algae of radical Suns

where the unconfinable

blazes as radiance

as a river of flashing mountain shale

sparked by the waters from great nuclear lakes

these being

interior signals from emptiness

from genetic transmigrations

forming re-implanted soil from the inevitable

the yield from my skin

from its tragic ethos in the Congo

reveal in my soma an auric medicine well

a scorched chrysalis

a great medicinal acreage

being a ghost from a sacred lava hide

I also dwell in post-aquatics

perhaps

as electrical lakes in Tibet

existing

& re-existing

through strange expansionary realms

beyond the characterological

which reflects itself across post-existence

not yet a coding

or an inflammatory number

but a merger through deafness

through holographic conservation

being a geometric figment

flowing from the water of meteors

flowing in simultaneous vacuums

being neither flame nor salt

neither henbane or sapphire

all these tendencies

being sigmas

& pions

& muons

not particles

but hyphenated cauldrons

being vertical tribulations

haunted as spirals

such is the state of flame through self-feeding

 through strange exclusionary cycles

as if feeding on the paradox of matches & sugar

I've evolved from a seeming singular realm

as human consequence through human consequence

my skin being barbiturate in Blackness

with my angular rotation as law being flight

I have taken on the dreadful oasis

the arcane barrier as reasoning

not as paradigm from Hatshepsut

but as lion maker

as agrarian builder

living in the want of the many

I

whose never been born or been dead

I

of the granular being

I

of meandering solar fumes

always knowing my body as blazing occultation

in contradistinction

the inveterate pogroms of the Portuguese

always knowing the secretive African in their

blood

hiding their invidious outcome

through their ruthless occupations

of Argium

of Santiago

of the castle at Jorge da Mina

they

who blinded bodies

who crafted hulls from darkened flesh

who honoured strangeness by barbarity

by reversing the living system

by attempting to forge power in barracoons

throwing my body in quarantine

like a cave dog

like a disease-ridden civet

my spirit narrowed

into the 'lower decks of ships'

sailing to Pernambuco

to rot in sullen labour fields

this being

my pre-birth

the cursed seasons before my waking

yet I

the shaman

as crypto oneiric bird

weaving my way from the darkness of wells

sending up signals

with the sound of each wingbeat

like the sound from random electron leakage

wingbeats

darting through cyanoethene

sending code through the complexified as Ground

whirring

which de-reverses & reverses

so that it permeates & permeates again

being as infectious kind of grenadine

which arises from burning indigo basins

being simultaneous with integral spores

looming in outer planetary fields

floating as orange-red spectra

an unimpeachable violet

mixed with curious dust from Uranus

counted by mono-meters

exquisite as rays

under too much angularity

certainly this is not the source of Imperial tension

of the way war transpires

of the way glances submit when fused

by violence or bribery

the latter being thoughts

which hover in cacti

which pose themselves in multitudes of sulfur

thereby submitting to dark illusional strife

all of this being a fragmentation of who I am

as Aguirre de dos Santos

as the sub-fields of the aforesaid

Aguirre de dos Santos

I exist

by shift as sorcerous acuity

by nova as multi-directional implanting

in this regard

I am subjective

my genetic ambulation

not strictly of human amperage

or of acutely staggered hummingbird's braille

but a mixture of hydroxyl & voltage

of dark adjustments in the vapour

so therefore

I remain manifold

elusive

eclectic in the vastitudes

of course I speak by delimited inferno

by the various shadings in Lobito

as if I were African in the Alentejo province
of Portugal

then knowing myself through the cane fields
of Fortaleza
scrounging dead millet & boar
my shamanistic sable
like blackened rays between Lobito & Fortaleza
beyond soma & its resonance beyond the
serpentine as spectrum
with its plasmatic shiftings
with its phantasmic isles
continuing to roam & create within themselves
because I am these isles
these strange surveyor's flames
from my nest split apart & rejoined into pions
which de-resist & regather
as numerous swarms of the Chilean Gigantus

which means
I relate these swarms to comets
as utter circulatory ranges
being beautiful squalls in the void
listening to themselves
as though fertilized by neurology

erratic phosphene murals
ambivalent compensatory fires

allowing me to weave & electrically merge

with myself

through odd participatory rite

as protractive rotation

adding

& ceasing to add to my substance

which reveals in my mind an alphabetic substrate

a language through charged tornado chasm

seen

through these exhaustive equilibria

through this series of resonant Sun quakes

there remains the ice from broken electrical snow

creating a paradox which is life through

new exhaustion

a curious polar ruin

electric interjacence

a somnolent rose oil gone bad

again

I

as Angolan in Alentejo

being the slave who crossed the sea mounts

as the baffling figment in Palmares

who wafts

who plagiarizes quicklime

434

who amazes by juggled addenda
both known & unknown
across the province of implication

its subtle acts
its anxious & meditative cruelty
grown from vacuums
which is my body as indentured data

going
from cellular form to cellular form
being
a telepathic light
always at one
with ignited vertigo rivulets
rivulets
being that plane
& that plane
& that plane
shifting
with electric variations
beyond mass & energy as mass
with shifts taking place
between Luanda & Lisbon
between Lobito & Fortaleza
the latter four enclaves
constructive social histrionics

all four constrictions

condensed in the posture

for the enslavement of melanin

their prototypical outline

to keep the 'beast' at bay

to keep its motions alchemically squandered

to keep its offspring psycho-socially deflated

they cannot know

that I breathe inside the Sun

that I exist as a-particulate ray

as ferment

as occulted hydrogen

as fervid helium spring

as bird

I bathe in radiant helium deltas

my shrillness de-exists

& re-evapourates

& regathers momentum through glyphs

which magnify & re-penetrate

each letter or glyph

each oxygen symbol

be it sapphire or algae

it inspires a trance of living normative equilibria

somehow equated to 90 million años

the latter being a transparent scan line

which empties & reconjugates

as shamanistic interjacence

436

between Hillstar & vacuum

between itself as bird

& illusive witness on this plane

not as commercial simulacra

or combat society

or broken planetary fiefdom

but as one alive

throughout

horrific a-activity & flaw

throughout 500 years of the purgatorial

as presence

I remain

the centripetal holocaust native

unclaimed as sub-divisive

yet knowing the Portuguese inside their skulls

knowing their delimited psychic compression

knowing their regime which lingers in the

bitterest hunger

their legacy at best

as embattled plagiarists

as swine

as deer headed monks

vicious

as shaman

as Angolan

as semi-Angolan

I know the planters

the railroad clerks

the stay at home philanderer's

all of whom consume

all of whom kill for profit

trading bodies for sugar

gold for parts of limbs

I the leper who mines the Mayans

through psychic palabras

who kindles Baktuns out of bread

I

the scribe

as host informant

who sculpts

an incantatory treatise

from entangled neuro-biology

so that estrangement insists

magic inscribes its grammar

which partakes of each phoneme as velocity

thereby transmuting glints form the abyss

each condensing fire:

chlorophyll

each grain as great electrical spore:

blaze as mantric electrical salt

which in an a a-classified manner

invigourates as lustrums

as hydrogen utopias

of depths of cinnabar & vapour

being moisture

as bluish sub-electrics

giving a kind of reign to flaming indigo spectrums

I

who have never not existed

I

who understands dying by having never been born

I de-exist as gravity

living the life of inveterate expansion

yet I am pressure

as pre-cosmic intaglio

an observational pre-histrionics

a respiration being body in emptiness

being life as contagion throughout nothingness

nothingness being

the preternatural substance

the primordial habituation

compounded

before arrival at singularity

before methodology or magnification

because of this

I exist as differing pressures

& pressure of pressures

creating scatterings & phases & unreasons

living beyond death

beyond the point of a fixed obstruction

where realia shifts & blinds & disintegrates

of course

I am not a courier from the Rhineland

or an old Dutch geriatric

spinning implosive yarn

on a turgid anthracite wheel

no

I am not a general existing

with a failure to report my own habits

or to expose a reckless culinary yield

affirming to myself soured fragments & boar

then perhaps scraps of lynx with shark & bread

perhaps simplicity

perhaps peppers with rice & oil

simmered to uncommon astringency

because a ghost does imbibe

because a ghost is a double body

he extends his substance

by eating wine & corn & molasses

440

& ignites his rice on strange argento benches

while leaning against a stunning coral shadow

counting to himself

unscripted cinder

aligned with wayward Microscopiums

both parallel & perpendicular to the species

a seeming exercise in particles

alive

as teeming aural neutrinos

at times

they occupy a strictly conducted sensory

conduction

& I hear them awake & withdraw

I hear them sing through exculpatory windows

through a series of drifting nerve extensions

like a dharana of crystal

or an extract from Hillstars

purified

as though harmonized reception

were explored as though a fire descended

by means of auric or transmutational tremendums

suddenly existing

as Phoenicians in the Hebrides

or Nubians in the Pacific being of strange

particulate renown

perhaps a trace from the dead in Lobito

perhaps measured by signs from uneven rain

which is a listening out of balance

a precarious phonemic response

frayed

by the pull of suggestion

dazed at odd advance

murky as ventriloqual blizzards

at another level

they persist

as vapourous astronomical lions

suggesting

by their angular aurality

Bellatrix

Orion and its forces

the Dogon star called Sirius B

keeping

in their ocular sieves

a magnetic field strength

a dazed endurance

a combustible celebration

this is where I exist

at a remove above ether

above the 100 trillion cells

known to be the body as matter

not that I am not Aguirre de dos Santos

not that I haven't formed for one time

as human generating field

as astronomer

as thinker

as listener from Namoratunga

announcing echoes from suns

as a sun astronomer from Mali

transmuting

each of the body's neural rotations

each cell

a simultaneous extension of itself

hovering

in its inner electrical lakes

with their various parallel dimensions

the latter concealing their quivering parallel

anarchial

thereby

knowing the body as a neuro-botanical archive

a substance which spins by reiterating gnomes

as an a-priori leaven

forming from itself a stark projection through

neutrality

not that I don't breathe

or witness the boat of the Sun in the darkness

but now

I am cleansed

of each corrupted signal

poisoned by duality

as if

I am listening to rotation

ignite itself through magnetic arousal

me being an auric substance

floating

through bickering & disunion

through illusive documents of dread

where the hearing recedes

& comes forth

always listening to vitality

like a fabulist

or haunted moral ascendant

singing

like a griot in a darkened cinder garden

working at differing removes

by gregarious motivations

& these haunted motivations

as invisible types of carbon

as anatomical simulacra

as physical registration

wrought

by genetic monsoon

therefore

as shaman

as Aguirre de dos Santos

I know the hybrid leaders & their essence

their reptilian mechanics

their policies condoned like ice against blood

like the force of stones which break against cycles

as if I were hoisting fragments

poisonous notions of death

knowing the latter

through human suffering as abscission

what I can say

is that the leaders of the Earth

have harvested contagion

have conspired against the salubrious

constructing nuclear pelts

in lieu of kinetics

& these pelts

as inertia

as pyretical imbalance

as warped & downward arc

this being

wavering

uncertainty

pulmonics

this being

fervour of flag versus fervour of flag

this being

admitted slights

saprogenic pogroms

territorial marcescence

me

the animist beast

against the Jesuit Fathers

then the Anglicans

the Methodists

the ruinous restraints ruling the Congo

the latter being

the lizards who pose as Africans

who mismanage our resolve

our forthright claims to compensation by injury

in this regard

we are always abandoned

disabled by bandits

claimed by the world as deficits & cadavers

I who brew

in the braille of snow & starlight

who builds

from each asylum of wounds

a masterful substance of thorns & resurrections

my 4 times as dying

my earthquake as human delivery

through a doubled zodiac of hunger

through abandonment as conundrum by despair

as to actual account

all resurrections & deaths have imploded

& spawned as spurious testament

a holographic mural

which attest to my arising & re-arising

at the portal of the spinning horizon Sun

which spins

which matriculates as chaos

which is departure by ordeal

understanding

that there exists by exhaustive strength

that there exists by kinetic encryption

inveterate meteoritics

numerations as sign as rising sunbirds over Saturn

creating as their symbol

mystic circular delay

so that Saturn

seen from spiraling mountainous caves

blaze as Jupiter/Saturn

& merge

as a strange interior protein

in terms of complex distillation

as if such cinder were a new photopia

again

shaping in the eye through botanical displacement

through

the fonio seed

through

the Digitaria exilis

being parallel

& knowing of themselves as parallel

thereby

knowing themselves on Earth

to be Syrian

& of the Syrian flood system

a flood beacon

which enables the grains to grow through

a-systemic ratio

such is life on Earth

as 2 systems blur

& create status through the improbable

Saturn/Jupiter

being lynx

448

& grass

& sable

& flamingo

these being nothing more than illuminated flecks

enrichments

linkages

patterns

charged with the azuric significance of magic

each code

each sigil

each fundamental rotation

being a spell

over & beyond the rotation of zodiacs

& by this latter summation

I suggest the scope of quantum proto-living

with its heavens

spiraling

out of deluge after deluge

being arcs of the unconfigurable

darting

& moving

like a drawing which blazes as spellbinding bones

I am

emigre from Nigredo

from a stark & roaming hiatus

Kemetic

in the sense that I've risen from black soil

from essential diamond & guano

so that I ceaselessly see inside myself

constructive ravens rising

from the light of rotational hogans

as living being in a hogan

I do not impose upon my life

a stark or a doctrinal menace

as if

I could alter the Cuanza

according to sources advanced by the strategic

of course

speaking with a stick of braille

leaning on precise photons

having broken in two a reasoned leprosy scale

so my mind by its bursts

plays ghosts with itself

with its incomplete strata

seemingly sculpted

by cyclically farming dictations on Venus

being an animus of minerals & flight

I am ultra-pasar

I am chama as voltage

as great carrier of sigils

as feldspar fragments

as burning with interior water

I am like the oral game of words

never ending in a word

supplying letter after letter

always treasonous with completion

always altering

always in-stating lingual migratory flames

in Portuguese

the word

recomecar

beginning & beginning again

leaving various phonemes awry

further inflaming themselves

as new forces of sufficiency

as various ghost around flames

being various flames around Sirius

being various suns of vigourous lunar integument

& these suns

condense inside a circle as my name

with always one sun blank

one sun missing

a shadow

at precipitous illustration

as aeolian remnant

a volatized feather

a herbivorous hissing

like a sunbird singing

amidst shafts spinning lunar fields

I

the blank Dominican name

I

the Angolan seismological telluric

whose essence is 'Year Star'

is Ganymede & its brightness

so I am mind at the essence of mind

I am knowing at the essence of knowing

vivid

via glints

& mirrors

& cycles

which means

I know of Arguin

of Santiago

of the Gulf of Guinea

of the plantations of Sao Tome

which ignited the 'rise of Brazil'

I am entangled in these motions
in these fissures & isolations
in this deafening sun complex
bing kinetic as bodiless discipline
as that which responds to savoir at the precipice

because I live & breathe as revolving sonar body
as cryptic distillation
which blazes
which is seen & unseen
which allows calligraphy through disorder
as puzzling nuance & dialectic
as consequence
as inveterate non-proposal

not that I have condoned myself as theory
or as a séance of particles splayed by abstraction

no
I remain
Aguirre de dos Santos
body connected by fumes
by evolving indigo slate
writing from bereftness
the old colonials as Gargantua
vis a vis
the Dutch/Portuguese & their standards

the old Spanish motives

the talismanic acids of the British

as old omnivores

they are suspended

& the Dutch remain ciphers

at the same time concluded as the nomos of Satan

they

who speak through salt & terror

through suffocation & cruelty

from Cape Verde through New Spain

they cause sorrow

they negotiate abuse

they enslave as order of property

they promote at essence the very motherhood of Satan

me

a hostage in wailing compounds

in the heat of open corrals

in the passage through mire

sleeping in foundations of wastage

I knew the maximum oeuvre of infra-dark

the sparks from dazed leakage

yet knowing

the hieroglyphic union

between each star & infinity

454

which allows me to live in lexical curvature

soaring above a vault of fractions

knowing the power of loam

to cast its rays

as frayed electrum & ennui

which analyzes twilight

akin

to the spectral exhaustion of current

which percolates

which drizzles inside the opening of ravines

such are

the elliptical states

where I see the Portuguese as lizards

as abandoned doubles from Oporto

feeding upon themselves

by reflexive mendacity

& this mendacity

come from a stock of jailers

from entombed & perfectly limitless marauders

frustrated

relentless

eccentric in their bloody fantasias

they are vicars self-condoned

creating blessing in crushed diamond

in sustained living opposition

who rule by chaotic feral command

it is within this wayward unnerving

that I unfold in bodies

that I live by bursts & kindlings

& so I affect

I suspend events

I penetrate systems & history

so as to extend a draft of auras

to reshape inactive iridium

knowing in myself that I re-contain old novae

one could call it charisma

or Chemotaxis

or the shape of lightning as guide

this being

the aeronautical as implosion

announcing new implosional causes

not as raw notational motive through burden

stance

but as tough through magnetic emotional mysteries

far beyond the vitreous

turned to the outward dust of visibility

again

me

456

sigil

isolate physical maladjustment

slander persistent at the fulcrum of magic

the body then

as great nuclear gust

as eye

as weather

as curvature

as act

possessing

the odour of great rainbows

transforming the static from the depths

of nervous ravines

for instance:

tornadoes from the lungs

living cycles from the spleen

then

the skeletal frame

a voltage ladder

an invisible thunder soma

translated

as quintessential seething

a greater more surreptitious complex understanding

a hypsometrical electrics

a hypsographical solar plasma

which shifts as migratory protein

as precarious discharge vacuum

which just as quickly

returns to its power through telepathic crowding

through the prismatics of merging

such a body being of galactic mean

as converse & activity

alive through numerical charging

thus

the body etched with hydroxyl

etched at the juncture of interstellar reddening

where the bells begin to hollow & blaze

through differing quanta as methodology

these bells being suns

being connectives to trenchant rotations

to trans-junctional proclivities

to trans-spatial statics

remaining in reduced transfunctional continuums

in & out of the mange of counting

this is where the logos is leaped

this is where the respiration transfunctions

which includes

the orphan

the slave

the inhabitant of baixadas

yet of Lobito & its ghosts

& Luanda & its parallels

living as translatable voltage

which

at minimum there exists

double observations

in rotations with dark eyes

with change in actual chemical coloration

this being the fierceness

the Uranian charisma

the stratospherics

the interior registration

as volcanic attractor

I live in the gulfs

before the Earth was born

before the eras from the prior Sun

before the universe that we know has come to be

knowing in sum

the black waters of the firmament

being a yield of sand

a reversive ghost barometer

speaking to myself

as if engulfed in a sudden asteroid sea

so I am claimed as the uninhabitable

as the 100 billion cells

as the body in post-recurrence

as I've come to endure

its very imminence & scattering

uprooted

since the Earth was provoked

I live as presence

beyond 'spurious signals'

beyond particles of ghostly showers

'produced as they perish'

being a bird across glassy eclipse phonations

being fabulous radii through turbulence

drinking great drafts of ether

as myriorama

in universe after universe

as rotational angularity

as substance

as cipher

what has evolved from such quickening

finds the human maze alive

at dark balletic perch

& at dark balletic perch

a transitional Hillstar singing

tenebrous variations

tenebrous micro-cores

responding as it does

to the respirational as helix

according to upright posture as flight

even when wandering through broken star formation

flight ascends through opaque comment

through that which conjuncts with the holographic

nursery

where the instantaneous writhes

where physically derived activity is reversed

where its properties are explored as unutterable

fluidity

telepathics

potentia

evolvement through concealment

these are planes

akin & non-akin

to Earth as we know it

to oxygen

as it relates & non-relates to Mars

to intermingled properties as distance

yet merged as utopian carpentry

perhaps

in a lake of blind regions

at the Venusian equator

yet

I'm never summoning

anthropomorphic residue

or the mortal as incoherent judgement

as if argument consisted

of the stony colloquial gaze

riveted at the level of the artefact

at its peculiar delimited rhetoric

operant

as a dark foundational terror

always in awe of any movement

always structured by the in-celestial as acid

evolving out of mayhem

always tested by conquest

extinguished

re-exhibited as points

as squalls

at the very nadir of endurance

462

as vanished form

as palpable re-occurrences

I

Aguirre de dos Santos

brought back to the colour of oil & shale

again tested

by the epics of hurricanes & pressure

yet I occur at that pitch

over & before the unforeseeable

in the green flash

in the day to day kin of the Maya

so whatever I reveal

concerning Phoenicia or Chaldea

or the Sun myths of Angola

I have risen to the juncture of the iconic

evocative

as neural combustion

as nigrescent interior combining

being the double pole

the isolate spell

always filled with contagion

& each of my subsequent

echoes through ensorcelling

diagonal

wavering

displaced throughout Andean misnomer

because I am stray

I have no dates to advance

no diary which reads

1545

1222

or 1346

I am never of carnivorous testing advancement

or subsisting in motives

of Saxon calendrical myth

I have never condensed as soldier

as dealer in capes & weapons

I've always appeared

as the non-descript formation

as the odd & anonymous deficit

as the bi-pedal specter

half-divided at the horizon

yet alive

at the southern half of the Congo Basin

feeding on crops of cassava & cane

fending off locusts

advancing as fluidic compression

gravitized

& at the same released from gravitization

so I am able to hover

to bend by suggestive anagram

like a molecule

buzzing

seeing & re-seeing my own function

464

understanding the gulf between being & not being

between dissonance & its ongoing dissonance

for instance:

observational ruin

chaotic sepulcher in movement

which amounts

to disruption I de-possess

to the ice & the shores of the world I co-inhabit

tracing my own neutrinos as current

as eccentric spectation

transmuting the moans of an Owl

hidden in the salt

of an old microbial telepathy

inside spontaneous stratagems

which a-light

which take on curious respiratory auras

which is asymptotic electrum

creating curious pauses & ignitions

precipitous drops

quantum pre-imbalance

in-parochial de-adjustment

animistic confine

living at the source of the unmeasurable

not just flint around my waist

nor my index voltage

stunned at ballistic sub-surface

but arguable cretinization

placed as a dark echinoderm in motion

as coronal sparks

as copious intuition

I cannot give as trance

a sequestered camouflage through old dichotomies

to old neural symbiotics

where each synapse sparks

the vitreous of old candelas

so I remain in a state of blankness

where states coalesce

where scorpion transmixes with ubiquitous stellar

hypnosis

I

being ember as body

as positron

as black electrical ravine

as osmotics from prior parties

being

Aguirre de dos Santos

as blaze

as ingeminated trace
hyper-dimensional at each one quarter angle

at collapse of partial zeniths
being one in the being
at the source & transmixture
at Ganda
Kikuyu
Kongo
& Rundi
all of them
alive in living sub-vapour
in combustive sub-raven

as if inscribing initiatory vitae
with silicon pyres
with osmotic Indian oscillations
part Macuni
part Lobito
part of a group of green incendiary planets
speaking in proto-Mande
creating integers from dried script
making up ink from 'soot & liana'

being the Sun Ghost
I am threaded with silver & fever
feasting in trance
off manioc as braille

part Angola & Saturn

part Recife through batuca & Ceres

with a blank frequency of vowels

read 'right to left'

& within & without

as code

as syllabic dictation & stress

a fugitive through space & distance

being noun from inundation

I gamble as spore

as smoke & utter residue as fragment

part patience

& oracle

& dust

as signs

as cryptos

as drainage

I

Aguirre de dos Santos

as suffix

as strange ballistic abbreviation

as phantom

as spark

as solar bodily grace

intrinsic

coterminous with exploration

with dialectical aquatics

468

which roams the higher elevations

through electro-botanical conjoinment"

The Ganges

The fifth-century Indian philosopher...considers
the faculty of speech to be an instinct or
intuition. He compares it to animal instinct and
does not believe language is learned.

Routledge Encyclopedia of Philosophy Volume 4

Lamas...are not so much monks as priests
and ghostly warriors who understand the
art of fighting with demons.

Sir Charles Eliot, *Hinduism and Buddhism Volume 3*

...a race of gnostic spiritual beings.

Sri Aurobindo

The Rig Veda was composed by the Brahmans...
and represents the sum total of the early
Aryan experience. ...it is absolutely rampant
with violence and racial overtones. It is also
in the Rig Veda that we find the first documentation
of the racially oriented caste system.

Runoko Rashidi

"I've come to these waters
as Shūdra
as hallucinated lama
as spellbinding dictat

in this regard
I am not a mahatma
nor a spurious intrusion
singing in mystical parlando

me
I'm an old Dravidian from Goa
spectral
velvet
discussing motions concussive with sand
discussing the body as a vernix riddle
or a poem sourced by cholera
or formations tense with blue rotational acids

perhaps
I am not more than a ghost
or a villainous discovery
or a gainless instigation
based on a set of rivalries with absence

perhaps I've come to these waters
to craft my own tremendums
to walk outside my noumenon

to blur my trans-identity through culture

perhaps

this is how blood works

how audition reacts

& stages itself

through reactive physical conflagrations

have I come to view to simply foil myself?

or to ignite my force by regressive combining?

as I react & speak as I react

I've come to hover at the ghats

the colour of a psychic Kashi

sometimes sable & liquid

at others

solferino & volcanic

as I respond through parallel as persona

there is Benares

& Varanasi

& Kashi once again

as if synergies were overactive with agua

as Buddhist

as Dravidian sprung from Goa

there is English voice mixed in Kanada Hindu agua

plunged in the depths

then exploding

476

as unquelled power as in the purity of ravens

& I see boats burn beneath an unstable Sun

ghats waver as strange proportional Richters

as ciphered monsoon epics

as blank emission misfocused

& so the maharajah's walls

take on a cunning electrical rate

as collapsing body self-moored to an unsteady balance

I am different

I make no offering of 'jai flowers'

or make as my form philosophical unraveling

to evince a kind of portion

forced from the gullet as mountainous prayer

perhaps firewood on the ghats

perhaps corpses piled as conflagrant in-audia

& perhaps my heresy of claim

is more that entranced moaning

more than something beyond intransigent chakras

for instance

my psyche swims through neglected alter currents

as if I'd stumbled on a feast of vermin

on infested sugar hamlets

& for those who declare themselves through samsara

I've risen to no more than the status of a ghoral

or a pangar

or that at best I'll live a million times

& never subsist as a purposeful vahana

I've never sat in posture

chewing on Channa

or invaded a dharmshala

speaking quietly to myself through immolated frenzy

when letters burn

when rocks fly in from the heavens

they are signs of bats & thistles

their kinetics internally stung by solar incandescence

these being kinetics

between the Varuna & the Asi

as if I were speaking of a liminal Varanasi

felled

& brought to life again

by rays form the great Surya

from solar form as shard

as cosmic spiral

as situational treatise

as looking glass spawned from complexification

& sulfur

thereby listening to suns as scorching indigo & silver

what I am able to do
is to translate
is to merge samsara with ghat after ghat
yet all the while barred from the crypto-Brahmanical

ah
but I know the very summoning of phenomena
& the Ganges reacts as luminescence through
nothingness
through a spell of transverse murmurs
calling
& taking away
the purest patterns of breathing
being colourless amethystine which emboldens
itself through rotational blinding

errors are seemingly embodied & drained
yet what has always concurred
is the body as wooden abandonment
as exhausted coronation
as sensate stained through providential inversion

so if I pick out points in time
it creates no ultimate significance

& if on such inscrutable date
a certain sari was stolen
if peculiar Yaks were transmogrified

life could build as no other outcome

being nothing in itself

being energy randomly exchanged

as say

tsunamis in Lisbon

so nothing would burn at that hour

therefore

the listless feuds

the pointless tiger cats prowling

alit

by a carved & tattooed lightning

these are fires which create of themselves riddles

imposed

& superimposed

so that

in the shape of the being no structure exists

no animal can live or be brought back from thinking

if vultures crawl & exhibit no response

I call them

naked

fraught with competitive cremations

& there must exist from this

a flicker of understanding

within the fuels which are considered transgression

480

much in the manner of the torment of owls

or hornets which gather affliction

& then revert in themselves

to a scorched or empty preludial

this is how hawks grow empty of their optimums

of their twists

of the writhing nature in their bones

at times

I make sport

by rivaling certain bodies

immobilized

on a curiously saddled sheep

or taking codes from Mongolian ponies

transposing in my sleep sudden eras of waking

not that I contest my own substance as law

of that I've reached an effortless fissure

that thoughts from certain Gods can't bury

because I've lost my thirst for the heralded soma

or for the image of myself

that nothingness can inspire

perhaps

the rats condone me as vapour

or as a scent which kindles venoms

or encircles itself with envy

as if I'd tangled myself with sounds

with unsuspected clauses

with rifts in the motes of cyclones

as if I captured dust from fractured 'tidal heating'

as if my strange basaltic wastes hollowed their

way through captured foundations

as lighted prows

as blazeless forts

as monomial stealths & tensions

not that these wastes are cold tellurian rapids

or that they exist as forms peculiar & mixed

with carnelian

as heightened waves delimited & sterile with

fraction

beings exist

they descend from ghat

they descend as moral plesiosaur's in crises

as those who emote by proportional stain

I cannot say

that the Ganges contains no suffusion

or that it has no effect on birth

or that it doesn't provoke human insular navigation

I am not saying

that this water is not of summoning

482

or has never existed

that is monaural worth has not blossomed beyond

the music of the Vedas

beyond its stones of sacred writings

this watcr

perhaps fumes from a stored up sun

or from a moon

which has fallen from itself

as response to halos seized at ironical limit

as lama

do I seek to extract from these waters the

flow of Tibetan sound?

or to give them the means to work through

proportional tenet?

because I remain anonymous on the ghat

I am never seen as alien

splashing its impure waters

not am I seen as witness

according to astrologies

poised as they are against dominance & forgetting

if I can call the Ganges

a lake of therapeutics

or an unraveled hollow

or a tool entangled with stricture

let me say

I do not spite its rivers

or seek to denigrate its form

or its birth in regions

which erupt from the sources of mountainous

parturition

for me

the Himalayas whirl

& carry no structured pitch

or static inference

because

I've flown inside their climates

& known their assignations

their riddles

their conditions

which substantiate a fulminate or sacred subspecies

saying this

I wear no rivalrous wool

I station none of my lore within the source of

Tibetan conflict

as ghost

as Shūdra

as Nilotic & Sino-Tibetan

I know bold & progressive detail

I know that perniciousness extends

& shifts continent to continent

484

of continent

through quarrelsome states

through perilous in-dynamics

the waters blaze

as parallel insignificance

as wandering on a stretch of land gone bad

which means

the divinations tangle

the rainbows merge & travel through peripheries

boats are dazed

hawks de-occur

dis-established monsters through bleak or

aggressive grammars

this I may say is the Ganges

as if

there existed no proof

no simple formula or reign

for various background calculations

for pilgrims

perhaps verbs burn

perhaps a circuitous séance instructs

perhaps chakras subsist by bold & carnivorous

exam

yet I

as one tested by remoteness

by slurred tendencies through speaking

know the crows which remain in Goa

who signal to themselves

as if appearing as forms on Sirius

as in-derived from manna

as in-volitational ink

as transmogrified embodiment

haunted by shifts

which seep from transgressive kingdoms

by shifted states in the Pleiades

on various afternoons

I attempt

to pose certain signals as if to interrupt

spectrums

as if to correct myself

as if to fuse all circular forms of deliverance

my training has been through the art of dissonance

through hypnotic purges

through thought which has languished in combative

meridians

so I ask

is that & that crow exclusive to Lhasa?

to something blank & generally Tibetan & un-beastly?

or is this lot by right possession?

or increased philosophical incensement?

is this exercise?

is this trebling the effects of the Sun by

divination?

or is this absented flaw?

or disappearance by various thought adjustment?

say

if the sun erupts from old asterisk thought as emergence

& doubles itself by means of the thorax

the Ganges will teach us

that it's never existed

that it's luminous in-exposure

that it's tremulous cusp

could never concur as luminous conflagration

being sudden escape through moral in-specifics

so the question now arises

have I risen from fatigue

have I haunted dishonour

just to rise to distinction as a powerless &
pointless master?

as a crude & depressive alloy?

perhaps I am he without sleep as machination
as he who thrives through cunning
who slips through the core of the equinox of rising

as a 3rd or 4th body
or bodies clouded in terms of astral dispensation
or utter effects
or breathings as taught by various practices &
resolutions

these are bodies at differing neural junctures
as voids or exhibits
come to judge my assignation
by creatureless form
by love in the form of bubonic exhibit

perhaps to this degree
a sadhu could see me
as a body condensed from the vapours of Saturn

this is how trees swim
how labours ignite

how the great intestinal forces

claim their ascent at the borders of dying

not the violence of mangled doves

or inclement demonstrability

but flaw

as persona which withstands the corona of non-

exposure

so de-limit exists

& the result

increased or compulsive wavering

first

there is the condition of weather

the difference shadowing of birth

then the living state as the calliope of indifference

then the next remove

as custom

as post-positional inurement

reverential with concern

never through noted utterance

has the Buddha desisted his yield

or embellished the prayer wheels with ice

or created error by lost concrescence

or invigouring the sonar which thrives through

proportional tribulation

something has happened

I survey as ghost
as eaten or eclectic principia

yet I do not seek camaraderie by poison
by triangulated hulls
by tragedies which consume by scope as self-
engulfment

which means
that they resolve themselves
as extinguished rate
as fastidious annulment

because I allow myself as Thutmose
as Dravidian conjoinment
creating judgement by means of stark or phantasmic
wiles

I could accuse my compatriots
of allowing gates to burn
of allowing forgeries to ensue
yet I cannot allow
thought of such saturation
yet I cannot allow
such separative conjoinment

at times

owls ignite from my fingers

& I witness in my sleep Yaks which drift in rain

if indeed

I have a double persona in Hindu

let him speak

let him consume his own merit

let him subside as angular deductive

because I have talked to snakes

& created rodents from ash

I condense no singular merit or honour

I am simply lama as self-sufficiency

which opens the Uranian

through inferential metal

for instance

my powers allow me pillage from ghosts

from the moats of 3 women who inscrutacize

their negotiable warrens

by means of curious & inevitable seduction

yet I cannot accuse myself of being maimed

& partially Hindu

having the authority to cook ants

or seize the property of those who live by

enlightened study

I do not denigrate the Hindu
or bypass the leanings of Shiva or Brahma

I simply state
seminal grasp & extension
accusing the human species
of electrical malfunction
of living according to superficial transfunction

just to say
that I cause glass to burn
provides no functional glance or exhibit
giving me no power to speak from refined pagodas

never glancing this way or that
I cannot speak to the Ganges
as separative fault
as protracted peregrination

I cannot reduce its force to residual day star
to habits which produce inevitable shunting

it has pauses
& currents
& the sadhus cleanse
& cast themselves through mystery

so to speak of dawn as gold & rivers

would only result in partial illumination

in doling out conventional day crafts

say

my body was of braised & wooden character

could I impress my sources

to conjure prayer out of glass

or retrieve silicates from rain

under such circumstance

I could never provoke a series of buried orations

or ride a sacred wraith

coloured by purplish mandalas

yet the vertiginous does not lull me

does not kindle my blood

as strength through non-event

which holds my inevitable disorder

for me

the pole star wavers as inevitable disorder

as reactive disservice

as cloud which trembles as ironical dis-identity

because I've trained in negation

I've been purified by blaze

by perfect crows of misperception

narrative does not consist

the soul blazes as mark through strategized

dysphonia

through roots & beasts

through defective laterals

which means

I've leapt the nest of increased fate

which means

I no longer exist as majority by way of person

the root is empty

yet the ground has not been broken

I've staged no belief

in a sky of buried ponies

in sight which masquerades as register by blinking

wolves

I've come to absence

by explored generosity

by nothingness traced through points in emptied

dietary seed

I neither accept

nor dis-accept myself as beast

as to function

I cannot say that I subsist as territorial

or omnivorous

or as coercive opposition

who ceases relations

who funnels speech

who opens the onerous as mystery

I can say that I hover above instigation

above crude & enforced transmixture

above the game of war

of monsters & their fiefdoms

having broken through relic of transpersonal

reduction

have I unwound the coil

creating blizzards in its wake?

or have I taken a stark approach to assassinated

feeding?

nothing marks me in this regard

I am summons who leans through drafts at

carnivorous juncture

who arrives at spells as approach derived from
singing

as extrinsic conjecture
one could evince me as magic or luck
or a conglomerate of cinders which transacts
with dust

of course
I am more than the bone field
more than harvested cholera
more than eroded moral ravines
this is not destiny which leans on itself
or burns or is silent & listens to lost
trajectories

this is how gold can bloom in darkness
how interlocuters rove & revert to origin

an in-grown thesis
heritage as anonymity

because I do not build adversarial declaratives
of the Buddha versus Shiva
or the Bön desires against primeval Brahmanisms

again
not here to uproot
496

the fables of Ajanta

or seek

to de-beatify the means of the sculptings at

Ellora

I do not carve on my table

a series of potions

or seek to induce grafts

by restating merits of sudden sadhu instruction

I do not mirror destruction

to mix one state of eras

& degrade another inclemency

just to provide a dialectic for summoned thought

or prayer

in this regard

I've abandoned discovery

& because I've abandoned discovery

my fate casts no ink

nor does it erupt from my indicatives

the sulfurous tools of monster or spider

because birds kill

this does not distract me

 or de-enlighten me as witness

one does not have to listen to me

as a treasonous or mournful idiophone

as a blasphemous jackal vomiting in the grain stores

no

not speaking in bubonic ideograph

I have reached the state where no transforcives apply

where I cease to unite strength with breathless

criminal value

therefore

I do not respond to osmosis

or deliberate its lone eccentrics

other than in a state of séance

because

I'm not given victories to preach

or prior sources to unravel

I

exist

burdens release

chasms are broken

as archetypes waver

strength detaches itself from personas

nerves filter back into darkness

into types of suns & forms

which inevitably lose their aim

498

this is other than the luminous

other than the victory

of one challenged form ascending above

another

this is the vertiginous solvent

the gesture which embodies meritorious cyclones

a shift

a depth of baffling leaves

a flight beyond triangular optometrics

then the ground breaks

noises occur

the serpent inside the spine begins to hiss

with other statics

not statics concurrent with hell or illusion

but independent monsoons

stirring wastes across the cosmos

these are spells which concur

which animate a type of feeling

so it occurs to me

that I harvest with my symbols

both bullocks & glass

gryphons & cranes

& other animated monsters

therefore

I've overcome response to apparitions

to remedial force

to vernacular opposition

in Varanasi

I live as no more than figment

& because I lie as no more than figment

I seem to challenge my self-abandonment

I seem to scroll

within old lamaic record

which accrues within subtractive inversion

true

at times I am stunned

my formation withdraws as oracular majority

yet my energy persists

by spell

by indifferent water

by salt which resists the engenderment of curses

because I do not engender old laws

I can tell you how the Sun is spun

how its bodies occur in bodies

how there de-exists a glossary of sins

how there de-exists motion spun from a galaxy

of dying

these are conditions

which do not form the absolute

nor do they issue in the flames which seeming

nothingness extends

never as a thief on an abstracted plane

nor a wooden bear

buried as a mis-focused purpose

because the void

& absence

& infinity

all swallowed by the Ground

by trace inductivists released beyond brass or

contained motives

there is no one beside me

I call for help or strength

all the Gods dis-provide

all the zodiacs seem scrambled

like scorched announcements

of implied duration

sparking

in an occulted sense

the fuel

of the soil

which increases the fact of in-celibate devolvement

these zodiacs

being traces of the Ground

not in terms of matter or ornament

but of the energy which raises itself

& signals mountain faults

& signals unbalanced rites through eclipses

which means

I'm not claimed by intention

by pre-thought frontality

or by modes conveyed by an elevated means of

abstraction

I could be

some smoke from the ghat

some priest gathering relics

or some thought unto itself

in solemn struggle with embittered singing

orchestral Sumerias?

Indus blending & chanting?

listening to partial thought occurring?

as it continues to thrive as peripheral

elevation

502

there comes to exist the blankly invaded mind

the social concertina

thriving as electrical potentia

at best being a soul from Harappa

melanotic

pre-Aryan in dispensation

I

who arrived from crepuscular tectonics

opposed as I was to Indra called by Indra Dasas

I who was seen

as rancid or cold memorial

as something other than the Sun from which

I'm carved

the Aryans

whose lies enkindled castes

who set up toil in pointless ether

who created for my living untold documents of dread

what of the power of King Ganges?

what of the Ethiopians

of the beings who drafted mangers

who explored the first soils?

so does the anonymous apply?

& do the galaxies concur that the anonymous applies?

saying such

am I placing daunting cinders in my hand?

or am I streaking across a journey as a haunted

template filled with salt?

or am I merely surreptitious?

or weight which inculcates strife as embracing

mission?

it could be said that I've drowned in galactic

waters

that I've tumbled from myth

from altitudinous riddle

from Fallopian suns

unobscured by the intentional

mystic on the one hand

land bathed in nerves on the other

of course

not proscribed

or medicinal in the Earthly sense

but let me say

even the sky burns in winter

the inscrutable turns

the matchless protracts

the cinders create themselves as bodies

which doesn't reduce to morbid integers

504

or to something counted

according to which the skeptics insist

is dazzled germination

is mirage

is inversion which seeks no balancing addition

under such circumstance

I leave no chronicle of ciphers

no events which register through the rational

so my thesis seems ruptured

my embankments broken

without established form

without deftness as a form of discipline

there is no science

no roundabout manner

in which the nerves can be chronicled for strength

this is why the pilgrims bathe

this is why they stroke themselves like fish

first

there is invisible dictation

there is preliminary contestation in the heights

dictation

being the ultimate soil of transparency

which traps monsters

simultaneity hovers

which transits the cells

beyond the spell of its defeatist intentionality

an ideological panopticon?

mantric ambiguity?

dalliance which ignites the necromantic?

which answers different stealths & disburdens

so that there exists whole panoplies of ambrosia

as if a sovereign delicacy were scrawled

in insistent shapes of misnomer

& these shapes

are of an alphabet of crystal

as if my double were explored by Indus nuance

by mystical physiologies

freed from the very Sun which inflames them

I can say

that I've become this heir

this alien sentinel

this curious voltage body

this primeval reconnoitering

alive

by telepathic quadrant

by algebraic volatility

certainly

not as mechanical substrata

or by forces which claim abjectness

or cling to energy as a poverty of habit

so I reach into scorching research

into scolding delimitation

perhaps provoking in my reach

penultimate Samadhi

through phenotype

through paradox as the partially conjoined Ground

as if I were a partial ozone keeper

as if I were alchemist aggrandized as dust

& no nefarious claim can withhold me

or subject me to cleansing other than I'm due

thus

I de-persuade those emboldened by cataracts

by practices akin to extrinsic testing points

I can promise you no prior or sustaining logos

I can promise you no yield from failed motifs

nor will there be growth as emitted from unguided

principle

I simply state my own suspension

knowing that my cells

pontificate & riot

that they state both resolved & unresolved quintessence

 my spirit

not unlike the Cholas

the Pallavas

the Pandyans

& in Funan

& Angkor

& Champa

the Buddha fused with my plasma

with my aerial fulminations of dust

never null or bereft of enlightenment

born

within a triune hull of concernment

I have never have understood conclusions

as core from unscaled geometries

as certainties linked to paradoxical zeniths

as of now

below the water's surface

deities have no power to renew me

to free the conflagration of my spiral

which scatters

beyond the eclectic surfaces & schisms

508

yet I do not deny my psychic relation

with Kanada

or Tamil

or Telugui

or to the remnants

of Kuki

of Manipuri

of Naga

again

being Nilotic & Sino-Tibetan

I condense these states in my ether

as for lanterns

as for clay or brass pots

I am weightless

I am pre-systemic & neutral

as if spun by impalpable ampersands

as if I spoke in pure tellurian tangles

I cannot say that my body hails from exhaustion

from lost or invisible smoke

matching its original blueness

yet this blueness occurs

because blazes exist

because fevers erupt from ingestion of the Kangyur

from scriptures from protracted Shen-rap

I am searching for a blank or nostalgic assertion

proceeding on a path to reach an adhigama

to reach pre-ingested extreme

perhaps

I have not ingested prajna in its purest form

or provoked analogous living

so as to circumvent ontology

I have understood

The Jewel Garland Sutra

where 'every point in space' & 'time'

its motions being refracted

like a hexametric meteor

igniting its range

outside the palpable cosmos

a meteor which protracts as roving synapse

as respirational occlusion

as tendency to mask itself through temperamental

atomics

which is not a trans-didactive

or wakeless error & explosive

therefore I draw blanks

make riddles

& listen to the Ganges through telepathic

re-occurrence

all the while grappling with vertical migration

I'm speaking of fumes which rise outside appearance

which emit through other vistas

amounts which seem as regressive transposing

I seem lone in this regard

connecting the Ganges to refractive cosmology

as I am watching its waters

until the Sun unreservedly expands

until its powers teem with ungovernable authority?

so the Titan will teem with beings?

so that Titan & Uranus & the code of a psychic

Ganges

unalterably reconnect?

are these canals upon which I insist?

& by canals I mean connection

in which Tibet & the Nandas

& all imputed risks will have merged

with loams in the magic of heaven

say the Ganges transmutes to Io

or to unknown occurrence within environs on Uranus

will the Ground transmute?

will its alien relief begin to in-gather alphabetic
definition?

as lama
as Nilotic & Sino-Tibetan
I can never seek frontality
or condone the rectilinear in my findings
there is never result
which I calculate through the porous
or argue as summation through indefinite
hull or property

this not being strain due to tedious instigation
or argument which propagates by means of Buddhist
duality

I am not looking at the Ganges
as illusionistic rector
or crowned exhibit
or scrolled exhibit which breaks demonic intent

I poetically scatter criteria
& un-procreate its life as lingering dissolution

the Ganges absorbs wisdom
it forms a black alter current
as emptied a-positional dilemma

its abductees

many times braised

many times debauched

yet

for others

it opens the portal

to Fana

to obliterate mystical laterality

to cleansing rays

to flashes from lightning in water

I do not quarantine its waters

through territorial mis-comment

through harangue

in order to battle its powers by number

or report its scenic view by monaural generality

yet I do not impugn myself with chronic or

objective impeccables

with chiseled or studious credentials

classifying wonders

as if I summarized a bevy of ocelots on fire

perhaps a summed effect

a misplaced ignition of sigil

or a circuitous resistance to a mis-heard

secondary ringing

this is why I cannot speak of Megasthenes

of Strabo's objectification

of Herodotus as pure & embrangled witness

as harvested Mediterranean's at the Ganges

burning in their truth through grammatical

papyri

this is why I can speak of Patna & Delhi

of Allahabad & Agra

according to the Arthashastra of Kautilya

the Ganges during drought

it is the...Hindu pilgrim centre

& where the Ganges 'enters the plains'

Pliny states

that 'it rises from unknown sources'

like Hiuen Tsang

I've arrived from other sources

Sino-Tibetan & ghost

consumed by acetylene & ferment

according to Hiuen Tsang

the water of the Ganges 'is blue'

'its waves roll as the sea'

'it is cleansing'

'it washes away sins'

'it is the safety of the other side'

514

unlike Arya Deva

I don't incite the crowds

I don't pour bread & line its steps with feces

I do not argue just to unsettle myself

by dazed or polemical crowning

positing in myself

dazed infection

populist fragmentation

forcing myself to unstructured anaemias

I cannot invent catastrophe

or mime statistical problematics

of order law as a face of systems

therefore

I can't compare intrinsics

I cannot build the Ganges according to sovereign

abstraction

according to distant sedentary likeness

according to verbs of unstated exposure

which cleaves by ruination

as if before calm

horizons were shattered

& the water of lepers was transfused with suns

say

I've come to its waters to collapse & implode

to advance my condition as miraculous incitement

I would merely take up my gait as inferior

fortune

as vertiginous holographic

suddenly grappling with unintended states

invisible dyzgotics

stricken vehicular dossiers

gambling

immersing themselves within carking ranges of

matter

as lama

as Sino-Tibetan from Goa

I carry power as regards the reaches through

undue deception

for instance

by making gold appear

I presume

pleasurable terminations

sedentary outcomes

creating the Sun as a lazy dragon

blurring & co-appearing in oneiric shrines

or perhaps

I could appeal to instigation

I could make through insignificance

a sub-atomic force field

with different firmaments & badgers
with different owls & strategies of dialogue

with virtues
& doctrines
& clairaudience

but the depths go much deeper

there are enigmas
& disciplines
& fates beyond disorder

there exists the improbable
the music which lives beyond danger

I have broached the in-saturate
I have given rise to my Dravidian co-mingling
with my electrical scent
rising to non-approach
an archipelago of pillage?
of distracted impecunious gain?

no

privately
there are phosphenes analogous to alterity
no more invoking domesticated ground

no more invoking ionized inversion

forestalling the higher exhaustives

where shadows fall as abandoned paranoia

as inference invoked by suggestible debris

I'm speaking of something

which leaps beyond grasp

beyond the in-resolved as property

yet invigourates the body with intangible

scintillation

in this regard

fana is property

fana is liberation

say I am Bön

I am habituated as Sadhu

I am proficient as my own ambrosia

as my own typification is to breathing

as if focusing my breathing

from the air of eclipsed wrens

& this

is not critique of proficiency

summoned from recognizable chroma

it is the Ganges as seen through tangible

referent

as in-locked body

518

as watery provincial glottic
as post-intrinsic reduction of itself

am I pronouncing the Ganges & its gifts
a rural state of authorship?
an unintended equilibrium?

or am I missing its inscrutables
its epics
its multiple condensations?

perhaps I'm reading its realia
as a vanished streak of manganese
or a series of blank cognitions
as in-irruptive transpositions

perhaps I huddle myself in mania
perhaps I am locked in a Spanish caja
isolate
stark with nomadic ocular yield

yet within this cajas
the galaxies avert
& re-suggest their yield
as brevities
as trances brewed on new coronal planes

the Ganges

as meteors

as dust from imploded signals

as open kind of warren

as germinal verticality

as interval

as conjured miraculous insistence

much like herding falcons in my sleep

rising from burning mirrors

so as to mimic extended form

& in this paradise

the Ganges turns orange

& absorbs

& agitates

so that the falcons drown

& resurrect through flight

seeded

like flaskless water rising

beyond desire of flawless mission

which means

the Ganges burns

as incendiary cipher

as inferential credentials

as a moonless ballet of signets

520

say

I was no more than colloquial isolation

the great rising could never subsist

could never evince from its power

the beauty of sea ravens singing

as something other than sulfurous diagonals

as something other than dangerous effigies

again

I see sadhus rise from the water

as shapes

as vertical regia

battling with wooden lightning bolts

like optic titans

gathered from scattered phosphenes & demons

conducting war

reclaiming fumes from the waters

as if

a battle over ice & last droplets

philosophically fingering

a sudden noose of draughts

an element harking back

to prior bursts

to sparks before Brahma

before the wounds of the unalterable first struck

not the 33 Gods of Rig Veda

not Brahma

nor his progenitor Prajapati

but something over & beyond Vishnu & Shiva

something over & beyond fatality as index

this being the source of error in this life

I've been born as unreason

miming unskillful diplopia

mingling inexpedience

so much so

that I'm always subject to vanishment

to reassertion by disappearance

blazing & retreating

as bicameral teratology

do I garishly blaspheme?

do I meretriciously bemoan the 9 incarnations

of Vishnu?

his power

his endless will through resurrection as boar?

of he who slays demons

of he raises Earth from phantasmic floodings

am I that rouge

that stormless emanation

that harried tiger in entanglement?

as Ganges

perhaps the water is partially Vishnu

perhaps its range extends as blank identity

through cycles

these cycles

supernatural in extent

as Ganges

perhaps the water is partially Vishnu

perhaps its range extends as blank identity

through cycles

these cycles

supernatural in extent

as something other translatable granite

as something other than energy beyond the kin

of what iridium endures

at a certain extreme

I can say that I am Ganges

that I erupt as transitional ornament

as a depth where nothing obtains

my breath being nothing more than a valley

of inscrutables

which illusively amounts

to planes closed off from planes

be I who worships wasps

who casts his ironic weight through Vishnu

or Shiva

feeling multiple frenzy as inward ark of Shiva

with its skulls

& its bones

with its blood consorts & Saturns

perhaps worship of Vishnu as boar

or Vishnu as heightened tortoise

or as Valmiki in the Ramayana

subsumed

in the 'nine incarnations' of Vishnu

as Dravidian & Sino-Tibetan

I feel alone as an element in a transfixing

Ganges

as its deft & immortal weaving transference

because

I no longer expiate as sin

as encaged by a self-existing mean

I am water

I am the element which ignited the transpersonal

Himalayas

the gulfs

the atmospheric distensions

absent the desire to bathe & caress Lakshmi

I who accrue

as curious meta-circumference

as flow as magic meta-warren

I

of the cursive states

where the Ganges exists

as curious parallel perpendicular

thus

the flowing meta-conjunction

the meta-ray

the open meta-osmosis

de-occurrence as blizzard

ruined symmetry as focus

if I listed

800,000 beliefs

it could never deride the proto-sum of the ozone

or send the chemicals of the Sun to depletion

because

I in no way imply weight nor height

nor the material as stricture

I am saying

that the Ganges is more than belief

more than intoxicant ferment

spawned by mythological herds

& sparks from nullified sub-hedrals

according to various colloquies of depth

its scales of fish

giving off burning monologies

giving off noxius territorial inscription

which certain underwater scribes

have surveyed as oblivion

the Ganges

brewing itself as glare

as strategic interior strata

as imperfected laterality

having fallen from aboriginal splendour

as inferior Uranian placebo

according to the Mahabharata

its waters transmix

as saviour of generations

as mirror of harmonic galactics

as endlessness by means of 'Bhagiratha's long devotion'

it has raised by means of Shiva

'Sagar's sixty thousand sons'

from the ashes of torment

into what the Hindus would call

transfiguring explanation

as element

I am Ganges

I am monk

I am 3 scales of lightning

I am gulf transmixed with the Sun & extra

solar masses

no

I am not a storm obscured by vigourous wastes

& acids

descending

to 'streams'

& 'lakes'

& 'seas'

as 'compressible liquid'

as 'solvent'

as 'ionizing agent'

but perhaps

I am 'lavender'

'camphor'

as flowing diamond through smoke

unlike the cobalt traced as eclectic rigidity

unlike a sullen scorpion miner

I do not hope for better outcome or caste

aspiring like the youngish Dhruva

conspiring at the river Jumna

for result from higher carnage

& no

I am not the lizard at the Gomti River

awaiting outcome for my sins

as seeming Chandāla

I am exposed to other substances & orders

to other burnings

to other chroma

lower than vicarious mirage

all I can say

is that my sources blaze

& I agree to no outcome

neither

am I karma marga

or bhakti marga

or he who dwells as gyāna marga

fabricating stars through philosophical

inscription

in this

there is nothing outside

my own electrical momentum

nothing outside

my surge as intransigent optics

in this

I am neither moth

or substance of a moth

by which to exercise loss

or partial embitterment as loss

because I have not yet collapsed

by whispering gain to myself

I tend to combat restitution

for the 'eight million four hundred

thousand' parturitions

which claim the self through suffering

if I am figment of the Ganges

I exist as no more than hyper-estrangement

unknown

to oblations

or personal sacrifice

or pre-engendered mantra

again

as to castes

being Dravidian & Sino-Tibetan

I am at one with the Shūdra

at the lowest cycle

at the sullen rank scorched by immobility

as for the Vaishya caste

or the other double rungs

such as the Kshatriya's & the Brahmans

nothing exists

in this regard

I am electric

feral

roaming beyond pre-thought conclusion

so if I am water & sin combined

how do I rectify

& conform to gross entropies?

how do I agitate other than by causation?

how do I claim as other than disharmonious

the realia which now seals me?

& I mean

the Gods

the demons

the godlings

the formed & disposable rishis

at initial view

I inaugurate death count

I move by disadvantage bubonic lettering & waste

the sullied as hyper-annealing

as cause unknown to Brahma

as nauseant outside of Indra

of course the Gods accuse me of acataphasia

of in-nimble surfeit

keeping company with the unordered

who am I to say that the Ganges is invisible

to its warren

to its creation of believers

to its correction of avarice & venality

all the while in acknowledgment

that something has settled inside my derma

misplaced resentment?

volatile reminiscence?

maybe I take into account

worship of Shiva & the 'daily slaughter of goats'

of the 'social pressure & imposition of varna'

forbidden to enter temples

or walk down certain passageways

because my 'shadow defiles'

I can say

that I maximize seclusion

I practice in-born honour

according to hidden blazes

according to mercurial salt which extracts

noise & error

the Ganges

being human

& heaven

& star

yet

it de-exists

as total restitution

what of other than North & Northeast India?

what of other than East & Eastern Pakistan?

provincial?

Gangetic?

of some other order than is swallowed by ascetics?

according to honed believers

I cast the cosmos as dispersion

as would a nephritic monk

or an unclean camel

as Shūdra

as suspected Chandāla

I am not worthy of induced electrics

532

not worthy of any form of expiation

to rise above doubt towards partial exaltation

if any Brahmin knew that I bathed as Shūdra

Indra would alight

to erase my noun as heir

to explode my coil of thinking

so that nothing is left of any subtle symbiosis

so infra-quakings

seismicity spirals

never at one with the Hindu's sketch of Mount

Mandara

as the churning pole

as the hydrosphere in torment

where sharks

& riddles of riddles

gain impartible touch with evanescence

through gnomonics

I have no response

as pre-existing trance

I am coded by dazed behavioural option

in terms of deafness or disorder

I am neither partial or totalic

nor am I standing in silt

with despair being vertiginous optional release

& so since I am water

I am myself who is standing in water

standing

syntonic

diagonal to terra firma

as optional hydronics

would it be possible to conclude

that my body partakes

of the Yamuna

of the Luni

of the Sabarmati

of the Brahmaputra

or does remain as optional theoretics

or water given speech

through falsely kindled quanta

a horizontal lalophobia?

an audacious parallelogram?

flash from blue neutrinos?

then again the Ganges

as red & green blindness

as after-shock

as underlying yellow

so if I say

looking glass law

lowest audible procedure

diffusive lumbar brightness

sand

blind meridian observation

fatuous amblyopia

I could nakedly be condemned

by intra-ocular modification

by ambivalent logorrhea

or reacting to zoopsia

by means of meta-suggestibility

as if in part

I rode a ram

or circled a lizard around a star

I might for a time

take shape as a blurred Garuda

or see myself

separate & apart

as hexane

as incombustibility

as a-chromatic & xanthene

then seeing its flow

as Tangier ocher

as nervous froth

as a form a daylight blue

then perhaps reseda

or solferino

or cineritious

or realgar orange

these exist

as blank derivative bodies

rising from glaucous solar pigmentation

as Sino-Tibetan in glaucescent

how do I arrive

as the shape of a great Chandāla in heaven?

how do I rise

as indanthrene blue?

as another sub-ingemination of a kind of azurite blue

existing beyond all the replicas of wattage?

I am consumed

by marked explosive hamlets

by invidious agitation

as if I'd opened myself to the pull of multiple

deficits

to compound ire

to ectoplasmic spasms

in this regard

I am not the Ganges

not its 3 billion lives

its habitat of ghosts

its black amounts of ochre

you see

my spillage

contains no electrical amount of odour

no blazes from the ghat

no widows crawling at the brazen edge of Suttee

this is life living in a water of riddles

as indeterminant

as nature revealed through ghostly Garhwal

exposure

as driftage

as cinders falling from strange inversional

singing

these are prior cuneiforms

yet I function as one always inciting their parallel disregard

therefore

I am pendulant

somehow swallowed by unused blazes

being officious as underactivity in abeyance

dissolved

interrupted as repeal through insurrection

which amounts to uttermost imperfectives

to maundering

to sesquipedalian flaw
to monolingual dysphemia

this is why my person has been so imperiously
debated

the wolves once spoke of trauma as my form

my substance in the woods:
anarchic fever

& so I
as each one of these debacles
is anomalistic slate
is compromised & incidental
is cupreous in colour & dissembling

an energy from the sky which bickers in the timber

in-culminate
viscous
as mirage which descends through tremorous atomics
so the weaker wolves would bestow me
would convince me
would give me parallel primevals
knowing as Shūdra
that I have fallen from blank Uranian lands
that my waters are marked by epic struggles

in my living solar minimums
all the while knowing that these energies
are prior to Vishnu

& being prior to Vishnu
they are prior to the Vedas
prior to all detached containment
being life as curious legendary omen

prior
to the one thousand cycles
of the four ages
being the Krita
the Tretā
the Dvāpara
the cinerous hail of the Kali

& according to the curse
'the inhabitants grow more & more evil'
& like the 'Yavanas of the Greeks'
secure pestilence as discovery
which means the 'Shūdras' ignite & 'become prayerful'

& I am essence of these 'Shūdras'
as specific compulsion
outside of the Sun
& all the forces of the Sun
prior to enacted grace

therefore I exist as a poorly known symbol

as poorly known stammer escaped from disappearance

being dormant near Uranus

I've hovered

in dexterous near ammonias

at invisible perigee

inducing the first verdurous vapours

in contact with Earth through incidental blackness

as Shudra as comet

I am charged by black ice

by a core of confrontation

transgressing incessant study

& so from fire

the ammonia scorches & unearths

& the Himalayas rise

& the glaciers in their subsequence begin speaking

in non-arrival

in religio-ballistics

as if water could mass function

& blaze as narrowed extreme

I've not come as pure water

'to overthrow Indra'

or to captivate the Pole Star

flowing in these times to retract Dhruva

or state as my power foreign eventuality

540

it is not to contend

with Vishnu as the Sun rising

or Vishnu as lizard

or Vishnu as burning meridian

again

I've not come to plague these 3 -kinesias

of the Sun

or pour from eruptive hails

a special torrent of glare

these 3 -kinesias

something of a spinning tribal furnace

poised at some brink

between malevolent insistence & aristocratic mantra

& so I have appeared in this test

as a summary of regions

which blurs beyond surname

much like the creeping of microbes

other than the seven continents

the seven seas

other than the incarnations attributed to Vishnu

other than the seeming sorcery of Shiva

other than the worship of a solemn & fixed agnosia

being the imperiled anagrammatic

wandering around a rishis' state of projection

as if peering at a statuesque motion of archers

aiming at diagonal droplets & vultures

the latter attempts movements through blue ash

the forest vipers

listening to the arrows whistle & curve around

the Sun

& one by one

the vultures imploding

& re-igniting as the never before seen

become curiously anointed stellar rotations

& the archers are amazed

& create comment

as if they saw Sirius matching itself with the

heliacal rise of the Sun

& so

by heliacal rise

half the moon is scorched

& its numerical properties makes of itself

utterance of the unexplored

& each southward facing rishi

proclaiming

that the good has been broken

that the solstitial has been flawed

by obscurantist's invective

'tell me

says a northward facing archer

that the birds have ceased exploring

that they face new states in hell'

the rishis

in response to the extra solar

in response to new sedition

because causation collapses causation

for the rishis

there exists no lateral fray

no tense or imperfected portion

at perfect parturition at the birth point of Brahma

do I blaspheme?

do I carry in my heart the micro-toxics of law?

perhaps

infra-rational substrate

spiral through foci as leakage

I can say

that I am replete with quaking seismics

listening to psychic crevasses

so Vishnu

through single proliferation

creates from the vantage of Shūdra

indefinite hallucinosis

eruptive phantastic regression

because I resist of such scale

I am maligned

I attempt myself as self-scattered in darkness

yet

I am never one with the impossible

never haunted or self-inscribed

by dour & repetitive oblation

I do not doubt the critical blazing

which erupts on Mount Meru

with various Gods

bellowing above demons

with their ochre brews

with their blank osmotics

mingling among themselves through splintered

suggestibility

me

a mangled motion on Mount Meru

me

inducing poison out of glass
making rain from the loins of dead tigers

& who has instructed me
perhaps the wolves who've consumed
stolen amrita?

or perhaps anger in the form of a desiccated
spirit?

or as energy of Yamma playing dice
with the ghosts?

I've wrenched the castes
I've known in myself a castigated brightness

one could say
that I speak through intentional litmus
that I've parceled my stratagems
through involuntary yeast

yet I am ghost at the shores of the Ganges
with my filigree & tooling
negated by unconquerable blinding

I am less to the dazzled
than rusted silver in basins
than photonic cells

my spiritual spectrum

roving as cinereal ray

& my eyes

like a threatening Roman umber

or Malaga red

or Indian Brown

or perhaps others would see

sorrel

sepia

castaneous

bay

all glinting

purely penetrant & burning

& so I see

all the higher defamations

the risks

the lower form of animal as alacrity

because I am other than didactics

other than maimed horses

or smoke from kindled pigeons

I am other than vexation

which burns itself by belief

the structures of war

replete in my view

as general aegis of the Gods

all the structures:

gazing derivatives

structural semi-weight

luke warm melancholia

death

a stationary flux as industry

argument versus lucid theatrics

as old Dravidian from Goa

I've absorbed the spectral

I've had encounter with its posed incarcerations

so that

Dharmaśāstra

temple building

earlier Puranas

without countering poise

without codification by iconography

as Shūdra

I am null

I am void of balance

I am integer of cacophony

the saint-singer of the Vaishnava Alvars
or the Saivite Nayanars
want no dealings with my roughage
with my body as subordinate delta
cast outside the absolute Nirguna Brahmin
outside the sampradayas
outside the Sun god Surya

the images come in swarms
Krishna's childhood
Rama's miraculous birth
the powers of monkey's & demons

certainly
I am not the caste
made totemic in the Gita

I
who was born to burn offal
to stuff in my shirt the dropping of pigs

I
being the lowest ambition of drought
of regressive exercise as rebus

never fueled as to sanctioned learning or prayer
I've simply arrived as hidden dust
as Sino-Tibetan on a porcelain camel
548

I am without what the rishis would assemble

as the mystical-amalgam of war

of heavily willed oblation

of struggles waged in a saltless optical lake

I make no claim to the ambrosial breath

of unharried sources

to energies accrued from non-isolate havens

to voices minus the unclean as aesthetic

yet I can claim by my genetic

'advanced scripts'

'urban dwelling'

'agricultural science'

my pedigree in Asia

'Iran to the Philippines'

Arabia to unknown drafts of China

as 'Andamanese'

as 'Kada' & 'Uralis'

as body from the Bay of Bengal

in Thailand & Malaysia

I am Sekai

I am China in the Yunnan province

I am Austric & the Ainu of Japan

as I now exist & feed I am Kolarian
my noun transmixes with the 'Veddas of Sri Lanka'

as Al-Jahiz insightfully mentions
in the islands of the seas
the 'Blacks are thriving'
from Hindustan to China
I trace my latter body
to Phoenicians in the seas
to susurrous recognition in Uganda

I am the fumes of the southern Arab
in the Hadhramaut
as a residue which ascends from ghosts

which means
I am electro-Dravidic in origin
swept like a spore to Tibet
where I hover
with all my histories
prior to being in being

so if I have come before Brahma
why wherefore do I argue with Brahma?
why wherefore do I sustain his misbegotteness?

I am not speaking of my source
as a system in terms of mere terrestrial primevals

550

of generated gaps
of frustrated settings

but let me be of a mind which tends to pioneer
old 'Mahra'
& give rise to the presence of spoken 'Galla'
in Abyssinia

I am speaking of connectives to deep
Kushitic alignment
there is Mohenjo-daro in Sind
there is Harappa in the western Punjab

& from these zones
arose Dravidian Brahui
circa two thousand four hundred B.C.

& so the Indus Valley
with the city of Lothal
with the 'oldest operant dock in the world'

all this prior to the Veda & the Ganges
all this in keeping with sources of King Ganges

let me say that the violence in the Veda
seems strictly Hurrian in origin

if I say Brahma is a Kassite?

is Dorian

is Mitanni

he is subsequent

he is 1500 B.C.

thus

he claims ascent through the impure as range

this is not a winding

through dazed or uncritical assumption

true

one can accuse my subjection

as being nothing other than the trans-typical

attempting to reverse my interior

to points of objective mass

condensed

say

to India as unarguable conduction

with its 3 water masses

the Arabian Sea to the West

the Bay of Bengal hovering in the East

& the giant Indian sea native to the 'Deccan'

& the 'Southern Plateau'

perhaps one could bear the rays of my nervous

approach

if I were trapped by Kanchenjunga at the border of Nepal

or if I spoke of the plains carved by the

Brahmaputra

or of the Northern Plains

or of the Deccan Plateau with the Krishna & the

Mahanadi Rivers

& if I spoke of mangoes

or jute

or millet

all description would be approved

& should ginger or turmeric appear

no established order would decline

as sudden spore in Tibet

if I spoke of Gar

of spectral blizzards at snowrise

of peaks of the Kunlun Range

of unfarmed gravel

of gazelles

& tigers

& panthers

I would seem to be contiguous

as if speaking no more

than through a maze of separations

as though etched by salt

& timber

& wool

yet my spirit consumed by explosive mystical

eruptives

by solipsistic mood devices

by that which assents to squalls which extend

across differing terrains of treason

because I am not haunted

not spellbound by Varunas

I am able to speak of the Kassites

of their bio-informational toxins

they

who gave Indra the power to slay Dasas

to drive Dravidians to oblivion

the nature of castes

an electrocuted summons

a divided

multi-dimensional despair

artificial bounding

pyrotechnical torture

Brahma condemns to hell

those who consort with Shudra

those who aid Shudra to escape the compunction

of fate

554

Hurrian racial imbalance
the social cyanide of colour

more effectual than murder
the effect as gratuitous inner corruption

thus
Varna in montage:

the void:
sullied

emotional depravation:
honoured

intra-psychic deformation:
never subject to contestation
chaotic generality:
purposely incurred

each impeachable offence:
practitioners of enforcement

the cleaning of offal:
demanded

emblazoned mental disturbance:
fitting

state of memory:

marred

incentive:

destructed

general cultural body:

condemned to the immobile

yet I remain

unpillaged rhinoceros

invading ghost in the city of Gar

as parallel embodiment

above the wastes of Uranus

& if the Sun remains an aperture a quarter

of a meter in guidance

it remains the Sun

blazing through the heresy of dimness

as influential etching

as musical drone

burning by minor awakening

a power

a penetrant occultation

a seal which spins in orbit

as if I had tossed from cosmic scrutiny

totalitarian pyosis

blockage

an uneven candle door

vertiginous non-forces

no

I am not an apomict

lulled by botanical conscription

nor do I face the praxis of a tribal alterity

linked to demanding forms of methane

I am something other

I have broken with bodies

I have embraced my own logistical solace

never am I shadowed by the stain of disregard

by deposed & philosophical diadems which loom

which enlist me in spasms

in cold lamentable training

taking on a turbulent self-mechanics of dishonour

I am neither of these gulfs

neither of these schisms

breathing within myself through self-suspected

alveoli

I breathe

but not through the pores

of expected human transmission

of course

there is voltage across the roving outer domains

as astonishing insurgence

across an uncanny region of habitable ices

& because

I know the hypo-electric

I can outlast the dharmas & the dramas of Brahma

no

not speaking in the flux of numerical condoning

nor of the 'fourth age called Kali'

nor of the age of Dvāpara

nor of the age which is called Krita

I am speaking of the bottomless

of the nth dimension

of life not referred to in systems

I can say in this Uranian Gar

that the Sun is spinning sideways

that the 27 moons are blue

that rotation remains occulted

in service of a stark intransigent inscription

again

this Gar is blue

the one solar mass elliptical & dim

& the forces thriving as a thin & unknown species

my hypo-electrics

not a sullied arboretum

or a void

or a misplaced current

or an indifferent suspension

perhaps

you say

a Potter's Wasp

in an enigmatic circus

or cattle risking through old enormity

the blindness of an unclean bondage

the manacles of karma?

associational purgation?

neither of the above

I am sigil

I am Uranian

I am Buddhist without transposed electrics

being other than kindled narrative

I have never enacted

rules

or laws

or enveloped salvation

having never broken with my power

I have sustained myself

as other than hermetic fallibility

as other than negative forms

dazzled with invective

I have studied aboriginal locution

broaching its standardized bereftments

& I say

that there exists no operant grasp as Shūdra

or as Chandāla

born of upright beast or bear

the Aryans

would pronounce me as bodiless

or unruled system

blinded by loam & anomaly

I

the Ethiopic as Buddha

as 'Nanda'

as 'Ashoka'

in the eyes of Arya
I was bred as 'Mauryan'
as dust
as ruse
as unrighteous combining

am I speculative?
loose?
injudicious?
tedious?

there are currents inside me
I am not without life

because
south of this Uranian Gar
there exists the unsurveyable
plains of escaped electrical transition

there exists no analytic shifting
no frail or errant consummation of habit

I am something other
than a crude or totemic pilgrim
something other than a body
bartered by a blizzard of whims
taught by ruined eclectics

thus

I do not react through modes

associational with lessening

always beyond the diagrams that model

always beyond negation of maimed & disfigured

sutras

so I am able to immerse in this Uranian Ganges

without form as aspiration or station

again

no death

no cups of burning mice

no arrangements through strife or debasement

if I were painting from an in-descriptive

leper's hut

I would invite my own dissertation

I would model myself on miscarried leanings

again

I would suggest to myself that I existed as soil

as nothing other than terminal demonstrability

as Dravidian & Sino-Tibetan on Uranus

I understand myself as formless form

I've come to experience

562

the alphabet of leakage

leakage as uncommon osmosis

& this osmosis

being of other submissions

of other gists

of other varieties

called at certain strata the non-existent

behaviours

which claim no fulguration

which claim no name

speaking through mirrors in Potala

not of course by regimen

but by despair

over & beyond circumstance

which kindles other lateralities

other quickenings

other chromatics

other shifts

other parallels

other spirals

being height in another median field

being fusion of 3 or 4 interior mandalas

I see

yes I see

that all the saddles are broken

that the storms are unlocked

that the wars have been stolen

there is blankness

& because there is blankness scotomas explode

the sensate extends & turns around & goes missing

& what exists as this vanishment

a central square

a geometry which lengthens

a calculus which points to unspoken spillage?

let me say

I do not claim the extinguished

I do not chant to myself to embody dereliction

so as to breed within myself Nirvanic encipherment

so if I am spore from the mirrors of Potala

how does this link to Gar

to astral addenda on Uranus?

how does this link to simultaneous steeds

to electrical salvation in rivers?

say

if I'm timed by Indra's endings

564

ambling on broken horse shoe carats

I am chasing my own persona

always wary in life like a targeted fowl

it is like Rama on the hunt for Hanuman

always listening for my scent

always taking into account

my listless carbon pulsation

in this condition

only a prayer to grounded dice

only a prayer with which to save me

through fortuitous synesthesia

if all has gone blank

if all of life's powers have been flooded

by non-arrangement

the Gods can no longer swear inside themselves

or pose themselves as figures as if wrought

by pictorial suffering

for instance

as opinionated waifs

as in-illuminant boars

perhaps they claim themselves as pythons in

waiting

as posed or intrusive scarabs surrounded by

splinters

this is unreason

yet this exists

as emotional errata

as wavering unascended moral emotive

not structuring the winds

of the solemn outer worlds

one can speak of dazed gauntlets on Neptune

or symptoms within Uranian holding moons

I've practised my gaze in the form of a Yak

I've taken vapour from my eyelids

I've come to think of myself through

a-symmetrical disservice

therefore

coiled in my own panic

leaping from the mind

never thinking of the Sun

never humbled by specific tenors that

I've known

this is power in a curious field

never quantic jactitation
never proof as fielded by untold number

if birds dry beneath several solar rays
I do not count their feathers
as though I gazed at a city
structured by portent
by numerical view
one seems cleansed of boredom
due to frightening mechanical operation

this means
a higher height
a more intensive data
the real as no more than numerical progeny

then
there are figures laced with enigma:

the sudden loaves of karma

the 'four thousand million years'
in the day of Brahma

the 'eight million four hundred thousand
births'
as equal to the 'burden of each soul'
the legion of panicked worshippers in hell

then Indra

with his untold number of deceitful assignations

then accruing battle scars collected

when fighting for the cup of amrita

& this being a certain splintering in being

a single or wrought projection in life

I do not option opinion

or speak from sectarian Buddhist alignment

to this degree

I do not search by tribe

or make of myself a denizen moved by forced

distinction

when Ashoka speaks of balance

I direct in this dimension

I emanate the indefinite

I infer from my leanings the bottomless

as proposal

I do not confer by broken angst

the fabulous & inscrutable as agenda

never commandments in ink

scribbled at a conference of boars

for me

odyssey across Uranian Decembers

wandering the nomes of Eris & MakeMake

none of them haunted or contrived

reacting to threat through psycho-physical

negation

I have not responded to aural shrines

sculpted to a peculiar scale of scorpion sonics

or carved a set of wizard's teeth

in a Yak's bordello

no

I have not laced planes laced with salt

& attrition

so what I challenge is the Ganges & its rule

of sin in scorched accent

of the code of the body as broken chariots

& rubble

being parallel with slag

& burning ghosts

& insubstantial monsters

personas

from the Bardo wheel

from after-encounters

from the moans of the self?

at such obscure scale

this could be reason

or the state which in-scales transitory ruin

the doubt

the agony

alighting from distance

the body as a corpse in thirst of prayer

yet there is never the overwhelming

never that experience which captures in itself

the whole which is born from actionless being

not action as kinetic against kinetic

or rivalry as gain against gain

since I exist as spore

as soldier of the intransigent

I contain as my essence no political sarcastic

no model as extracted from 8 million corpses

the Dharmsala does not know me

does this mean I eat water

or soak my bread in various inks

or bake as my ointment excretion from bricks?

does this mean

that my skills are surreptitious

& persists by melancholia?

further

am I intangible embryonics

or ascetic exposure at the sunrise of kilns?

let me address this ascetic latter fervour

supreme toil

instigational pneumonics

spent wood

abrasive schist

yet to Rama & the Brahmins

I rank less than an owl

I rank less than particles of dirt

I am banned by withdrawal

by a series of stains due to partisan disclosure

to tampered spells

to exclusions voiced through tainted opinion

if I held a log by the strength of three fingers

if I broke a stone by the thinking of my heart

Indra would deny me

bringing baneful gifts produced by staggered

feeling

a cleft eye

blistered limbs

neurotic tornadoes

he would give me none of the merits of birth

none of the wonders reaped by ingestion

only me

as benefit by staggering inclemency

as Shūdra

as particle outside the main

as particle outside the palace of hoaxes

so by ringing a bell with my eyes

by describing the world through solstitial

verbing

I would arrive at nothing other than death

at in-transcendence

as voice in a sepulchre rebuffed by lowly spirit

which turn to wrought lilies & chaos

& I am not fighting from opposing views

mixing chaos with chaos

dye infested

scrambled

imposition has been placed upon me

rival drafts

inculcated candour

& this not only according to turbulent gain

brewed by contiguous reason

but by all the minerals within this reason

which seeks to haunt

& clarify response through vernacular didactics

what I say is not a social script

or postures carved on a-priori porcelain

or weight erected by external hexagrams

through integer

so that there exists within such

self-destructive structure

a privately hexed coronation

this is treasonous instruction

which simulates law by previous invading

perhaps I am teaching the proper skills of sin

perhaps a treatise on collapsible menace

full of green & black teeming

this being a point of observable blood concern

where a type of reflex is condensed

by rarefied solemnity

let me digress

let me come to the point of embittered declaration

of foils

let me dwell on the species called flaw & misnomer:

first: blackened conjugal marks

          disfigured striving

          social illegality

at next remove: kinship broken

                    the general given marred

               the Sun no longer witnessed

               by the power of astute example

as penultimate phrasing: black remarks

                         ill begotten lanterns

                         bodies stored & re-stored

                         as movement by ashes

never fused by morbidity

or strict fiduciary ember

removed as I am from Augustinian stain

from the energy disrobing Anselm

in his shocking denial of infants

dense & inevitable root work?

source as esoteric confinement?

so do I descend to radical evil

to what Kant begins to rationally

conjure in his focus?

as the 'peccatum originarium'

somehow upholding linkage

to Augustine & his aconite

pathological kindling

no known remorse for failure inside one's person

instead

their seems struggle through fatal mechanics

through misspoken substance

through the body as unacceptable notation

the latter

tainted by inevitable judgement

& not the karma as spoken by Yājñvalkya

or type of conflict

issued in The Mahābhārata

when the Pandavas regain their kingdom

from their 'cousins the Kauravas'

I gain no power from these origins

no resolve of duty

no example of form

as Shūdra

the Dharmaśāstras

do not perceive or build respect in my being

my body in death not even a draft of mausoleums

always equated with omens

with incumbent fetal assignations

thus

I am absent of categorical pomposity

akin to shepherds scattered under rainfall

I know no celebration

I know nothing of the consequence

of what royal personae emit as liberty

so I persist as black example

as spark which never approached the good

as shadow distracted by lost embodiment

I am mortal clothed by locusts & dust

by a glossary formed by uneven motives

yet giving me the power to listen to free extremes

to listen to views which pour from the posture

of emptiness

void of interior penance

unleashed

from superfluous registration

so the schools

the logics

the tenets

vanished

which casts no aspersion upon the Gelukba

upon the Sagyaba

upon the Nyingmapa

when they take into view

organic sūnyatā

I am at the source of the Ganges Uranus

I flow as the Ganges Uranus

I am replete as the Ganges Uranus

an apparition?

a beast?

delimited fuels?

unappended atoms?

a mirage?

a tropical pilot in a stunning hyper-sea?

never as sum

prior relational wantage

 breathing condemned strata

I do not eat myself as prior abomination

as stillborn crow

as Dravidian as judged by Kassite

no

I no longer practice my skill as sobering

detonation

as obscure wattage

as inactive calling broached by false experience

I relate to all my sources

to my mysteries

to my unencumbered principles

shunning 'intentional ignorance'

this is not

simple civil registration

or aggregational procession

in agreement with Dorian hypnotists

under Kassite provision

I am granted

neither horse

nor woman

nor cow

I am granted none of the scruples

except propulsion by warrantless chaos

always amiss

as if staggered by invisible deception

according to the Aryans

the lice know higher laws than Shūdra

lower than the trance which emanates from rubble

no assurance

no bonding with forces

no empathy from creation

yet I ask

how can all sums remain sprawled in dissension

submitted to less than refuse?

how can the universe breathe such dazed existence?

as if the interstellar sugars

possessed no treatise or condition

as if the zodiac were condensed of strained

or ideological carbon

because I know from my sufferings

trace amounts of these sugars as coffins

yet because I know these trace amounts

I know the Uranian Ganges as spillage

I wade in its auras

as anomalous trans-person

as disappearing Shūdra

in parallel Lhasas & Gars

say

if I presented to the world

a dossier on bullocks

or reported a complex moon

flooded

& rising on 3 horizons

there would never exist comment

as to my angular drift

or my gift of brilliance

or my conduction of insight through forces

at best

I receive no more than silence

being no more than fixation

condemned for my in-born opprobrium

as Shūdra

nursed by unhappy rhinoceri

by unstructured poisons from cobras

strictly known by disease & its bottoms

I have no need to convince myself

that I am absent of failure

that I carry no false incision in my thinking

deposing myself

according to central imposition & dread

I mean

voice as mass scale

as agreed upon divisives

as Kantian transposition bending to Augustinian verdict

me

creating from the Uranian Ganges

another scroll for lepers

creating for myself a roving source for the

in-divisional

perhaps

I'll mark these lepers' names

on horses' skin

blending my own embitterment at root

I've known the Sun to be broken in parts

to glow as strange impersonal staggering

self-absconded & taken away from itself

yet wading in this parallel Uranus

speaking code through greenish harmattans

making from the methane uncivil welters

junctureless?

barren?

un-ascendant?

no

I am not seeking to typify injury
or re-invigour the Aryas
splintering the galaxies at this root
at times
I consult in myself
trinitarian pulsation
a de-possessive streak which argues
its self-nativity through sound

I never naively configure wholes as oneness
or meditate on flaws to partially scramble
the mind
so as to comfort my skill
flanked as it is by discomforted acid

I can say
there is the one substance
the one performing principle
which blazes
which arcs
which spins
throughout spiralling
stellar confinement

as an nth of an nth of an nth
let me speak of the 6 trillion miles

of the clouds of Serpens

with its neutron implosions

with its frayed event horizons

the whole which supersedes a billion compressed suns

with all the galaxies spinning

above doubled focus as being

as riddle which spills through epic centreing properties

this being reversal which blazes

which connects with itself

inferring in the process

an omnivorous othering

reaching other states

which live at a higher form of council

stars have no form

experience convenes through multiple de-existence

this is more than sterile complication

more than collapsing parable through leakage

first:

let me quote from my own cavernous phantom compression

where numbers avert themselves

& part through elliptical double movements

so that half of halfs of halfs

merge

& become copious

as each half of each half

takes on sufficiency at differing proto levels

following this:

levels which implicate

a hovering interjacence

mingling with increments at conceptual solar rise

these increments

the Northern Uranian Ganges in movement

unlit pollen

flowing through the wastes

searching as implausible hypothermia

wading without argument

cleansed by dartings

by suns which weave through the amorphic

transmixing non-belief & locale with origin

yet I believe in my body

the script of early Indus locations

the body being baffling

inching inside itself

through moats of the indecipherable

being both Earth & speaking Indus emplacements

I am both remote & ulterior as remote

wading the Uranian Ganges

584

I wade as pure electrical sheaf

purged of neurotic estrangement

transferred persona

zeros which flood

aporias which explode

this being a Ganges unscorched

by prescient lateral mechanics

by drift which condenses itself

through pervasive assumption

deathlessness builds

entropy recedes

one then freed as viator

as innate noctambulist

listening

to the nuance of every nuance

thereby understanding

that every spell has levels

that conditioning respond & de-occur

going deeper & deeper

into the sigils of potentia

levels

which issue honings

which allow through greater feeling

sudden form

through inner issuing respiration

ignited papyri

great alluvial metrics

heightened levitational bodies

the latter being forays into solution

into the answers of cracked rock

which precipitates hesitation

I

who've explored the death rounds

who's brought to my own tenor

aboriginal electrics

power by means of advanced consumptives

in this regard

I am replete with non-dilemma

with doubt & its model obscured in a withdrawn

oasis

as Shudra

as hallucinate

as Chandāla

I am lama

creating through tense primeval

a kind of contained tablet

being figment

being deafening origination

so in Uranian Gar

the history of the Sun flows backward

& its Ganges extends

as a greenish percolation

in Uranian Gar

I seem blank & abolished

nullified

yet privately kindled

assembling dark advance through hidden topics

to the common mind

they are barriers which consort with symptoms

always stating to themselves concurring

omissions

as to true concussive fantasia

I have greeted Hanuman in the woods

& by consorting with tailors

I am disguised in strips of raw metal

with a headdress of bamboo

my flanks surrounded by fumes from green cobras

I tell him of my lifetimes as weaver

as weaver of Uranian mayflies

as constructor of the telepathic throughout

scent

he knows by my symbols

that I have outlasted floods

ranted in from of assemblies

& assembled a choir of fowls

so as to emanate intuitive candelas

& I'll admit through Uranian parallel

that I've existed on Earth as a wild red dog

that I've existed in the brush of Borneo

that I've hunted bears

that I've opened wounds

that I've cherished monsters

but as an odd red dog

I've been open to a flight of falcons

having left the pack

& roamed the Narbada River

having once consoled my apprehension

by transposing my skills through Manchurian tigers

to Hanuman I say

I am he who has braved battles

& lifted invisible mountains from wrath

& Hanuman in his glance agrees with my bravery

that I of the burning lakes

588

of untoward suspension

of the unsummed sums of the unsullied am valid

I call this dialogue by vapour

by unruly wind song

by plight beyond torpor as setting

but from another degree

one could call this brokered estimation

or range which opens to wishful accommodation

yet

as Shūdra

I have no mission

I always cling to regression

which imposes salt

which redefines one's fury

Hanuman

who gifted the failing of Rama

who fuels the lesions in the gifted monkey race

thus

I speak

as unenviable begetter

as a double whistling of pheasants

as a blinded gull or a spider

perhaps I have crowned all manner of mammals

with my scrawl marks

with my paean to precious labour

perhaps I've suffered through only 1 million bodies

perhaps I've reduced my occupation to non-admission

& the absence of killing

perhaps I've employed in my cycle

perpendicular beings

who've outlasted nature

rife as it is with common begetting

on old Earth

war by green error

territorial ascendance

all assumed by the Ganges

its mud which registers

its dazzling location

as if I could evolve from singular ruination

a rishi

suspending himself

so as to speak as an owl

as an 'Asiatic pangolin'

turning his sins into gryphons which vanish

which brings me back to my substance

over & beyond empirical geometries

590

being none other

than the faultless applicative of the Moscow Papyrus

extracting square roots from fractions

these are issues of ballistic trans-receiving

of something which eclipses

old monarchical re-authority

thus

I remain the scribe

who copies volumes & slants

& double remens & triggering

of the 'unitary radius'

superseding the thought of uprootedness

as tincture

as Chandāla

I've been listed as dispersed by blood

as energy spawned by the inactive

as a carking re-enactment on a double roof of tigers

as salt in a fresh abyss

as salt which de-covets the invisible

being a squall which listens

through instantaneous splinters

through plinths

& differing states of plinths

all the way down

to indecipherable resolution

as listed occultations

a vacuous rose

a vacant in-grandiose incitement

a falsely reactive distance

indefinite clonings

personification of nadirs

octosyllabic thought as reduction

scorched calendrical mesas

broken de-ambrosias

lists of skulls of skulls

in-dutiful cradles

perspectives

thrones

palms

branches

loss by causation of optics

thought through in-magnetized magenta

fervour as played by Ektaras

flotational moss

squalor

the unattainable

omissions?

episodic locations?

paradox?

I am here to evince

none of the above

nothing of the force of unbalanced notations

I am simply here as a source come to express my concerns

as would a nebula in the throes

of its erupting star forming regions

yet on Earth I sometimes speak with sharks

with haunted beings

with storks who hunt for sterilized explosives

which amounts to nothing more

thatn exercise as diacritics

linking motion to motion

somehow analogous to spartan stationary wrath

fixation upon sentience?

moral structuring?

transposed extrinsics?

perhaps I am leading myself

back to budding agronomies

reassembling themselves in themselves

as occulted mesons

as pions which emit themselves

as the ceaseless sparked by the ceaseless

murals

mazes which swim in embrace

is this now the human state?

do my eyes imply the structureless as medium?

or have I been simply soaked by the power

of trans-structural notation?

my energy allies with the oblique

which cannot be conveyed

by any countable pronation

or yield its captivation to the common aphoristic

of the greatest number in greatest agreement

believers

adrift with dazed incentives

with broken yields

with self-replicate annulments

I am replete with non-combining

with energies which dissolve ruinous salvation

for me

heaven is anti-critical

is belief by continuing negligence

so in this regard the Ganges breeds fever

breeds within its manta skewed or dysphoric

sensation

594

virtue

which seems to turn on itself

with the human womb now consumed by unheralded

palsy

by dominant form as error

the Ganges

under Aryan orientation

as lost

as tragic spell

as habituated novena

let me say

realia is beyond my stillborn body as ark

as irksome dissolution

emoting frames of social distinctives

I do not argue my legality

through false monarchical gift & authority

seemingly forestalled as light through

altered ray

I do not implore

I do not milk the flanks of a cobra

simply to prove myself

as a God against injustice

this being mirage

which falters as plebian centigrade

as code which surfaces as unbearable stricture

as if I fingered my shadow

so as to remove its scars

from the optical light of Brahma

thus I

I hover in Uranian Gar

with what the Spaniards call luz

& the inference of luz

with my astral yak

& this yak

reveals & de-reveals

solar mummification & its spirit

when the pineal eye opens

as a specific form of sigil

thus

there is writ

in the penetrant or invisible ledger

rays congealed & released

inside the human meta-vacuum

& this vacuum being body

as transfunctional meta-torrent

596

as totalic insistence on the transfunctional
as meta-current
flow as susurrus singing
where all the torrents coalesce
where all the tensions release
through in-abrasive balance

energy which surpasses itself
which surpasses
the laws
the whims
the isms
leakage is thus appended to something
other than endurance
to something other
than forms of stark excitement

again
that which surpasses raw deistical bodies
other than powers which gleam
as raw deistical bodies

above their raw chaotic surface
something other
than their conflicted surgical tundra
according to plotted stationary fractions

let us take the road of quenched syllabi

the road of exploded holding rails

let us come to rays of gnomic inner sources

whispering beheaded missives

forming structural paradox as ambrosia

at one level

this mixes with Lung-gom-pa

Tibetan psychic sport

yet on another plane there exists

subjective enrichment

something not to be confused with rustic

adjustment

with transpositional exploration

which comes from mixing a hoarse or brutish drink

a leap

a fuel

a diagrammatic emerald

unlike a copper melodiously stifled by contraction

being as immortal continuum

as imperishable suffusion

replete as riverine pneuma

breathing endocrine transfusions

& the Ganges in this state

being breath as awakened scroll

as something more than a somnolent drinking urn

as for myself

as lama at pneumonic transparency

the Ganges shifts to a river of levels

flowing as Uranian allotment

its sensate purity

missing & unmissing

without end

without the properties of limit

known to the King-Seers Jahnu & Bhagiratha

I

of the purest fury of blazes

subsist upon moons

which now breathe in my body

as an undying schist

perfectly balanced for all outcomes & summas"

Sources:

"Concerning the Henbane Bird"

Shamanism: Mircea Eliade

Dictionary of Astronomy: edited by Valerie Illingworth

A Dictionary of Psychology: James Drever

Encyclopedia Britannica; 1958 edition

Earth Ascending: Jose Arguelles

Grolier Encyclopedia of Knowledge

A Dictionary of Geography: W. G. Moore

Atlas of Plant Life: Herbert Edlin

The Myths of Mexico and Peru: Lewis Spence

Starlight Elixirs & Cosmic Vibrational Healing: Michael Smulkis & Fred Rubenfeld

Coastal Waters of the World: Don Hinrichson

Hummingbirds Their Life and Behavior: Text byQuesada Tyrrell & Photographs by Robert Tyrrell

"On Solar Physiology"

Great Black Leaders: Ancient and Modern: edited by Ivan Van Sertima

Angola Under the Portuguese: Gerald Bender

Africana: Kwame Anthony Appiah & Henry Louis Gates

Dictionary of Angola: Phyllis M. Martin

Dictionary of Psychology: James Drevor

Websters Third International Dictionary Unabridged

The Deserts of Africa: Michael Martin

"The Ganges"

Nile Valley Civilizations: Editor Van Sertima

Hinduism and Buddhism, Volume Three: Sir Charles Eliot

The Ganja Trail: Jagoham Mahajan

Along The Ganjes: Ilija Trojanow

African Antiquity in Pictures: Cheikh Anta Diop

Africa's Contribution To World Civilization, "The Exact Sciences": Essay by Cheikh Anta Diop

"The Nile Valley Presence In Asian Antiquity": Runoko Rashidi

Webster's Third International Dictionary Unabridged

Routledge Encyclopedia of Philosophy Volume 8: Edited by Edward Craig

Garhwal Himalaya Nature: Edited by O. P. Kandari & O.P. Gusain

The Mind of the Cells: Satprem

Tibet's Ancient Religion BON: Christopher Baumer

Myths from The Mahabharata Volume 3: Sadashiv Ambadas Dange

Probe in Early Dim History and Folklore: Sadashiv Ambadas Dange

A Popular Dictionary of Buddhism: Christmas Humphreys

Tropical Asia: Dillon Ripley

The Temple of Man: R.A. Schwaller de Lubicz

National Geographic: The Space Edition

Glossary

Concerning the Henbane Bird:

Cladistics- "A shared method of classification in which relationships between organisms are based on selected shared characteristics."

Hillstar- Next to the Patagonia gigas or giant hummingbird whose range extends from Ecuador through Chile, Peru, and Argentina. It survives in one of the most unfavorable nesting environments of Earth.

Shrillness- Hummingbird vocalizations are of a "high pitched nature" that includes the Peruvian Hillstar. One of the few species that has anything like a true song is the Vervain hummingbird in the West Indies.

Trochilidae- Latin term for hummingbird family.

turiya- Pure Consciousness.

Hirayama asteroids- 40 families recognized containing more than 70 members named after Japanese astronomer K. Hirayama. First families discovered in 1928.

2.7/1.6/1.4/3.7- Various background kelvins via which other universes may exist.

Pachacta Unanchac- Inca device for determining solstices.

Troano Codex- Story attributed to the Troano Code where war is portrayed between the brothers Coh and Aac in which the former is killed by the latter leaving the sister-wife Coh. Part of the Mayan annals named after Senor Troy Y Orotolano, found in Madrid in 1865.

Bat Hawks- They hunt for bats in early morning or late in the evening. Native to Central Africa and Madagascar. The size of their hunting area remains a mystery.

Heruka- Horrific Buddha who dances on corpses.

Atnongara stone- Magical fragments of quartz placed inside a shaman's body

Holonomic Equation- "Encompassing both the psychic operations of the human organism and the laws by which the phenomenal world makes itself known to us…"

Aayamis- Shaman's teacher/ spiritual guide.

Aksobhya- Imperturbable Buddha, cosmic Buddha of the east.

Oreotrochilus estella- Genus and species of Andean Hillstar

Ghats- Where Hindus burn their dead.

resustance- coined term aligned with the word resuscitation.

Altaic law- Initiation of the Siberian shaman of that includes the eating of their flesh and the drinking of blood by the spirits of their ancestors.

Araucanian Vileos- Great shamans who live in the middle of the sky. The Araucanian of Chile are always sickly or morbidly sensitive with vertigo

Huitzilopochtli- Aztec god of war associated with serpent and hummingbird.

Samoyeds- Siberian shamans whose supreme God is Num. If illness has been sent, he refuses to treat it. He ascends to sky to ask for Num's help

Tarsis volcanoes- Olympus Mons and three other great volcanoes on Mars.

Angakok rooster- Magical rooster of the Eskimo shaman.

Alnimlam- Blue-white supergiant 1600 light years away. Enhances one's ability to work with responsibility.

barymetrics- coined term alludes to weight or heaviness

baktuns/katuns- Mayan calendrical units

thirteen numbers/twenty signs- the Zolkin universal harmonic module is a matrix created by the permutations of these two key numbers. They are aligned with universal resonance accommodating every possible permutation.

mimosoid legumes- they include anadenanthera used for hallucinogens.

meteoritic- coined term for inflammation.

Bloodlight- coined term that implies violence.

Ipurina- Shamans who send their doubles into the sky to extinguish meteors that threaten to burn the universe. Part of the Manasi tribe that resides in eastern Bolivia.

Potasi- One of the highest cities in the world, it was a fabulous source for silver for the first 50 years after it was founded.

Pissac- Ruined Inca fort and observatory.

Toveyo- Toltec sorcerer.

Aranda/ Unmatjera- Indigenous magical tribes within the confine of Australia.

Ilpaillurkna- a famous magician of the Unmatjera tribe killed and brought back from the dead.

Warrumungu- Indigenous Australian tribe where the funeral rite requires removal of the shaman's old organs that are replaced while lying dead as a living snake is inserted inside his body so when he awakens he is endowed with the tribes' magical powers

Altair & Yahgan- the Altains of Siberia and the Yahgan of Tierra del Fuego ascend by vegetable ladder. An example of global planetary resonance.

Tusput- Famous Yakut shaman from Siberia able to hear great distances through dead shamans.

On Solar Physiology

Upper & Lower Egypt- Unification for the whole of Egypt between 3200-3150 B.C. achieved by Menes. Upper Egypt in its original state was composed of Nubians, persons of the first nation on Earth named Ta-Seti.

transmatics- coined term. In this context it is the nervous system infiltrated by signals whose origin remains akin to the intelligence that fuels our collective stellar system.

Kuroshio current- warm current that flows north-east from East Coast of Philippines along east coast of Japan.

Salazar- Prime Minister and dictator of Portugal for 40 years starting in 1932. He stressed the backwardness of African peoples.

Protaesthesia- Primitive sensory experience.

Mbuntu region- The savanna region south of the equatorial forest in Angola. Its people are extremely skilled in the rotation of crops, the working of metals, while possessing skills as potters. They resisted colonization from 1575 to 1902.

Mestico- the Portuguese considered Mesticos to be naturally inferior which many accepted yet many were also prominent in the liberation movements especially in Neto's MPLA.

Sao Paulo/Porto Alegre/Recife/Salvador/Fortaleza- Cities entwined by the Portuguese slave trade. Between 1450 and 1500, 150,000 slaves were active in Angola and Brazil.

Scorpion- first known ruler in recorded history in Ta-Seti or Nubia.

Bantu Pharaohs- A pharaonic civilization operating prior to Djer the second king of the first Egyptian dynasty.

Quilombos- settlements of escaped slaves in Brazil.

paranomasia- coined term that blurs the line between memory and word loss as distinct from the standard meaning of the word as a pun.

Arcturus- Yellow giant 36 light years away.

Almach- Group of four stars 250 light years away that assists in the transfer of energy from the mental body into the heart.

Ankaa- Orange giant 93 light years away that strengthens one's ability to survive, having the ability to create a powerful change in the physical body.

Adhara- Blue-white giant 650 light years away that enhances the absorption of minerals and food in the physical body.

Tzolkin- "a period of 260 days constituting a complete cycle of 20-day names with the numbers 1 to 13 that constitutes the Maya sacred year."

Pacal Votan- ruler of Mayan polity of Palenque in the late classic period of Pre-Colombian Meso-American chronology. Responsible for inscriptions and monumental architecture. Ruled 615 to 683 of the common-era.

Falarmos- Portuguese for to speak.

caliology- refers to birds' nests

lysophobia- fear of decomposition

anagogics- spiritual meaning of life or sense of the heavenly life

Monteiro- colonial minister under Salazar. He argued that colonization "required boundless pity for the inferiority of the blacks in the bush…"

Arabic or Bacongo- In this context it means whispering in an alien manner

Indus Valley- Referring to the deciphered script of the ancient Indus Valley civilization around 2400 B.C.

mulemba tree- associated in the African identity with feelings of nostalgia, disillusionment, and sadness

N'Dalatando- Angolan city known under the Portuguese as Vila Salazar neolalia- speech containing many words coined by the speaker

Ordovician sea floor- era of the rise of fishes 400 million years ago

Mane woodlands- south of the "Angolan Combo woodlands eco-region…mostly comprising Cuene Province,…but that extends across the border into neighboring Namibia"

voar- to fly in Portuguese

revoar- coined term in this context means to fly again

circumvoar- coined term means to circle in flight

Palmares- rice fields in Brazil between 1550 and 1737. I use the Spanish word quilombos to indicate the mess caused by the labour that was slavery

electrical lakes in Tibet- used in this context to indicate a pristine parallel dimension

Santiago- Old city of Mbanza Kongo, renamed Sao Salvador during the 16th century; a slave depot

Jorge da Mina- where slaves were traded for gold in early 16th century Brazil

barracoons- barracks for slaves

Namoratunga- observatory found in Kenya from 300 B.C.

"fonio" seed / Digitaria exilis- appellations for crab grass of northern Africa

Argium- Trading posts or factories established by the Portuguese at Atrium in 1445 in an effort to tap the trans-Sahara slave trade of the Western Sudan

Gulf of Guinea- The island Principe located in the Gulf where African slaves were harvested

sobadas- slave farms run by the Portuguese in Angola

Chemotaxis- movement of cells or organisms in relation to chemical agents

Ganda- Bantu language in Uganda

Kongo- Bantu language in western Congo and in adjacent parts of Angola

Rundi- Bantu language of Burundi. Also trade language of Rwanda

Macuni- spoken by the younger population in a few villages in Brazil it also goes by the names of Monaxo, Monocho and Cumanasho

proto Mande- Mande is "branch of the Niger-Congo language family including Malinke, Bambara, Dyula, Mono, Vai, Mende, Kpelle, Loma, spoken in French West Africa, Sierra Leone and Liberia with their center in the upper Niger Valley"

Manioc (cassava)- Tupian in origin, a food staple for Tupi-Guarani Indigenous peoples

batuca- Afro-Brazilian dance used to invoke and commune with divine entities. Batuca energizes a great poem by Aimé Césaire

The Ganges

Shudra- lowest of the four castes: Brahmins being the priests, Vaishyas being the trading classes, Kshatriyas being the warriors, and Shudras being the offspring of Manu, wife of Kashyapa, Shudra are the offspring of her feet

dictor- coined term variation of the word dictation

Dravidian from Goa- Southern Indian descendants from the Nile Valley historically. Their energy was located in the Indus Valley Civilization. The language spoken was Bruhui

Kashi/Benares/Varanasi- Synonymous names. Oldest city in India and one of the oldest continuously in habited on Earth. Located along the Ganges

Kanada- Dravidian language that also includes Tamil, Malto, Malayalam and Bondi

jai flowers- cast by Hindus into the Ganges so that their troubles will float away

ghoral- barking deer sometimes seen on the steep rocky cliffs of the Himalayas

pangar- light colored onagar in Maylasia

vahana- animal that accompanies or conveys a God

pureous- slightly tainted or polluted

Thutmous I- father of Hapshepsut, female Pharaoh of Egypt

Inscrutacize- coined term. In this context it means to be freed from scrutiny

Bon- dominant Tibetan religion until the 8th century that still influences death and marriage rites, oracle techniques, temple and mountain circumambulation, having much in common with shamanism in Mongolia

Ajanta- rock-cut caves in the Deccan contain Buddhist frescos and Buddhist sculptures

608

Ellora- Group of buildings in the Deccan, some Hindu, some Buddhist, all carved from solid rock

Idiophone- in this context impairment of the voice due to psychic forces

Harappa- capital of Indus Valley Civilization. Exhibited high level of city planning and cultural uniformity. Mentioned in the early histories by Apollonius of Tyana

Dasas- Blacks in the Indus Valley civilization referred to by the Aryans as (Dasas) enemies

King Ganges- Ethiopian King who led a conquering army into Asia as far as the river Ganges

defeatist intentionality- collective suggestibility of the negative. This being the microscopic whisper of fear fueling limitation in the physical mind that induces habit, frustration and death

Cholas/Pallavas/Pandyans- Dravidian kingdoms never conquered by the Aryans

Funan/Angkor/Champa- Dravidian colonies that reflect the latter's iconography and architecture

Telugui- Dravidian language

Kuki / Manipuri / Naga- Languages spoken along the Tibetan/Burmese border

Shen-rap- Legendary founder of Bon, native of Tarik in eastern Persia

adhigama- "…direct experience of reality, when the cognizer, the content of cognition and the cognition are identical"

prajna- transcendental wisdom or supreme knowledge gained in Buddhism through intuitive insight

Jewel Garland Sutra- A central pillar in ancient Tibetan Buddhist mind training

Nandas- Black Indian dynasty founded by Mahapadma Nanda who was Shudra. Fearsome collective and direct predecessors of the Mauryan dynasty made notable by Asoka

Megasthenes- Early Greek traveler to the Ganges

Huien Tsang- renowned early Chinese pilgrim to India wrote of detailed life as it happened along the river

Foshwui- another name for the Ganges, the river of religious merit and washes away countless sins.

Arya Deva- Buddhist scholar who renounced the Ganges, 3rd century common era.

33 God's of Rig Veda- refers to mind-born son Brahma, father of Gods and demons

Vishnu as boar- In the *Mahabharata*, earth appealed to Vishnu for help when he turned into a boar and raised earth with a single tusk to its proper place in the cosmos

Vishnu as…tortoise- enabled gods and demons to carry to successful issue the churning of the oceans for amrita. Vishnu turned into a tortoise and placed a mountain on his back

Lakshmi- Hindu goddess of prosperity

Chandala- offspring of a Shura mother who has mated with a Brahmin father

Katrina and the Brahmins- The supposed caste of Buddha

actaphasia- inability to connect words sensibly into sentences. In this context it means disorder

varna- Sanskrit term for caste

Mount Mandara- Mountain in the Ramayana, 77,000 miles high with an equal distance descending into the earth. Churned by demons in their search for amrita

Lalopzoopsia- hallucinations taking the form of animals

logorrhea- an incoherent rush of words

Garuda- great bird vehicle of Vishnu

Garwhal- birthplace of Ganga and Yamuna rivers has acquired status as land of the God's, its flora and fauna almost utopian in nature

Yavanas or the Greeks- according to the *Mahabharata* "Wicked kings" who were synonymous with the Yavanas

Helical rising- Sirius and our Sun as simultaneous rise on the horizon occurs every 1461 years

amrita- Immortal elixir in Hinduism

Vaishayas Alvars- 12 saints of south India from all levels of society between 7th and 9th century deeply immersed in God

Shavite Nayanmars- Poets of the 6th through 8th composed songs to Shiva

Nirguna Brahmin- Brahmin without qualities, impersonal and absolute

Sampradyas- Each of Hinduisms primary sects their rituals, deities, beliefs with one another

Iran to Philippines- referring to the first migration of blacks out of Africa to Asia over 50,000 years ago

Sakai- Negritos in Thailand and Malaysia

Yunan Province- refers to Black dwarfs in southern China whose presence persisted into the 3rd century

Ainu of Japan- of the same stock of Australian Aborigines. Their beliefs correspond with those of Ancient Egypt

Kolarian- Blacks of east-central India

Al-Jahiz- Black scholar of the 9th century himself part of the African diaspora in Asia, as were the Copts, the Nubians, the peoples of Sind, the Hindus, the Qamar, the Dabila, as well as the islands in the seas, all populous with Blacks

Susurrous recognition in Uganda- Robert Graves traces the origins of the Kanaanites or Phoenicians from Uganda

Hadrmaut- southern extremity of Arabia where Blacks exist. According to Major-General Maitland, this is where the Arabs exist differing from the Semite of the north, Arab by adaptation and residence by descent

Mahra- a kingdom of Blacks in southern Arabia

Galla- Black population in Abyssinia not unlike the Kushite nations of old

Mohenjo-Daro- Major Indus Valley city that possessed multiple level houses enhanced by sophisticated wells, drains, and bathrooms complete with toilets

Lothal- port city at the southern end of the Indus complex with oldest artificial dock in the world that measured 955 x 121 feet

Hurrian / Dorian / Mittanni- Aryan languages that emerged from Europe and south Russia

Kanchenjunga- Third highest mountain in the world on the border of Sikkim and Nepal

Gar- Highest city on earth at 14,060 feet at the north-west boundary of the Tibetan Plateau

Kassites- Aryan language/ethnicity

Dasas- appellation for Blacks under the Aryans

Ethiopic Buddha- Cheik Anta Diop surmised that Buddha was an Egyptian priest fleeing persecution of the Persian autocrat Cambyses. In Godfrey Higgins' Anacalypsis "Some statues of Buddha...exhibit thick Ethiopean lips."

Argation- coined term conjures both irrigation and breathing

phonomias- coined term conjures aural phantoms.

Eight million four hundred thousand births- Hindu cycle. Burden of each soul

Dharmasala- Rest house for Buddhist pilgrims

Peccam originarium- term offered by Kant as proxy for original sin it defines the human spirit as being naturally prone to evil

Gelukba / Sagyaba / Nyingpa- Buddhist Schools.

Dorian hypnotists- In this context refers to the Aryan mode that originally structured the caste system

Augustinian verdict- Judgement based on unrelenting schism

conceptual solar rise- in this context the theoretical component of Egyptian mathematics at the higher remove from the strictly mechanical nature of Mesopotamian mathematics

Indus locations- refers to the indecipherability of the Indus language. An ongoing mystery.

wild red dogs- Fierce and untamable, running in tireless packs, they occur in Burma, Singapore, Java, Sumatra, and Borneo.

unitary radius- trigonometric property invented after the invention of trigonometry by the Egyptians. The later fact is an example in problems 56 and 60 of the Rhind Mathematical Papyrus

Ektaras- Indian string instruments

Lung-gom-pa- Tibetan spiritual athletics

Jahnu & Bhagiratha- Instigated the Ganges to fall from the heavens